When You Care

When You Care

THE UNEXPECTED MAGIC
OF CARING FOR OTHERS

ELISSA STRAUSS

G

GALLERY BOOKS

New York   London   Toronto   Sydney   New Delhi

Gallery Books
An Imprint of Simon & Schuster, LLC
1230 Avenue of the Americas
New York, NY 10020

First Gallery Books hardcover edition April 2024

GALLERY BOOKS and colophon are registered trademarks of Simon & Schuster, LLC

Simon & Schuster: Celebrating 100 Years of Publishing in 2024

For information about special discounts for bulk purchases, please contact Simon & Schuster Special Sales at 1-866-506-1949 or business@simonandschuster.com.

The Simon & Schuster Speakers Bureau can bring authors to your live event. For more information or to book an event, contact the Simon & Schuster Speakers Bureau at 1-866-248-3049 or visit our website at www.simonspeakers.com.

Interior design by Jaime Putorti

Manufactured in the United States of America

10 9 8 7 6 5 4 3 2 1

Library of Congress Control Number: 2023933047

ISBN 978-1-9821-6927-5
ISBN 978-1-9821-6929-9 (ebook)

To my parents, Jona and Martin,
for giving me care,
and my children, Augie and Levi,
for receiving my care

CONTENTS

Introduction: *Why Care?*   1

PART ONE: LOOKING OUT

CHAPTER ONE
Breaking the Glass Doors: Building a Feminism of Care   27

CHAPTER TWO
Social Housekeepers: When Women Embraced Care   55

CHAPTER THREE
A New Man: On the Rise of Male Caregivers
and How Care Changes Men   73

CHAPTER FOUR
Love and Money: The Economic and
Social Might of Care   105

PART TWO: LOOKING WITHIN

CHAPTER FIVE

Survival of the Most Sympathetic:
Rediscovering Charles Darwin and Our Instinct to Care   143

CHAPTER SIX

The Feeling Is Mutual:
How Caring for Others Can Better Our Minds and Bodies   161

CHAPTER SEVEN

A Philosophy of Care: Through Caregiving,
We Can Encounter Big Questions, and Big Answers   191

CHAPTER EIGHT

When Revelation Takes Place at Home:
Care's Spiritual Potential and Why It's So Easy to Ignore   223

Conclusion: Interdependently   253

Acknowledgments   273

Notes   277

When You Care

Why Care?

AN AWAKENING

I went into motherhood determined not to lose myself in it. The obliteration of who I was, or thought I was, who I could be, or thought I could be, all felt inevitable without a conscious defense. When my first son was born in 2012, I believed I was ready.

By then, I had spent over a decade reading, admiring, and aggressively underlining many feminist, marquee-name books, by the likes of Simone de Beauvoir, Betty Friedan, and Virginia Woolf. They were all different thinkers with different agendas, living in different times and circumstances. But it didn't take a particularly careful reader to detect a common thread among them: Caregiving gets in women's way. A woman must find a way out of the home, away from the kids and older parents and anyone else who depends on her. Only then will she have a chance to find deep fulfillment and enlightenment.

"There is nothing more boring for an intelligent woman than to spend endless amounts of time with small children," Nobel Prize–winning novelist Doris Lessing is reported as saying. Lessing sounds a lot like many of the bright, accomplished moms I've read about or met on playgrounds and in school pickup lines. Nearly all of them declare a distance between themselves and motherhood, a shadow space of detachment or alienation. Often, these confessions are followed by declarations of adoration for Rachel Cusk's 2003 early parenthood memoir, *A Life's Work*, in which parenthood and selfhood are presented as a zero-sum game. "To be myself I must let the baby cry, must forestall her hunger or leave her for evenings out, must forget her in order to think about other things. To succeed in being one means to fail at being the other." A woman could either be herself, or be a parent. Never both. Never at once.

In case I had any doubts about which to choose, the internet made it clear. Caregiving, Facebook, Twitter, Instagram, and a million blog posts informed me, oscillates mostly between tedium and nightmare, picky eaters and sleepless nights, with small breaks of sweetness now and then. There were the occasional exceptions that proved the rule, like the meticulously curated prairie moms of Instagram, who showcased their wholesale embrace of parenthood through earth-toned linens and rosy-cheeked kids—never a sock or feeling out of place. Clearly far more interesting, far cooler, than either of these options is what comes before or after a period of caregiving, the untethered unpredictability of life on one's own, ignited by that bright blaze of independence.

I wasn't subtle about it. In my attempts to protect my non-mom self from disintegrating into the sludge of motherhood, I took the kind of absolute and petty measures that would delight a self-important CEO or bossy first grader. Rule #1: No one was allowed to use the term "mom" except when in direct reference to my relationship to my son, or my son when he finally got around to talking. I, respectfully I'd like to believe, made this clear when pediatricians or preschool teachers or tot music leaders addressed me as such. "Elissa," I'd interject with a smile whenever they called me "Mom," an attempt to inform them that all of me, not just mom-me, is standing before them. Rule #2: No engaging in non-mom activities through the prism of motherhood. I didn't drink "mom juice," have "mom friends," or participate in any activity organized around the category of "mom" like mommy-and-me exercise classes, support groups, or even a self-conscious "mom's night out." Could a glass of wine not still be a glass of wine? Could a friend not still be a friend, regardless of shared reproductive status or the shared proximity of conception? These phrases weren't only irksome because of their meme-able, Etsy-able cuteness. They were proof of how easily my identity could tip too far in the direction of "mom," so far I'd never come back.

I was an ideologue, but not without my moments of doubt. One weekday afternoon when Augie, my first, was around three months old, I took myself to lunch at an Italian restaurant around the corner from our apartment building in Brooklyn Heights. The place was almost always empty during the day, but its then au courant industrial decor and thick marble bar made me feel like I was somebody going somewhere. A lonely, wintertime maternity leave can make one grasp for relevancy.

I had been there a week before and the waitress, business slow as usual, had offered to carry my baby around while I ate. I knew not a single detail about this woman, nothing about her past, her temperament, or even her name, but I said yes. I wasn't going to refuse a chance to chew, swallow, sip, and breathe free of the threat of infant fussiness. Over a decade later, I still remember that lunch: a large bowl of hot minestrone soup followed by a poached pear with vanilla cream and a decaf macchiato for dessert.

This time, however, when I arrived at the restaurant for my lunch, there were voices, lots of voices, all amplified by that industrial decor. A dozen women were sitting around a long table, speaking over one another while tending to their babies. It was the neighborhood new-moms group, likely the one I could have joined, talking loudly about breastfeeding and diaper changes in between forkfuls of spaghetti. The waitress was too busy to carry Augie that day, leaving me to balance eating my pasta and tending to a newborn all by myself, without anyone to commiserate with.

I didn't want to join the group. I was absolutely certain of it. The taboos against bottle-feeding and pushing your baby in a stroller were strong at the time, and I did both. I wasn't opposed to breastfeeding or babywearing, but my boobs didn't make enough milk and my giant baby strained my back and neck when strapped to my torso. Joining such a group would be an invitation for disapproval or judgment, I suspected, and I had no evidence to the contrary. As I listened to them speak, I became ever more certain of my position, and a not not-misogynistic hostility consumed me. There are other things, so many other things, to talk about! I thought while they compared diapers, strollers, feeding struggles, and sleep schedules. They put on supportive faces for one another in the moment, but I knew, *knew*, that the majority of them interpreted news of a better diaper, bottle, bath, swaddle, whatever, as a personal attack or an occasion to spiral into self-doubt. A report of a better eater or sleeper was an act of war. Right there in front of me, women were losing themselves to motherhood. They had come in search of support and understanding but would leave with worries. Over time, these worries would metastasize motherhood into an outsize purpose, an outsize identity, stifling everything else.

Or maybe these were the deranged musings of the woman on the other side of the restaurant, sitting alone with a baby, watching a new-moms group interact as if she'd been hired to write an exposé on it, skeptical that caring for a baby could make for interesting conversation. It was all a little lonely if only she'd admit it.

I'm not sure my husband knew the depth of my fears. He understood that I wanted equality in childcare and domestic work. But he seemed mostly unaware that I believed my future best self, a woman who is wise, charismatic, and sexy, was at stake. Either way, and despite our good intentions, we were nowhere near equal as parents. He did what he could, driven by his instinct and my prodding, washing and washing bottles and onesies, shushing and burping the baby and waking up in the middle of the night. Unlike many men, he acknowledged that caring for a baby during the day is work, and that his office job didn't give him a pass on 3:00 a.m. feedings.

Still, in the morning he'd head off to work to a job that didn't yet offer paternity leave and I'd stay home and care. A painful situation exacerbated by the fact that, like me, he is a writer, who, pre-baby, was financially and professionally better off than I was. Nathaniel was a staff reporter for the *New York Times*, where he wrote about finance. He regularly fielded meeting requests from powerful book agents and offers for lucrative speaking gigs. I was a freelancer who wrote about women's issues, a beat for which there were few staff jobs, though many, many opportunities to pour one's heart out for $300 an essay. He brought our home a steady, and relatively substantial, paycheck and health insurance. I brought flexibility, the ability to press pause on my work in order to provide care.

Eight weeks after Augie was born, we hired a Jamaican-born woman named Carole to watch him, first for ten and then, a month or so later, twenty-five hours a week. She was a mother and grandmother, and former longtime nanny for one of my husband's colleagues at work. The ability to trust someone with my child was a gift, one that, for the first time since becoming a mom, made it possible for some of my anxiety to deflate. Someone else competent and nurturing was in charge. We tried to let her know we saw it this way, making sure to show her kindness and respect and taking the fact that she was our paid employee seriously. We paid her a living wage, gave her paid time off, confirmed she had decent health-care coverage, and contributed to her retirement.

The part-time working schedule itself didn't bother me. I was never someone who needed to work forty-plus-hour weeks to feel like I mattered, and there is only so much writing one can do and do well. Instead, what stung was the fact that I was spending that nonworking time caring: I was yet another woman whose new baby made her a willing accomplice in the gender pay gap. I was semi–opting out, letting feminism down, the face of a problem that economists, journalists, and activists rehashed time and again. As Nathaniel's career grew and mine slowed down, I couldn't help but internalize our weekly schedule as a failure for all women, everywhere.

The shame and fear about letting motherhood get the best of me in my own life metabolized into rage in my essays and blog posts. I became one of those journalists whose work filled me with guilt, writing often and furiously about the perils of caregiving and the ways women suffered as a result of doing it. I pushed for changes to individuals, men in particular, governments, workplaces, school schedules, and whatever else stood in the way of women freeing themselves from the grip of care. I raged about the way mothers were discriminated against when seeking out paid work, and how the demands of motherhood made it hard for women, from all income brackets, to achieve financial independence. I called for better policies, things like paid family leave and universal childcare, in order to free mothers to pursue financial security alongside other ambitions.

On top of this, I wrote about the internal experience, encouraging women not to let motherhood colonize their otherwise wild and interesting minds. My overarching thesis, the spirit behind much of my work at the time, was that motherhood is perfectly fine as long as it fits neatly into the gaps of a noble and multifaceted life. In a perfect world, a woman would be able to be a mother without sacrificing whatever splendid existence she had long imagined for herself. We didn't have to let motherhood change us or alter our fate if we didn't want to. We just needed to make sure the gaps into which we placed motherhood remained separate from everything else, distinct and well maintained, so we could physically or psychologically step away whenever we needed to go and live freely. My pieces on the subject received lots of page views, comments, likes, and tweets, and I got the smug satisfaction from believing these web metrics meant I was right.

What I didn't say, certainly not in my writing, and not even to myself at first, was that parenthood was far more compelling than I had thought it would be. The older Augie got, the truer this felt. And then even more so when my second son, Levi, was born four and a half years later. I always anticipated feeling some amount of joy as a parent, and, after making it through the dark and narrow tunnel of the first four months of parenthood, I found lots of it. Children, in flesh and spirit, can be a wonder. But what I discovered was something more—and more complicated—than just joy.

The world suddenly looked very different. *I* suddenly looked very different. I saw openings, possibilities, internal and external, and not only could I not look away; I didn't want to. Keeping parenthood in the gaps isn't just impossible, I'd come to feel; it's undesirable. The experience of care had seeped into everything, provoking me and enlightening me, and I liked it. I had put so much energy into figuring out how not to lose myself to caregiving that I completely ignored the possibility that I might, in fact, find some of myself there. That complex, wiser, more interesting person I had wanted to be, the one whose growth I presumed would be impeded by motherhood, was emerging through care.

The changes brought on by becoming a caregiver began on a subconscious level. When people asked me how it felt to be a mom during my first six months of motherhood, I told them I felt like an animal. Despite my general loquaciousness and instinct to interpret, I had nothing else to say about the experience, no way to articulate this deep need in me to care for my child. Whatever was happening between Augie and me felt hardwired, outside the realm of reason or conscious thought. Over time this primal response became ingrained, like a new limb I managed to incorporate into my gait. Only then did I begin to notice other creeping and articulable changes.

One of them involved a relinquishing of control, imagined and otherwise. A big-sister-for-life type, I have long lived with an irrepressible instinct to fix everything, even when no one asks; "shit happens," as a worldview, had never come easily to me. Thus, I used to see life and the people in it as a document that not only required but also desired my constant editing. After kids, I started to see that one can also experience others as a book: bound, predetermined, and there for observation and engagement but not regular meddling. With constant intervention off the table, I began to realize that I was paying better attention to friends and family, gaining a deeper understanding into what made them, them—and, in the process, what made me, me as well.

Franz Kafka said: "A book must be the axe for the frozen sea inside of us." Care did the same, unleashing a torrent of feelings and delusions that were sometimes easier left buried inside. Easier, but far less interesting. Raising my children has been a nonstop exercise in learning to sort out the shit I can clean up from the shit I need to accept and learn to live with. With time, accepting the idiosyncrasies and complexities of others allowed me to accept my own idiosyncrasies and complexities as well as those of life in general. People return from weeks-long silent meditation retreats or vomitous psychedelic journeys in the desert with these kinds of personal psychological epiphanies. I got there through care.

Eventually, the questions and epiphanies that caregiving provoked in my personal life spilled over to broader categories. Philosophically, spiritually, socially, even politically and economically, I had thoughts, new, sometimes big ideas that I arrived at through care. I reflected on what it meant to be a good person, to both the person in front of me and the world around me. I considered what it means to believe a divine force created the world, and what our role is in the act of creation. I thought about why so much of what ends up being women's work goes undervalued, and how caregiving helps men be more vulnerable and accepting of human dependency. Sometimes these shifts in my perspective were gentle. Other times they were painful, like when the demands on my independence were greater than I was prepared to give, or when long-accommodating delusions about who I am or how the world works were snapped in half. None snapped more loudly than my misconceptions about care.

Caregiving was not, it turned out, an end—the parking of the car after a long and exciting journey. Instead, it's been wild, a transcendent experience that has challenged me and enlightened me, while going straight to the heart of what it means to be a human. It's some of the truest intimacy I have ever known, an intimacy that has brought me closer to others, and, ultimately, myself.

Why did nobody tell me it could be like this?

It wasn't long before I began to see the power of intimate care in our collective existence as well. The caregiving I gave to my kids was not just good for them, or me; it was good for everyone. Care as a powerful social, economic, and political force was never something I encountered in college courses or, until very recently, political speeches. And yet it requires so little imagination, so little mental energy, to consider a world without care and quickly come to understand that our society and lives depend on it. Care is how future citizens and employees are created. Care is how we maintain dignity.

Aside from these loftier outcomes of care, it's also a crucial piece of the economic puzzle. If there are children or dependent adults around, some adult has to care for them. Perhaps this adult is paid for providing care, or, as is often the case, perhaps they are doing care work instead of participating in the labor market. Either way, their work has financial worth. Whether I am writing an article for an editor or caring for my children, I am participating in the economy. Historically speaking, economists only paid attention to the paid labor. Today, largely thanks to the prodding of feminist economists, they're increasingly putting care into spreadsheets and databases too.

There is, I realized, a clear and reciprocal connection between our inability to really see and acknowledge the complexity and richness of care in our individual lives and our unwillingness to support care and caregivers as a society. If we really valued care as individuals, then we might start valuing it as a society. And if we really valued care as a society, then we might start valuing it as individuals. One by one, we would see how big care is, and, from there, begin to contemplate how it can enrich us and challenge us for the better. We'd also see how easily care can become too big, too challenging, and, together as a society, commit to providing caregivers with more support. We'd know that caregivers consumed by care may be ruined by it, and the recipient of their care will suffer as well as a result. And we'd know that if we gave burnt-out caregivers societal support, the potential outcomes would look very different. The caregivers themselves would be positively shaped by care and the people they care for would be positively shaped by care, creating a ripple effect of social, political, and economic benefits for everyone. We all, I promise, want to live in a society where good care is big, possible, and abundant.

Our narratives about care have been so one-dimensional, so lacking in curiosity, so influenced by the patriarchy's simple algorithm in which anything female equals uninteresting, that we've failed to see this. If care were men's work, there's a good chance it would already be seen as inherently valuable—a major plot point in the human story rather than the footnote status it has long held. A version of this book probably would have already been written. By a man. Instead, we live in a world where a mother has "the most important job in the world," as Mother's Day cards have informed women for decades. And yet the title has never translated to tangible respect. If motherhood is really the most important job, one we admire in all its depth, then why hasn't a mother been president of the United States? Why aren't, more broadly, caregivers being looked to as leaders outside their homes? Why doesn't the U.S. government guarantee paid leave for caregiving? Why aren't we doing more to help caregivers do their jobs well? Why aren't we more curious about their work and what we can learn from them? And, the biggest question of them all, why aren't men lining up around the block to get in on this very important job?

I FIND IT WHOLESOME TO BE ALONE

The answer to these questions can be found, in part, in almost any high school English curriculum. It's where I first encountered the abiding belief that wisdom, enlightenment, and growth are best pursued on our own outside the home. I read books, *great* books, by *great* authors, and bought what they were saying. If only I could get it together to free myself when I grow up, I thought, I'd also wake up. To what? I had no idea. The point was to leave it all behind and then everything else in my life would fall into place.

"If you are ready to leave father and mother, and brother and sister, and wife and child and friends, and never see them again—if you have paid your debts, and made your will, and settled all your affairs, and are a free man, then you are ready for a walk." When my eleventh-grade English teacher read this passage from Henry David Thoreau's "Walking," her voice deepened and her meter slowed. This, we were to understand, is the work of a genius, a true American original who found it "wholesome to be alone." To really walk, to really live, Thoreau argued in this essay, as well as in his far more famous work *Walden*, one had to live a life unfettered from everyone and everything but one's own thoughts. Only then can we begin to understand who we are and what we're doing in this life.

American literature is lousy with similar tales of mostly white men heading to the big out there to find their way. This is a central theme in what literary scholars often consider the great American novel, Mark Twain's *The Adventures of Huckleberry Finn*. The book begins with Huck informing us how "rough" it is "living in the house all the time," and how he fears that he is being "sivilized" by the Widow Douglas. "I got into my old rags and my sugar-hogshead again, and was free and satisfied," he tells us, representing a nation of men, past and future. We hear more of the same from the other marquee writers of the twentieth century, including Ernest Hemingway and Jack Kerouac. Epiphany could not, would not, take place in anyone's living room. It could only be found by striking out on one's own, away from the mood-killing vibes of familial responsibilities and obligations.

Of course, one need not be a high school lit nerd to encounter these messages. Maybe we grew up on stories about mystic recluses like Saint Anthony the Great, a man who locked himself in an abandoned fort for two decades only to emerge, the story goes, healthy, enlightened, and, in time, the father of all monks. Maybe we believed that, given the opportunity, this kind of solitude would make us lucid and transcendent too. Or maybe our fantasy life leans more toward the win, victories achieved by heroic figures. We read biographies of great men, and the occasional great woman, and cataloged all the personal and familial sacrifices they made for the masses. The *greater* good, we were told. Maybe we got high on the vicarious power and came to believe that we, too, should be fighting our way to the top. Or maybe we're not quite that ambitious but still can't help but feel seduced by modern-day productivity culture in which long hours at work, or long hours training for a marathon, or perfecting one's meditation practice count as doing something important when caregiving does not. As different as all these lifestyles are, they're still undergirded by the same fundamental conceit: We can only become our truest, realest, best selves on our own.

For a long time, these narratives of getting away from home in order to self-actualize were mostly limited to men. Men went away and discovered big truths while women stayed behind and cared for family and home. It took until late into the twentieth century for women to tell these kinds of going-away stories about themselves and receive mainstream attention. Two of the most popular books of the past couple of decades, Elizabeth Gilbert's *Eat Pray Love* and Cheryl Strayed's *Wild*, are about women who left home and loved ones behind to figure it all out. These books were major bestsellers, made into equally popular movies, and inspired a generation of well-off women to find themselves—on their own. In 2017, the most purchased photo for the search term "woman" from Getty Images, a stock photo service, was of a woman alone, hiking in the mountains. Pam Grossman, a director at Getty, told the *New York Times* that people are drawn to this photo because it "really feels like an image about power, about freedom, about trusting oneself."

The image features a woman at a distance, walking along a craggy precipice with a long and confident stride. She wears a red down jacket and a wool hat, pom-pom on top and curly hair tumbling down her back. We can't see her face. I suspect we are supposed to think that is a good thing. She is there to be, think, and observe in her own body, on her own time, and not cater to or care for us, not even with a gesture or a smile. She is away, on her own. She is her own.

After centuries of forced intimacy, it feels marvelous to see women out of the home, alone, high on self-determination. I wanted this too and spent much of my early twenties in search of the great out there—and the great me I thought I would find out there. I crossed South American highways, meditated in a Thai jungle, picked oranges in the Australian outback, and slept on an ottoman in a cramped Tel Aviv apartment, all over a few years in the early 2000s. The epiphanies were few, but the joy and sense of adventure were great. I am glad I got to go away.

I'm also glad that when it came time to stay, married with kids, I knew to be wary of care. Beauvoir, Friedan, Woolf, Lessing, and the internet moms were not altogether wrong. Caring for another is often boring and depleting, and for too long the larger culture ignored this. When we become parents, our individual desires and needs, the ones that took decades to properly tune in to—if we ever got the chance to tune in to them in the first place—are supplanted by the desires and needs of another. The to-do list is long and plays on loop: feed, clean, nurture, and, the most challenging, listen. The fewer financial and social resources one has, the harder it is. My fear of self-effacement by way of motherhood, fueled by their warnings, pushed me to keep the non-mom parts of myself alive. I remained committed to my work, friend-ships, relationships with siblings and parents. I catered to my need to wander city streets, lose myself in concert halls, and follow along clum-sily to whatever dance I decided to learn. Not a metaphor. If I needed to leave home to travel, for work or pleasure, I did it without guilt because I knew, like the stock image woman in the pom-pom beanie, that there are some things I could only discover on my own, where no one could see me or needed me to smile. This, in turn, helped me shed my defenses around motherhood and be more open to connecting with my children and, ultimately, finding more meaning in care.

What I am asking for here isn't for us to deny women the power of going away or to deny the difficulties of care, but for us to see both going away and staying home as sometimes challenging, potentially life-changing experiences. What I want is for someone to also describe a picture of a woman doing care as "an image about power, about freedom, about trusting oneself." Or, even better, a man. Women get to do the things they never used to get to do, like travel, have careers they are passionate about, and revel in the pleasures and insights those offer. And they, now alongside everyone else, get to explore the potential in long-belittled, long-reduced, long-ignored care.

I've had days when I felt sure about this, and days when I've been riddled with self-doubt. Again, Cusk, Woolf, Beauvoir's writings, the "candid" Instagram posts about the bleakness of motherhood that get millions of likes, the increasing presentations of motherhood as costly, painful, escape-worthy in novels and essays, had me questioning myself. Movies like Maggie Gyllenhaal's *The Lost Daughter*, based on an Elena Ferrante novel of the same name, brought the punishing side of motherhood to the forefront, all while making the potential rewards of the experience hard to detect. "Children are a crushing responsibility," quoted nearly every single reviewer, this line representing the long-hidden and indisputable truth uncovered in the film. The more complicated truths about the push and pull of motherhood explored in the novel had been written out. One writer I read went so far as to compare caring for children to sex work and surrogacy; in her eyes, caring for others was a purely physical endeavor, both commodifiable and distinct from the life of the mind. The writing I encountered about eldercare, caring for people living with disabilities, and paid caregiving wasn't much better. Most of it focused exclusively on the opportunity costs involved in caring for another; always what we gave up, never what we gained.

It's not that I can't see the truth in those arguments. There is, without question, a lot to complain about when it comes to care. In the United States, caregivers are often left to fend for themselves without financial or institutional support. Under these conditions, care can deplete you, your body, your bank account, and your soul, and a reprieve is hard to find. Conditions can be even worse for paid caregivers, a largely immigrant women and women of color workforce who are often underpaid and taken advantage of on the job, in ways both subtle and overt. Then there's the indisputable truth that, even in ideal circumstances, care can be backbreakingly, soul-crushingly hard. I can't imagine there's ever been a caregiver who has never experienced a moment of ambivalence, of wishing more than anything they did not have to meet the needs of another right now.

But my issue, the cause for my doubt, wasn't with the writers' talking about care as hard work. Instead, it was how care was solely presented as hard and, therefore, finding anything good in care was surely an error of judgment. Caregiving isn't really interesting, I told myself; it was my native Californian optimism or, worse, Stockholm syndrome that was deluding me. I was too sentimental. A good girl. A victim of the patriarchy. If only I could undo the repression and social conditioning and tap into my rawer, wilder self. Sometimes I'd read conservative Christian mom bloggers just to be in the company of others thinking about the good side of care. I didn't agree with them about Jesus, gender roles, or abortion, but, oh yes, yes, caring could be sublime. This didn't help me feel less dull or boring—my quietest, deepest fear—but it did make me feel less alone.

But in moments of clarity, I saw things differently. I realized that while we used to diminish care with shallow, sentimental praise, we are now diminishing it with ceaseless complaint. Where is the acknowledgment of caregiving's complexity, or caregiving's might? Care can be enlightening, challenging, and, yes, sometimes, excruciating; a fiery furnace that might sting and singe while revealing what's underneath. I wanted to talk about it, unpack it, examine it, to take it apart and put it back together all with the goal of better understanding how care can change us and the world around us for the better, and why it's been ignored.

A NEW STORY

This book is my attempt to do just that. Here I combine reporting on care's value in a variety of realms, including economics, politics, philosophy, and spirituality, with some digging into why the people in power have devalued it for so long. This is woven through with my care story, as well as the care stories of a wide variety of caregivers whose backgrounds are very different from mine, and caregiving experiences often more challenging. I spoke to old and young, full-time and part-time, paid and unpaid caregivers to old, disabled, and ill individuals along with other parents, with the hope of broadening my perspective as well as discovering the universal themes in care. While each caregiver's situation is different, there is, I discovered, a widespread hunger to speak about care in all its depth and see these stories, their stories, get more attention and praise.

"Care" can mean a lot of different things. Same with "caregivers," or "caregiving." In this book, I am defining caregivers as those in intimate, ongoing relationships of care. This includes parents and caregivers to children, old, ill, and disabled people, relative and nonrelative, paid and unpaid. "Care" and "caregiving" will be used to describe the emotions and labor, cognitive and physical, these relationships require.

I'd love to help more people value care and make the world a better place for caregivers, which must include giving them more dignity and support. I hope it speaks to the believers, the ones who, like me, have been stirred by their roles as caregivers but could use some help figuring it all out. And I hope it speaks to the skeptics and haters, the people who just can't imagine that anything good could come out of care, as well as any partners and supervisors of caregivers who have the mistaken idea that time off to care for a dependent loved one is a vacation.

Such a reckoning with caregiving is important on more than just a personal level. We are, according to a growing number of political leaders and experts, plunging headlong into a caregiving crisis. This is the situation for parents, many of whom are not given the option of paid family leave, adequate paid sick days, or access to affordable and reliable childcare and after-school programs that make parents' professional lives possible. On top of this, it costs more than ever to raise a family, while expectations for caregiving are higher than ever. It's no wonder parents feel like they are failing at everything. One of the reasons fertility rates are at an all-time low is because many people don't think they have what it takes, temporally, financially, or psychologically, to raise a child.

Just a century ago, experts advised parents not to spend too much time with their babies, fed in part by the desire, and seeming necessity, of raising children who were self-sufficient from an early age. "Handle the baby as little as possible. Turn it occasionally from side to side, feed it, change it, keep it warm, and let it alone," read one manual from 1916. Today we know how crucial the parent-child bond is and that the way we care for our children will affect them for the rest of their lives. It's easy to mock the "helicopter" and "snowplow" parents, and indeed some parents' behavior is worthy of mockery. As are the expectations set forth by certain popular parenting experts who demand what I've only ever found impossible: a perfect balance of alert watchfulness and gentle affection. In other words, freak out on the inside while maintaining still waters on the outside. But the overarching reality is that we are all parenting more than previous generations, and sometimes for good reason. Cultivating empathetic kids for an uncertain future is hard and important work. To do it well, parents need more support.

Eldercare is also facing a crisis. By 2034, older adults are expected to outnumber children under the age of five. In 2020, roughly 42 million Americans provided unpaid care for an adult over the age of fifty—up from roughly 34 million in 2015. Caregivers to the elderly have, like caregivers to the young, no social safety net and must make hard decisions that pit their financial, emotional, and physical well-being against their ability to care well. Many have no choice but to cut back at work or leave their jobs altogether. Compounding the emotional and financial stress is the fact that a growing number of Americans are caring for two generations at once: their children, whom they are increasingly having at an older age, and their older relatives. People faced with this are known as the sandwich generation, representing, according to the Pew Research Center, 30 percent of adults with a parent over the age of sixty-five who "say their parent or parents need help to handle their affairs or care for themselves."

To make matters worse, there is a shortage of paid caregivers. Because of a combination of hard work, low pay, low status, better opportunities elsewhere, and pandemic burnout, there are fewer paid family caregivers than ever. Meanwhile, demand continues to soar. "There are people going without baths," Jason Kavulich, who has worked in this field since 1999, told the AARP in 2022. "This is the worst ever."

Feeding this crisis is the fact that we are spending more time alone than ever before, and as a result care, whether giving or receiving, has become a less organic part of our lives. For much of history, it was difficult for humans to go it alone. Goods and services were more expensive in relative terms, and running a house was extremely labor-intensive. It just wasn't economically or practically feasible to view success, or even fate really, as a party of one. But in the twentieth century, changes in manufacturing, technology, and our culture made it increasingly possible and seemingly desirable to make a life of one's own, on one's own. We gained freedom and, as a result, started spending a lot less time together.

Up until the 1960s, single-person households were rare. Now it's the second-most common household type in the United States, more prevalent than married families with children. This is in part because of the decline of marriage over the last sixty years. Today half of American adults are married. In 1960, that figure was 72 percent. Cohabitation has risen, but not nearly enough to offset the decline of marital partnerships. There are also fewer people having children. Fertility rates have steadily declined in the last fifty years, moving from a global average rate of 4.7 children per woman in 1950 to 2.4 children per woman in 2017. These figures are a response to changes in our economy as well as our attitudes toward family life and togetherness. A large portion of Americans today lack the financial stability to build a family, and there's little interest from the powers that be in helping them out. Another, sometimes overlapping, portion of Americans simply don't want to have children.

This is part of the reason why we are, according to public health officials, in the middle of a loneliness epidemic. According to the Pew Research Center, the size of the average American's "core discussion group" shrunk by a third between 1985 and 2009. A 2018 study of twenty thousand Americans by Cigna found that only about half reported having "meaningful, daily face-to-face social interactions." For some, loneliness means social isolation; for others, it's feeling disconnected from the world around them. Either way, the effects are grave. Loneliness is a similar health threat to substance abuse or lack of access to health care, and a contributing factor to the spike in suicide rates in recent decades. Even if someone doesn't consider themselves lonely, they're still increasingly likely to be feeling low. General happiness among American adults has declined since the 1970s, as anxiety and depression have increased among adolescents in recent years. Just as they did with loneliness, experts point to our decline in social connection and rise in social isolation as a major contributing factor to our collective struggles with mental health.

I'm not endorsing any particular family arrangement, or a certain set of life choices, or attributing all of the loneliness crisis to our smaller families. One can have kids and be lonely, as many mothers of young children well know. Instead, I want to make the point that there is a relationship between the loneliness crisis and the crisis in care, two social illnesses with the same root cause. A report on loneliness from Harvard states:

> Loneliness is a bellwether not only of our country's emotional and physical but moral health. In this age of hyper-individualism, the degree to which Americans have prioritized self-concerns and self-advancement and demoted concern for others in many communities has left many Americans stranded and disconnected.

Humans used to be surrounded by more people, family and non-family. They used to be more invested in community, which curtailed loneliness and benefited care. When we are other-directed, we place more value on acts of togetherness, including care, and we also invest more time and energy into caring for the caregiver and sharing the burdens of care.

To combat the caregiving crisis, we need to make big changes, from the top down and the bottom up. From on high, policy makers with the power to effect change should focus on building new infrastructure that invests in and supports caregivers. We, the ones down below, need to work on creating new narratives around, and understandings of, care. I don't see us succeeding in achieving one without the other. It's time to stop seeing caring for others as an obstacle to the good life and to start seeing it as an essential part of a meaningful one, individually and collectively. All of us receive care, and most of us, at some point, provide it. Many of us spend the majority of our lives at one end of a care relationship, including the two decades we spend as children, the other two we spend raising children, along with whatever time we give to the care of our parents and partners and being cared for ourselves toward the end of our lives. What if we saw caring well as more than obligation? What if we also saw it as a privilege, opportunity, and right? That will only happen when we acknowledge the power of care.

When we talk about caregiving, we're often quick to associate it with something akin to saintliness. There's a sense that only the few and best among us can make the sacrifices necessary to provide good care. This book will attempt to put an end to this simplistic and self-defeating point of view. When we view care as something we need to bear, we can only see what we have to lose. When we think of it as a chance for betterment, physical, psychological, philosophical, and societal, care becomes ripe with potential.

I honor and respect that there are a wide range of caregiving experiences, and that some are harder than others—and many are significantly harder than mine. For those who are caregiving in incredibly difficult circumstances, I hope this book will provide some context to what they've been through, helping them take pride in how it's shaped them. While this book will not ignore the challenges around caregiving, it will focus mostly on the potential for good within the average caregiving experience without accounting for all possible hardships. Sometimes caregiving is so hard and trying, it is beyond redemption, and when that happens no one should feel like they have to deny or justify their pain.

Overall, what I want is for us to be, whenever possible, more willing to see how the stresses of caregiving can sit alongside the good of caregiving. I can think of dozens of human endeavors, from physical endurance tests like marathons and long-distance hikes to psychological ones like English teacher favorite Henry David Thoreau living alone in a cabin for two years, that have all been afforded this complexity of thought. We are aware of such endeavors' capacity for pushing us to our limits, while at the same time able to honor how they create well-being and growth. How many big-budget war movies have I sat through in my life that demanded I understand that an experience can be both difficult and profound? I'm asking you to do the same for care.

It might seem paradoxical, ironic even, to want to better understand how care benefits individual caregivers. The idea that we should embrace care because it is good for us may seem like a strangely selfish case for caregiving. But this is only the case if we continue to stubbornly cling to the fiction of independence, one that is woven into the fabric of American life with the finest of threads. If we continue to measure our lives by standards of self-determination, self-actualization, self-reliance, self-betterment, self-care, if we continue to believe in the myth of the self-made man, then yes, caregiving just to get wiser, happier, and healthier seems like a strange path.

But if we change our orientation to one of interdependence, seeing humans as a web of twisted roots, the pieces fall into place. A vision of interdependence allows for us to see how when we engage with other people it helps us figure out who we are, what we want, and what we're doing here in this one and only life. In the inner sanctum of human interdependence, behind the doors, sit the quiet acts of care. The lunches and baths. The listening and letting go.

Interdependence can feel suffocating—I know. Acknowledging how much we are needed by others, and how much we need others, goes against everything many of us have learned about the good life in the West. But eventually the gasping stops, the distance between the seemingly sublime and the seemingly mundane shrinks, and a slow-forming awareness settles in. We begin to see and feel the transformative power of care.

I have mom friends now. They are not, as I once feared, women with whom my main connection is the fact that we live close to each other and have similar-aged children who like to play with one another. In fact, these friendships aren't tethered by our children at all, who, for the most part, met through us and don't always connect. Nor are they women with whom I primarily discuss how to parent my children, things like Halloween candy management or discipline strategies, though there is some of that too. They're mom friends because they are the women with whom I regularly discuss what it's like to be a mother with the same intensity as our discussions about other intimate relationships in our lives along with our favorite books and movies. We sit together at restaurants and, in between forkfuls of pasta, discuss how caring for our children has challenged us and healed us, sometimes at once. The fear of care taking over my identity that I had over a decade ago when I sat in that restaurant in Brooklyn has been replaced by a piercing interest in how care is shaping me and everyone else. Caregiving, my mom friends and I understand, is a beginning, an opening through which new questions, possibilities, and powers can emerge. I hope this book can help take you there.

PART ONE

Looking Out

CHAPTER ONE

Breaking the Glass Doors

Building a Feminism of Care

THE CARE TABOO

I was about half a decade into parenting, mother to two very different kids who needed me in very different ways, when the urge to dive into how caregiving changes us arose. In my head and in my notes, I amassed an ongoing list of observations, anecdotes, grand unified theories, and inchoate feelings that I wanted to present and unpack to friends and readers. Besides that Hallmark bliss and meme-able burden of caregiving, I was discovering a vast forest of feelings, epiphanies, and psychological sleights of hand and it was all—the good and bad, easy and difficult, light and dark—fascinating.

I wanted to talk about care, and I wanted to talk about talking about care, and why it so rarely happened. I wanted to ask why even though we spend our lives tugging at the complex psychological and philosophical nature of our friendships, romances, and connections to our parents, when it comes to this other major human relationship our conversations tend to remain in shallow waters. Wasn't care, too, an example of two complex humans trying to find their way together? This desire to investigate didn't mean I always liked care—that I didn't also feel moments of despair. There were times I felt frustration and rage, when I wanted to drive the car far, far away from home or least feign illness to avoid yet another morning. But this despair interested me too, as it seemed to suggest depth rather than futility. Like writing and my marriage, all the things that bring my life meaning come laced with instances of hardship, and the subsequent tendency to make mistakes, or, worse, do nothing, in the face of an enormous task.

I wanted to talk about how I didn't like caregiving because it was easy. I liked caregiving because it was big, a galaxy of knotted entanglements, and I was in awe of this bigness and felt compelled to explore it. I wanted to say that caring for another person is like a hero's journey, a transformative experience. Except unlike in the common formula, one does not need to leave the home.

In the hero's journey, as defined by Joseph Campbell and appearing in stories throughout time, the hero must depart, or separate, from what they know, which has broadly entailed leaving home. Then they must pass through a threshold to a special world where they encounter a trial. There they go through an ordeal and solve a major crisis. After this, they return home, imbued with special spiritual or cognitive powers gained from their experience that allow them to enlighten others and help solve future crises. *The Odyssey. Star Wars. Finding Nemo. Moana.*

When I became an active caregiver for the first time, I experienced a separation from the world I previously knew: I lost my independence. Someone depended on me. Holy shit. Then I entered the new world: My body, my living room, my brain, and everywhere else were all rendered foreign. Tiny Augie, big as a loaf of bread, had shape-shifted all that surrounded him. The crisis: Who am I now that someone is attached to me? What do I do with this person who is attached to me? I experienced struggle—and then, finally, eventually, a return. I overcame the threat that was dependence, and I returned to my body, mind, and life understanding a little bit more about what it means to be human. All this, and I never had to leave my apartment.

For a while, I didn't talk about this because I didn't know how. There is no vocabulary for describing becoming a parent in its complexity and fullness without running the risk of sounding retrogressive. Be too positive and close ones and readers might think of me as sentimental; there is no greater insult to a woman writer than being called sentimental by her peers.

But where, I wondered, is the line? How many warm-blooded emotions could I include in a piece of writing and still maintain my intellectual credibility among readers and peers? I had no idea. I only knew that, as a woman, it was best to keep a safe distance from not only anything too happy, sad, or nostalgic but also from excess feeling altogether. Caregiving is a wellspring of feelings. "Today, often the appropriate stance expected of a thinking woman is ambivalence about motherhood. Intellectual and professional credibility means assuming a defensive stance with respect to it, protecting yourself from this potentially colonizing force," philosopher Anastasia Berg told me. Berg, alongside critic Rachel Wiseman, writes about the changing attitudes toward children, parenthood, and family in contemporary society, and the value of having children in an imperfect world.

There were numerous forces that taught me these lessons, most of which I wasn't conscious of until I began researching this book. Evolution, psychology, philosophy, theology, politics, and economics all write care out of the larger human story in subtle and not-so-subtle ways. Though before I noticed any of this, before I saw how the denial of care was woven into our most fundamental institutions and narratives, institutions and narratives largely made by and for men, I experienced it most acutely within the women's movement. I understand the irony of beginning this book with a critique of feminism. Feminists, it needs to be noted, were neither the main architects nor the main villains when it comes to our dismissive attitudes about care. What they were, however, was the first way I, someone who has long answered "feminist writer" when asked what I did for work, encountered them.

While I'm still thankful for the feminist writings that had me questioning everything, I now struggle with the limitations of their imaginations when it comes to care. From Marxist feminists and careerist feminists to novelists, bloggers, and random commenters on Facebook, everyone I came in contact with seemed to be in agreement on one thing: Care and women's liberation were in opposition. Some thought care was an oppressive product of capitalism, while others saw it as the impediment to there being more women CEOs; there were those who thought care was the impediment to making good poetry or art, and those who were mostly worried about the way care stops us from understanding ourselves. All true to a degree in the world as we know it—but what if the problem wasn't so much care as it was the circumstances within which we give it, and the unrealistic and emotionally hollow stories we tell ourselves about it? It was the rare piece of feminist writing that considered the ways in which liberation, or a woman being her fullest self and fully engaging in the world, can take place in part through care.

In her 1927 novel *To the Lighthouse*, Virginia Woolf writes about Mrs. Ramsay, Victorian wife and mother of eight, who feels she fully experiences the world only when away from her children:

> For now she need not think about anybody. She could be herself,
> by herself. And that was what now she often felt the need of—to
> think; well, not even to think. To be silent; to be alone.

When I first read this novel in my early twenties, long before starting a family, I immediately began gaming out how I would ward off such a fate in my own life. I wanted to avoid domestic confinement and thought that, should I have kids, I could incorporate them into a nontraditional, perhaps globe-trotting lifestyle that would help me avoid the inevitable tedium of motherhood. My kids would go with my flow, never intruding on my other pursuits, accessories to a bohemian and meaningful existence.

There were many other influences for me as well, some more severe than Woolf. In her 1949 book *The Second Sex*, iconic French feminist Simone de Beauvoir argues that women are raised to be inward, passive, inhospitable to growth. Men, meanwhile, live active, productive, meaty existences, which would allow them to extend beyond themselves and reach toward greater truths and richer experiences. The solution, as Beauvoir saw it, was for women to leave home and go to work, engage in intellectual activity, and fight for economic justice.

Decades later she told interviewers that she no longer thought it was impossible for a woman to be a mother and be transcendent. "Very difficult," but not impossible. "I think that motherhood is the most dangerous snare for all those women who want to be free and independent, for those who want to earn their living, for those who want to think for themselves, and for those women who want to have a life of their own. The conditions could be changed . . . maybe. . . . Let's hope so," Beauvoir explained. Sadly, my women's studies professors never mentioned this evolution in their hero's thinking.

Then there's the book that helped launch second-wave feminism, Betty Friedan's 1963 *The Feminine Mystique*. It begins with a list of domestic and caretaking activities, including eating "peanut butter sandwiches with her children," and follows this catalog of domestic tasks with the question: "Is this all?" This iconic opening set the tone and energy of decades of feminism in which Friedan's characterization of domestic life as a "comfortable concentration camp" framed the way many women saw their lives and choices. Women experienced "a deep-seated fear that our lives would be destroyed, we'd be ruined, if we had kids. At some psychic level we felt it was death," as a member of a New York feminist group in the 1960s put it.

Over the years, this fear of family life would take on many manifestations. Women embraced the sexy, single, and fabulous *Cosmo*-girl lifestyle, a vision from magazine editor Helen Gurley Brown that she first wrote about in the early 1960s and continued to cultivate during her thirty-plus years as editor of *Cosmopolitan* magazine. And, though less common, there were the more radical ideas of thinkers like Shulamith Firestone, who, in the late 1960s, argued for a future in which child-rearing would be "so diffused as to be practically eliminated." She thought babies could one day be incubated in artificial wombs, making caring for any individual child a collective endeavor, shared by many.

The feminism I first encountered as a teen in the late 1990s was the sex-positive variety, a Gurley Brown–inspired approach that largely equated a woman's true freedom in society with her true freedom in her body and bedroom. This focus on women's sexual pleasure dovetailed well with the other big issue of that time: the fight for birth control access and abortion rights. I supported the right to choose then and continue to today. I don't see how we can value something as rich and complex as care without trusting caregivers to make decisions about when and how to care.

As for the sex stuff, I tried my best, separating making out from love or virtue, listening to Liz Phair at maximum volume in my black Jetta, and taking notes from the then fresh women of *Sex and the City*. I had fun, some good sex, but stumbled a few times along the way, confusing self-sexualization with sexual freedom. Once, in pursuit of this laid-back, cool-girl energy, I wore a thin white tank top printed with the *Playboy* logo. Worse, I very casually referred to this style of tank top as a "wifebeater."

The wave of feminism that influenced me the most was the one that coincided with my early thirties, the period of time in which adulthood officially settled in and I felt as though my real life was at stake. This was the "Lean In" feminism of the early 2010s, Sheryl Sandberg's push for women's professional domination that spawned #bossbabes and #girlbosses, hashtags in which career and femininity were united triumphantly. That I never aspired to the corner suite or anything that represented professional domination didn't matter. This mandate to win at work set the terms of the feminist ambition for a generation. For my grandmother and mother, escaping domestic life and getting a job, any job, qualified as success. The point was financial freedom. Now, in this formula, women needed to have impressive résumés and a closet full of power suits, and family life was fine as long as it didn't get in the way of one's fight to the top.

It was Woolf, Beauvoir, Friedan, Sandberg, Carrie, Miranda, Samantha, and Charlotte that I found the most convincing recipes for smashing the patriarchy and living a fuller, more complete life. I am grateful to each and every one, whose advocacy, even if sometimes imperfect, made it possible for me and so many others to do just that. If their work occasionally suffered from shortsightedness, it doesn't negate the fact that the issues they took on were very real for many women. They made me and many others pay attention to what women lacked because they are women, the physical and material security, freedom and power, and everything else that existed outside the four walls of home. Over time, this attention translated to action and success—not all the way but enough for us to take on what I saw as the next step of the feminist project. It was time to freely, and maybe even enthusiastically, return to our homes and find the good in it.

Though the more I began thinking about the home as a place for hero's journeys and other such epiphanic processes, the more I began to realize that this distinction between what happens inside its walls and what happens outside them is not as firm as I had long imagined. Our domestic and public spaces, our domestic and public selves, have never been and will never be two entirely separate entities but instead are intimately intertwined. Women don't just live under glass ceilings. They also live behind "glass doors," as I have come to think of it, invisible barriers standing in the way of women's full expression of self and full participation in society. We will never value care, we will never solve the riddle that is feminism plus caregiving, until we smash them.

THE GLASS DOORS

At the root of nearly all the tension surrounding women and care sits our inclination to separate the public and private sphere, and our public and private selves. Here's how the myth of the glass door works: At home we give care, in a realm apart from politics, economics, and ambition. At work and in public, we hustle and compete, separate from our care obligations. Our private selves belong at home and only at home, pure and soft, and shouldn't expect any help or acknowledgment from entities outside those four walls, like our government or workplaces. Our public selves, on the other hand, the ones who engage in systems of money, politics, and justice, have no place within our homes while we care for our families. They aren't the ones playing music to a parent with dementia or waking up in the middle of the night to nurse an infant.

Well, it's all a big fat lie, one that philosopher Seyla Benhabib traces back to the birth of the fictitious "independent" man in politics and economics. "This vision of autonomy was and continues to be based upon an implicit politics which defines the domestic, intimate sphere as ahistorical, unchanging and immutable, thereby removing it from reflection and discussion," she writes in an essay titled "The Generalized and the Concrete Other." When freedom and independence are the most important things in our personal and political lives, then any place in which they are limited will, conveniently, be seen as inferior. Male thinkers over the ages didn't ignore the existence of the domestic space, but they kept it small, uninteresting, apart from the complexity and chaos that is real life.

We don't have to buy into that point of view. Care and domesticity, politics and economics, private lives and public lives, are all, intricately, irrevocably, intertwined. The people we are when we care and the people we are when we work or attend a city council meeting are all tangled up and this is a good thing. Exposing this truth should be at the heart of the women's liberation project.

Our capacity to give and receive care at home is affected by circumstances outside the home, be it workplace policies, government policies, or a culture that either supports or turns a blind eye to the needs of young, old, and disabled people. Our willingness to care is also influenced by the culture around us. Are caregivers acknowledged and exalted, or ignored? When it is the former, research shows that individual caregivers are more likely to feel good about caregiving. When it is the latter, they don't. Also, the way we vote, the way we work, the way we create, and the way we relate to our friends and colleagues and strangers are all influenced by our experiences with care. When it comes to children, our ability to care well translates to an emotionally stable and productive future electorate and workforce.

For decades now, the singular metaphor of the women's movement has been to look up, up, up at those glass ceilings blocking our way to the power and achievements long only awarded to men. Up is good. Necessary. We're more than half of humanity. Why shouldn't we have more money and more control? But we can't *only* look up, because up represents a world order and hierarchy created by men, for men—and one in severe denial of care. We are all, men included, suffering for it. A revolution focused on and fueled by care would aim not just to break glass ceilings but also to attempt to break through these glass doors that artificially isolate the care happening in our homes from the wider world without.

These doors convince us that our struggles to care must only be our problem, and that the solution must come from within. They partition care away, leaving us to buy into the myth that caring for another is something one person can, and should, manage on their own rather than something that requires support. Shatter them and we will see why we need to help caregivers and how helping caregivers has a ripple effect on our society, making it stronger overall.

Glass doors also convince us that the richness of the experience of care, and the lessons learned from it, have no place in the wider world. Not in political debates, or novels, or large-scale prescriptions of how a human should be. Glass doors are the reason we are still ashamed of a care gap on a résumé. They are why we hesitate to acknowledge the way caregiving has made us a better manager or writer or artist, and why we continue to denigrate domesticity and raise up professional success, no matter what effect a job has on our souls or the world.

Care has been a thorn in mainstream feminism's side for so long that a large-scale embrace of care within the context of women's rights can feel hard to imagine. But it is starting to happen, little by little, picking up where a lot of care feminists from history, mostly Black women, whose work is not on the mainstream's radar and that I explore in the following chapter, left off. Today a growing number of activists, thinkers, and artists are attempting to smash those glass doors. They are fighting for and alongside women who give care and are shaped by care, and continue to do so because there is no humanity without care. They want to free women to be their fullest selves, caregiver and non-caregiver, public and private, and, if all goes well, respected for it by everyone else. Not freeing just women either. Every person who cares.

A MODERN-DAY CARE FEMINISM EMERGES

Ai-jen Poo has been advocating for nannies and housekeepers for over a quarter of a century, fighting for guaranteed fair wages and workplace protections, benefits these workers uniquely lacked. According to the United States' labor law, domestic employees are not guaranteed sick days, a safe workplace, or legal protection from workplace harassment. This gap in policy is a relic of the New Deal, when these workers were excluded from wholesale labor reforms of the time, likely, in part, for racist reasons.

About a decade into her job, Poo noticed a trend. More and more nannies and housekeepers were being called upon to care for the old who had, increasingly, no one to care for them. She began to see her work advocating for housekeepers and caregivers as part of a much bigger story. This struggle shouldn't just be about wages and protections for individuals, but a broader fight against the economic, political, and social forces that make giving and receiving care, particularly for paid caregivers, harder than ever. Women, who used to do most of the unpaid caregiving, are now increasingly working out of the house. Economic freedom for women is a good thing, but few think about all the care work they left behind and no longer have time for. Families replace these unpaid caregivers with hired help, or, in cases when they can't afford to hire someone, less attentive care. When they do hire caregivers, whether in the home or out of it, they often can't afford to pay them a fair wage. Care as something you can buy on the open market just doesn't work for most of us—it costs much more to provide quality care than most people can afford to pay for it. As such, paid caregivers are often mistreated, underpaid, and in short supply. Meanwhile, many workers lack the flexibility and paid-leave policies from their employers to adequately care for their own loved ones and hold down a job at the same time, leaving them no choice but to pick between their careers and their ability to care well.

All these problems, all these strains on individuals, are of one piece, Poo realized. They are all rooted in our disregard of care, and come together to create a massive crisis in care felt by all. With this in mind, Poo went on to help create a coalition called Caring Across Generations, which brought together activists on all these fronts. Through conversations with eldercare activists, disability activists, childcare activists, paid-leave activists, and more, she began to see how this was a systemic issue that merited a systemic response. "Private" care, the thing happening behind glass doors, was failing because of a lack of public investment. "I started talking about these issues and thinking about what we need in the twenty-first century, and I realized that we need to think about care as an infrastructure, or a public good, that enables us to do everything else," she told me.

Just as we have publicly maintained highways, federal investment in the internet, government oversight and subsidies for agriculture, and a public education system, we also need publicly maintained and subsidized care. This could include universal paid family and medical leave; flexible and supportive workplaces with breastfeeding rooms and no big meetings scheduled at 5:00 p.m., when those with care duties likely have to leave; financial support for unpaid caregivers; and government investment in childcare and long-term and elderly care, which would lead to more relief for unpaid caregivers and better wages and work conditions for paid caregivers.

We all need safe roads, we all need to eat safe foods, and we all need to give and/or, at some point, receive care. The government could, and should, help ensure that we are able to provide that care without going broke or insane or burdening underpaid caregivers.

"Care infrastructure," as a concept, first appeared in Poo's 2016 book, *The Age of Dignity*. Though few people took notice of it until the COVID-19 pandemic showed us what happens when all of our preexisting, albeit unreliable and underfunded, care infrastructure is taken away. Suddenly there was no school or after-school care for the kids, home health-care workers and aides were unable to work, and many had to choose between keeping their older parents in homes and not seeing them for a long time and bringing them home and finding a way to care for them in addition to fulfilling their other responsibilities. In the years that followed, care shortages have continued, pushing many women out of the workforce, as they couldn't find anyone to watch their children or parents. Women found this experience so challenging that some took to gathering in fields and howling, a protest directed toward the invisible forces that govern the world, because the visible ones just weren't listening. With this rage came clarity of mission, and with this clarity came momentum for caregiver advocacy.

In 2021, a "Marshall Plan for Moms," which calls for government investment in care, was launched by activist Reshma Saujani and signed by a long list of activists and actresses including Charlize Theron, Amy Schumer, and Eva Longoria, alongside other Hollywood and Silicon Valley elites. This was one of many pushes for care-related reforms, including expanded paid leave, rights for pregnant workers, investment in childcare centers, and more investment in eldercare. That same year, President Biden began advocating for care infrastructure as part of his Build Back Better plan. It failed to pass but sparked serious debate and shifted the Overton window on the kinds of conversations we have about public investment in care. "This was really such a big moment. It showed respect and recognition for a workforce that has been undervalued and overlooked for so long," Poo said.

A common critique of feminism is that wealthy women's liberation depended on the "enslavement," as it is often put, of working-class
women. Essentially, in order for some women to be their fullest selves
and fully engage in the world, other women had to fill in for them and
take over the soul-crushing task of maintaining a family and home.
Taken to its logical conclusion, this means that women will remain
oppressed until none of us does caregiving or household work. It's a
shaky formula, one that dismisses the reality that such work is necessary for the functioning of society. It also dismisses the possibility that
some of these "enslaved" women don't mind the work itself and don't
think of themselves as "enslaved" at all. For many, caring for a child or
dependent adult is far preferable to and more meaningful than other
jobs they could have. They take the work seriously. They see their work
as essential and noble. What they want is for others to see it the way
they do.

Lourdes Dobarganes is one of these workers. Born in Mexico, she
described her childhood to me as a "mountain of responsibility." Her
dad died when she was thirteen, after which her family moved from
a small town to the capital city. Lourdes helped care for their home
while her mom was off at her job at a local butcher and, later, she
cared for her mom when she became sick. During downtime, Lourdes
watched television. One of her favorite shows was *The Streets of San
Francisco*, a 1970s detective drama starring Karl Malden and Michael
Douglas. She fell in love with the city and at age twenty-seven she
moved there, undocumented, with her husband and two daughters,
ages six and eleven months.

Like many immigrant women, Lourdes's most marketable skill set
was her experience in caregiving and housekeeping, so she pursued a
job as a nanny. She quickly learned that there is a real gap between the
inherent value of this work and what someone who does this work gets
paid. Her first job in the United States was working as a nanny for one

child, for which she earned fifteen dollars a day. In 1989, this was a little more than half the minimum wage.

Lourdes didn't get it. She believes that she has provided quality and meaningful care for everyone she has worked for, bringing dignity and stability to their loved ones and their lives. Personally, she has found great meaning in her domestic jobs, which have since included housecleaning and eldercare in addition to nannying. She marvels at the variability among children, how they "all learn differently," and enjoys the challenge of figuring out how to tend to their unique needs. She loves the way children "tell the truth," and feels like she had some of the most honest conversations of her life with the kids she nannied. The older people she's cared for have taught her so much, everything from cooking to the meaning of existence. She remains in touch with many of the families for whom she has provided care, sometimes decades after their work relationships have ended.

How, why, she wondered, is work as important as this not worthy of guaranteed fair wages or workplace protections? A lot of love can take place inside a home, but so can a lot of abuse, whether it's unintentional or not.

In 2017, she heard about the California Domestic Workers Coalition, a group advocating for more security and support for domestic workers. She soon joined their ranks and has since become an outspoken advocate, lobbying Sacramento lawmakers and joining protests for the right to care with dignity and safety, at work and at home. "We want to be paid fairly. We don't have enough to care for our own kids, while we spend our day caring for someone else's kids. We have to work to give them what they need, what they deserve, but aren't getting what we need. We want to be seen. We want to be able to not go to work if our own kids are sick, or we hurt our back, or are sick. But we can't because if you stop working for a day, they aren't going to pay you," she told me.

* * *

Contemporary care feminism has another face. In addition to the push for collective recognition and investment in care, women are also trying to change the narrative about care's impact in their individual lives. For so long, care and being a politician, artist, or good worker were seen as in opposition. A woman could pick one to do well. Never both. But now a growing number of women are questioning that paradigm, making space for the ways in which care may strengthen our capacity to create, cooperate, and innovate. Or, more broadly, to engage with people and the world outside our care relationships.

More and more politicians are now putting the fact that they tend to children front and center. This has long been a shorthand to signify one's moral compass, particularly among conservative women, but today's political mothers are doing something else. For them, motherhood is a shorthand for competency and creativity, busy people who know how to compromise and get stuff done. Congresswoman Katie Porter, of whiteboard math fame, makes her experience as a caregiver—in her case, as a single mom—a central piece of her public persona. It's part of what made her so hardworking and agile, and also what informs her sense of what Americans really need. "You have to be scrappy—as a working mom, a single mom, and as someone who doesn't have wealth and all these advantages. You have to fight to be taken seriously," she told *ELLE* magazine in August 2020. "That is even true in Congress, and I wasn't prepared for it."

Caregivers in Silicon Valley are attempting something similar. They're tired of competing with the industry's idea of an ideal worker—a guy who does nothing but work and is available 24/7, apart from occasional trips to Burning Man or a silent meditation retreat—and they're starting to tell another story. Amy Henderson is at the center of this movement. She is the cofounder and CEO of TendLab, a Silicon Valley–based incubator looking to improve lives for families, and the FamTech Founders Collaborative, a group of start-up founders looking to change the narrative on care. When Henderson became a parent while working in the tech industry it was as hard as she expected. But she also noticed that while her life was logistically difficult, good things were happening within. "I noticed I was much better at work. My ability to focus was much better. I felt much more competent. At first, I couldn't figure out how or why, especially because I had less time than I had before. It was clear, though, that my impact was much greater, even with less time invested," she told me. Surprised by this shift, Henderson began asking around if others felt the same. First informally and then through surveys and interviews, she discovered that she wasn't alone. Care, be it for children or dependent adults, had made others better at their jobs as well, more collaborative and more empathetic—both increasingly useful skills in today's workplace. Henderson put this research in her 2021 book *Tending: Parenthood and the Future of Work*, and now regularly speaks at businesses and start-ups encouraging employers to see the potential in caregivers, while also supporting them.

REIMAGINING AMBITION

"Ambition" has always been a barbed concept for women, and asking a woman if she is ambitious almost always feels like a trick question. Am *I* ambitious? Well, I don't make serious money, nor have I ever tried to make serious money. When I lived in New York City, the world capital of naked ambition, I failed to schmooze at parties or network in any meaningful way. I never get back on the laptop at 9:30 p.m. or on the weekends. I could absolutely put more effort into building what we today call a platform, courting followers on social media. In short, if I do make it big, it will have a lot more to do with luck than hard work.

And yet look at the terms I, and maybe you too, use to define "ambitious." I've totally discounted that I managed to make a career out of writing. Not to mention the intimate relationships I maintain with my parents, in-laws, siblings, and friends; or that I cook for my family at least five days a week; or that I'm raising kids who are kind and curious; or that I've indulged my younger son Levi's inborn and surprising passion for the cello and am now a full-on Suzuki mom practicing with him almost every night. You don't need to reassure me that this is a lot. I know that it's plenty. Still, when someone asks me about my ambition, the word gets stuck in my throat because the definition of ambition has, for so long, been limited to work.

"Women's professional achievement used to depend on being exactly like men. Female partners in law firms had bow ties; they looked exactly like men and acted like men as much as they could. They had to be ballbusters, tough as nails, and nobody wanted to talk about childcare," Anne-Marie Slaughter, the CEO of New America and author of *Unfinished Business: Women Men Work Family*, told me. She's one of a handful of unambiguously ambitious women trying to redefine ambition, a result of her own struggle balancing work and family life and a subsequent questioning of why a perfect balance between the two became the goal in the first place.

In recent years, Slaughter has been self-identifying as a "care feminist," a pivot from decades as a "career feminist." For her this includes the kind of work Ai-jen Poo is doing in getting more public investment into care, as well as a wholesale reassessment of feminism and success, or imagining "what the world would be like if women were truly in charge." She told me that when she first started talking about all this in the mid-2010s she met a lot of resistance. Her Davos-going, TED-talking peers couldn't wrap their heads around the fact that she now thought care could be just as important as career, and ambition could encompass both. "For my generation" [Slaughter was born in 1958] "embracing care feminism requires a deprogramming and reprogramming. I was programmed to think that my father's work was important and my mother's work was not, except for her professional work as an artist. A lot of the women in my generation thought I was betraying the cause when I began talking about care."

Seeing Slaughter's mother's work, and all the other caregivers' work, as important pushes us to consider, in all its Sisyphean fullness, the task of maintaining a home and family. In the past five years, a lot of women have been talking about this, labeling it as "invisible labor," "emotional labor," the "second shift." Sadly, many buy into the career feminist point of view where only the hard work outside the home should be celebrated and all the birthday party planning, well-visit booking, and new-shoe buying is a burden. But others, thankfully, find a way to talk about the immensity of caregiving and domestic work without degrading it. They want men to do more care because care is hard and because doing too much care holds women back from engaging in the world in other ways. But they also want men to take part in care because it's an important part of a meaningful existence. The moonshot: Convince men to expand their definition of ambition to include care, leading to a rise in men doing more care and advocating on behalf of caregivers.

Self-identified care feminist Eve Rodsky thinks while there absolutely are some men who are lazy and neglectful, this is not the driving force behind why women do more caregiving and housework. Instead, it's inertia, the fact that this is how it was in their home and this is how it was in their father's home, combined with the fact that we haven't taken this kind of work very seriously. "We've failed to see the home as an important organization, so to speak, in need of respect and rigor," Rodsky, cofounder of CareForce, a collective of political activists, culture makers, and businesspeople who work together to raise up care, told me. She is also the author of the best-selling book *Fair Play*, which offers a path forward in care and chore sharing among couples. The cure to the invisible labor gap is identifying such labor and then recognizing its value.

Like many women I've spoken to, the reason Rodsky wants her husband to help figure out summer camp is not because doing stuff for her kids is inherently awful. Rather, Rodsky's concerned that if she does everything, the unequal distribution of care labor will get in the way of her sanity and professional work and, equally important, her husband will miss out. The men she has worked with don't always see this at first, but over time many catch on and see the beauty in working with their child on a school project or holding their child's hand at a doctor's appointment. "When we talk about care as chores it can sometimes seem as though care is the worst thing in the world," she said. "But caring for other beings is literally the existential reason we are alive, and we can help men see that and what it takes."

SOURCE MATERIAL

The care bias that has haunted me the most is the one among creative circles. This is where my vanity lies. Can a woman be an artist and a mother? I may not have ambition in the Sandbergian sense, but I do find great meaning and a big chunk of my identity in creative expression. Not only do I want to think this is possible as a caregiver; I'd also like more recognition of the ways in which it is an advantage to care and create. While caregiving limits my time, it has dramatically expanded the range of answers I have to the eternal questions of how a person should be and what a life should look like.

What a relief it's been to hear more and more writers and artists talk about care as an opening and see this in their work. "I feel really nourished by stories of how they can feed each other rather than being these warring gods, motherhood and art," explained the writer Leslie Jamison in an interview on Artnet. "On a creative level, I feel like becoming a mother has totally deepened and expanded my writing practice. It's opened me up to thinking about caregiving as a subject with a new kind of focus, and not just caregiving within the boundaries of a parent/child relationship, but also thinking about it in broader ways, too." This reminds me of Brandi Carlile's song "The Mother," which deals with a subject that has been conspicuously absent in popular music. In it, she mourns the end of her independence, before exploring the "wonders" she will experience with and through her daughter. Success, she concludes, would not happen without her daughter. We aren't told explicitly what kind of success she is referring to, whether professional or familial, and I like to think that is the point. Carlile is blurring the lines around what it means to make it in "the big time," as she puts it. We, the mothers, the listeners, get to decide that on our own.

Atalya Laufer, a Berlin-based Israeli visual artist, likes to create art in response to the work of others. In the past, she's engaged in imagined dialogues with visual artists and writers, dead and alive.

In the winter of 2022, she showed up at a family-friendly artist residency in Berkeley, California, where, for five months, she would live rent-free in a Craftsman bungalow and receive a weekly stipend and childcare support. In the morning she or her husband, Daniel, would take turns bicycling their four-year-old daughter, Esther, to preschool, after which Atalya would retreat to the studio and begin to work.

As for what she would do in the studio, initially she had no idea. The plan was to take in Berkeley, visit museums, meet interesting people, read history books, and find, like she had always found, that one person to set her off on a project. She went through the steps, engaged in her process, but not a single artist was as compelling to her as little

Esther. This feeling, to her surprise, was first met with hesitancy and then fear.

Motherhood is a taboo subject for artists. Not a sexy taboo, a foray into the transgressive, but a patriarchal decree in which motherhood is inherently mawkish and devoid of compelling friction or universal insights. Work with motherhood and Atalya risked taking on that dreaded thing, a hyphenated identity like "mother-artist," or some such moniker reserved for those whose work is tethered to a particular subject matter and not otherwise worthy on its own merits. Atalya didn't want to be a mother-artist. She wanted to be an artist-artist, who explored children and motherhood. And she knew that whatever it was she created wouldn't be what those hyphenators thought it would be. The work she'd make would bear tension, pain, an atmosphere of the vulnerability and uncertainty she felt every day as a mother and which she wanted to transmute into her art.

"There is a sense that working with motherhood means that motherhood took over your identity. It is uncool. But, at the same time, of course having a child changed my life. And so I thought, Do I want to be authentic with myself? Because working with Esther's drawings was really interesting to me," she told me.

Like many of her preschool-aged peers, Esther's work had something otherworldly about it, the rainbows, flowers, and smiling suns executed with the swirling effect of an acid trip, or a prophetic vision foretold on a high peak. "She was at that point where she was in between abstract work and figuration, and there was something so interesting in that. She was so free."

Esther's work contained a sweetness and hope, but more than that there was a primary knowledge, a spiritual possession, evinced by it. There is an old Jewish myth that children are born with all the knowledge in the world, but then an angel comes and presses on their lips—*shhh*—and erases this knowledge. The philtrum, that biologically mysterious little indentation above the lip, is the mark. Some believe that it takes a few years for our children to fully forget everything, and so this knowledge lingers until their conscious minds take over, super-egos develop, and they forget.

Atalya began sorting through the art Esther made every day and choosing pieces that she would redraw in her own hand. Sometimes she would work on top of Esther's work, or collage both her and Esther's work together. Occasionally, Esther would have feedback about colors and shapes, and Atalya enjoyed these conversations. Other times, Esther would draw on Atalya's art, art that Esther felt some ownership over since it was based on her work. Atalya really didn't like that. She wanted the connection she shared with her daughter through art making, but she wanted separation too.

Over time, this process became part artistic exercise and part psychological journey. "She is my child and we are so close, and I was exploring these boundaries between us, and through that I began to realize that boundaries are a big deal for me and my art," she said. "It became a process of figuring out what is mine and what is hers. And acknowledging the fact that we inspire one another and are together, but still have our own lives and that is important."

While the hazy precariousness of boundaries is complicated for all caregivers, it was particularly so for Atalya. She grew up on a kibbutz in Israel where, in the name of achieving a collective existence, children slept in different houses from their parents starting from three months old. Family time was limited to around three hours in the afternoon. The rest of the day children spent with childcare workers, teachers, and their peers.

Atalya entered parenthood knowing she didn't want to replicate her childhood for her daughter. Her boldest and least subtle attempt to break with her past was co-sleeping with Esther every night since the day she was born. There would be no children's house, or even, in a way, a children's bed, in her home. Esther had her own bed but has only slept there a handful of times since birth. This closeness, the chubby, damp hand on the blanket, the unsteady rhythms of a child's nocturnal breath, were sweet. But the risk of Atalya's being crowded out of her own bed, her own life, was always present.

When Atalya returned to Berlin from Berkeley, she had a gallery show of the series of art she created. She named it Ma. Besides being a word we use for mothers, "ma" also sounds like the Hebrew word for questioning, translating to "what," "why," or "how much." Ma is also the name of the Japanese concept for the in-between space, whether the distance between two objects in a drawing or the emotional space between two people.

In her work, one can see a mother—though really the better word to use here would be "artist"—trying to get to know her child, and a mother trying to get to know herself. Sometimes Esther's art inspired large-scale black-and-white printed collages that contain more mystery and uncertainty than their source work. Other times, they inspired colorful dreamscapes, a sense of freedom and escape. Altogether, they are a study of the boundaries, the "ma," that intrigued Atalya, boundaries that she will never fully make sense of, but that's okay. The point isn't clarity but to keep dancing the dance that is one of the central dances of our lives. To understand ourselves in relation to others.

Atalya chose not to include any of Esther's art in her gallery show, but she did invite her to the opening. Immediately after Esther arrived, she saw the microphone and asked her mom if she could sing. Esther fell in love with a pop singer's version of "Hallelujah" while spending time on YouTube a few years back, and has looked for opportunities to perform it ever since.

Atalya said no. It felt risky enough to "out" herself as an artist who explores motherhood. No need to make this a cutesy kid thing. Esther, who in her five years had managed to create her own firm boundaries from her mom, felt as though she had her own, dissenting artistic vision. Toward the end of the night, Esther walked on the stage and began, to Atalya's chagrin, to sing. First, terror. But then that subsided as the attendees seemed okay with it. Even, somehow, the extremely cool gallery manager was not above enjoying it. Could Atalya still be the artist, even with Esther behind the mic? "It's not a cry that you hear at night / It's not somebody who has seen the light," Esther sang. You know the rest. Cold, broken—imperfect. But nevertheless, Hallelujah.

In the work of Atalya and these other culture makers I see an opening, a beautifully jagged crack in the glass door. Internally, sometimes subconsciously, they are rejecting the fiction that care can only take away from one's ability to fully engage in the world, or be a real artist. They are proof that it is possible for people to desire time to care and time to create, and that both activities can feed each other, often for the better. It's an exchange that begs for a metaphor, something involving light refracting and bending, illuminating new patterns and dimensions. Or maybe it is water, two bodies of water, which feed into each other and balance each other should they get too full or too empty. Currents that come together to form new patterns, dimensions, ripples, and directions that our care-ignorant, dependency-phobic culture has yet to experience.

This is at the heart of a feminism, my feminism, fueled by care. It's a mixture of reshaping the world so it accommodates the many women who are caregivers and reshaping our collective consciousness to acknowledge the fact that care is a worthwhile, profound experience that deserves our attention and curiosity. This curiosity promises to lead to more respect for caregivers, as the fullness of the experience is explored. And, I hope, a long overdue openness to the internal complexity and ambivalence surrounding care. We'll be less hard on ourselves when care feels hard because we will understand that care should be hard and there is no one way to do it. Those broken glass doors will reveal the love and the mess not only of our homes but also of our minds and hearts, all while we make our way through care. The messes aren't failures, but signs that authentic care is taking place.

Psychoanalyst Rozsika Parker wrote about the ill effects of denying these psychological messes, encouraging mothers to "own the malice, the hostility, the exasperation, the fury and dislike they feel—maybe only for a fleeting moment—towards their own children." When these feelings produce shame in the mother, though this applies to all caregivers, "a cycle can get going in which hatred really does end up outweighing love. The mother feels a bad, unnatural mother, her shame mounts and soon the child is perceived as nothing more than a guilt-inducing, hateful persecutor." But when ambivalence becomes an accepted part of the experience, our capacity to care deepens and love has a stronger chance of winning.

Of all the gifts my mother gave me, knowledge of what Parker describes is the best one. She never hid her ambivalence—not about whether she should have had us, but instead about how she felt about us—which was never long-lasting. We knew when she couldn't stand us, when she needed space, when we pissed her off. This might sound a bit much to those of you who grew up in quieter homes, but in our loud and blunt Jewish household it was reassuring. To yell is to love, as my friend Yael, who grew up in a similar environment, put it. The temporary lapses in affection made it so we felt like we really knew her and therefore could trust her. We knew that when she told us she loved us, when she got in bed with us and held us and laughed with us, she really meant it, and that those sporadic moments of frustration and anger were a small part of a bigger, unconditional tether, a love pact that could withstand her moments of ambivalence. She permitted herself complexity as a mother, and, relatedly I believe, she permitted us complexity as children. As a result, she never fell for overly prescriptive parenting advice when figuring out how to parent us. Each one of her four children were, in her eyes, their own people with their own sets of strengths and weaknesses. Each frustrated and delighted her in different ways, and each of us needed a different parent in return.

On top of this, she was emotionally unconflicted about the fifteen years she took off from her career to dedicate herself to raising her children. There was no ideology behind this, no conscious attempt to redefine feminism and place stay-at-home moms at the center of the narrative. In fact, my mom never entirely embraced feminism because of the sense that it was anti-motherhood. She didn't view her life in political terms, or believe that her day-to-day existence should prove a larger point. Rather, she was a woman who opened herself up to the possibilities of care, and, as she sees it, got so much in return. When she returned to work when I was fifteen, achieving success fairly quickly, she didn't feel as though the work was a reward for the time spent with her children, or that she finally had something to tout as an accomplishment. Both her job and her family were measures of her ambition, signs of her success.

These days when my mom calls me she is far more interested in my caregiving life than my professional life. She wants to know how the kids are doing, how I am doing, and if I have enough help. She wants to know what's hard and easy, right and wrong, the petty and the heavy, all at once. Sometimes I remind her I work too. "I just published something in the *New York Times*, isn't that great, Mom?" or, "A story I wrote got tweeted by a celebrity," some big name we both know and respect. She loves that too, but, in her vision of ambition the care wins out. It's the thing to work hard at, and to be proud of in moments of struggle and moments of joy. I get mad at her for this, again and again; her lack of interest in my career is a leitmotif of our mother-daughter fights. Still, to regularly experience ambition through her eyes and believe that caring well for another is a significant achievement, a mark of distinction, and good for all those who are willing to strive for its attainment is a gift. One that I've come to gratefully receive.

CHAPTER TWO

Social Housekeepers

When Women Embraced Care

Care hasn't always been a four-letter word among feminists and women's rights activists. There is a lesser-known feminist history, one that I never encountered in women's studies courses or in mainstream feminist writing of the early twentieth century, filled with women, often Black, who valued the breaking down of glass doors as much as they did that of glass ceilings. They saw a world in which care was not a hindrance to gender equality and women's empowerment, but a potential asset. Something to be proud of, and something to fight for.

One such woman was Rheta Childe Dorr, a white suffragist who had all the markings of a contemporary feminist icon. Born in Omaha, Nebraska, in 1866, she married young, had a child, and then soon realized that Victorian motherhood was not for her. At age thirty-two, she left her husband and moved herself and her young son to New York City where she took up journalism. She'd go on, as noted in her *New York Times* obituary, to advocate for the women's vote, write five books, and take numerous reporting trips to Europe, covering major events like World War I and the Russian Revolution. But while her biography might make her sound like the kind of woman who belongs on a *Forbes* magazine "100 Most Powerful Women" list, her writing, to the contemporary ear, at least, does not. In her 1910 book *What Eight Million Women Want*, she wrote:

> Woman's place is in the home. This is a platitude which no woman will ever dissent from, provided two words are dropped out of it. Woman's place is Home. Her task is homemaking. Her talents, as a rule, are mainly for homemaking. But Home is not contained within the four walls of an individual home. Home is the community. The city full of people is the Family. The public school is the real Nursery. And badly do the Home and the Family and the Nursery need their mother.

With these words, and while she never described it this way, Dorr is smashing glass doors. The expertise women gain in caring for all that takes place within our homes has immense value in the world outside our homes. Care is a necessary ingredient in public and private life, she argues.

Another was Mary Church Terrell, born in 1863, a Black racial justice activist and suffragist who saw motherhood and domestic know-how as a resource and a strength. Terrell came from a uniquely privileged upbringing for a Black woman of her age. Her father, Robert Reed Church, went from being enslaved to becoming a successful entrepreneur and businessman. Because of this wealth, Terrell had opportunities denied to the vast majority of her peers. She earned a bachelor's and master's degree from Oberlin, and then went on to a life dedicated to political organizing. She helped found the National Association of Colored Women, where, as president, her mission was to raise up Black people through raising up Black women and care. This was far more challenging to do for Black women, since the broader culture didn't see them as being inherently virtuous, domestic, or in possession of great moral insights from their experience as lovingly devoted homemakers—like their white counterparts.

What Dorr, Terrell, and other similarly minded suffragists of the time were fighting for was not the right to be more like men, but an ability to be like women—and by "women" they really meant caregivers—and fully engage with the world. More specifically, they wanted their domestically honed caring skills to spill over to their participation in public life and, ultimately, their vote. Care, they believed, belonged everywhere, not just at home.

Yes, by today's lights, there are problems here. Which women, and whose care, exactly? The servants? Factory girls? Or only the middle- to upper-class ladies of the house who could claim authority as care-givers? On the other hand, what if a woman excelled at work as a saleswoman or mathematician or engineer? Did her insights matter too? More upsetting were the many white suffragists, including some of the biggest names, who were only concerned with securing the vote for fellow white women. As a result, Black suffragists often had to go it alone.

Still, this approach worked. The passing of the Nineteenth Amend-ment in 1920—which afforded the right to vote to all white women and some Black women, depending on where they lived—was not solely based on the argument that women were the same as men. In-stead, many activists presented women's entrance into voting booths, public spaces, and halls of power as necessary for what they brought to the table as caregivers.

The need for this gendered special sauce goes back to the early days of the United States, when the founders imagined a country in which men would be free to act in their own self-interest. However, even the founders knew that there is such a thing as too much independence, and so they cast women in the opposing role: providers of selfless care. Men were the lead actors; women supported them behind the scenes. Men were reason; women were virtue. Men were public; women were domestic and therefore private. And so it remained until around the end of the nineteenth century when women and womanly virtues began to appear in public and political settings where they were welcome as long as they didn't directly challenge men and continued to bolster male independence.

Women's entry into public life happened largely through clubs, social and political organizations where they relied on their reputation as caregivers to advocate for change. They organized job and homemaking training and support for other, poorer women, fought for universal childcare, and organized their own kindergartens and nurseries. Black women also took on Jim Crow laws and the criminal justice system, all from the distinct point of view as mothers and homemakers. Overall, some of these activists' causes, including their fight against sex work and alcohol consumption, are less sympathetic today—while others, as in the case of those who supported eugenics, are unforgivable. But many, including separate prisons for women and juveniles, public playgrounds, labor regulations for children, clean water, better sewage, kindergartens, pensions for poor mothers, and oversight of food and drugs, are things we've come to expect from a responsible government. In time, this organizing led to increased support for the women's vote, as more and more women and men recognized how women and their perspectives should be represented in the electorate. Women like Dorr and Terrell, social housekeepers, or municipal housekeepers as they were also called, fought for suffrage because, as Dorr herself said, "Home is not contained within the four walls of an individual home."

Is it possible they were wearing the cloak of femininity in order to Trojan horse themselves into political power? Consciously or subconsciously, men didn't want to have to compete with women, nor did they want to be replaced, so the activists had to sell themselves as different and yet still useful. "I don't know if we can ever know for sure," historian Paula Baker, who's studied this period of feminist history, told me. "But I'm hesitant to call people in the past insincere." Historical records make it hard to believe that they all were putting it on for the sake of men. And how cynical does it make us to assume total insincerity? How little faith would we have in the moral reckoning and skill building that come by way of care to cast doubt? Wouldn't our world be a better place if we eschewed our independence and saw our communities and civic life as more of a home?

And the work of women like Dorr and Terrell paid off. They turned the country into a more caring place, raising our expectations of what a nation should take responsibility for. By the 1920s, due to a mix of success and failure, the social housekeeping movement had begun to fade away. Success: Their care agenda was incorporated into a mainstream progressive agenda, and women got the vote. Feminists of the Roaring Twenties began to explore what life might be like if they loosened women's tether to the home and family to get a taste of long-deserved independence. Failure: Sexism lingered, and women realized they would only get so far demanding equality from men by emphasizing difference. The social housekeeper's vision of motherhood, in which care could heal society's wounds, didn't stop mainstream culture from viewing motherhood as a biological imperative that forced women to depend on, and need protection from, men.

Historian Eileen Boris observed this in a paper she wrote on the subject: "Instead, the concept of women as mothers or potential mothers justified limiting women's labor market options without elevating the value of motherhood or nurturing."

Over the course of the twentieth century, the notion that a woman could be radical and invested in caregiving, and that those two identities may entwine, began to fade, until, eventually, many mainstream feminists forgot such a thing was possible. "So much of the women's movement ends up being written out of the history of feminism," Baker told me. We've forgotten about care as a guiding ethic, a driver for activism, as well as the fact that without care there would be no activism. "The day-to-day work of maintaining communities is what made their level of activism possible."

Inspired by the social housekeepers, I went in search of other times care was seen as a feminist objective rather than an impediment. There was, in the mid-1970s, a large, and nearly successful, fight for universal childcare in the United States—part of an effort to publicly acknowledge the value of care and support caregivers. Feminists were a major force in the lobbying effort behind 1971's Comprehensive Child Development Act, which would have led to childcare for all. Initially, they persuaded President Nixon to join their side. He told Congress in 1969: "So crucial is the matter of early growth that we must make a national commitment to providing all American children an opportunity for healthful and stimulating development during the first five years of life." But conservatives painted the effort as communist and Nixon, in an about-face for the sake of political preservation, went on to veto it.

Universal childcare "would commit the vast moral authority of the National Government to the side of communal approaches to child rearing over against the family-centered approach," he said. It's a classic argument in favor of glass doors, yet another endorsement of the myth that communal support for caregivers and an intimate family bond are inevitably at odds. Following this defeat, mainstream feminists largely moved on from advocating for support for caregivers in favor of causes like reproductive and workplace rights.

A year after the defeat of the Comprehensive Child Development Act, a group of radical Marxist feminists launched a "Wages for

Housework" campaign, calling for remuneration for domestic labor. For them, the struggle to get care and housework acknowledged was necessary for the undoing of capitalism and the power hierarchies created by the existence of unpaid domestic labor. The voices of this movement advocated for caregivers, but they didn't always have the nicest things to say about care itself. Silvia Federici, a founder of the movement, called housework "the most pervasive manipulation, the most subtle and mystified violence that capitalism has ever perpetrated against any section of the working class." Still, they were effective in reminding the Far Left to consider the home alongside the factory floor when reimagining the redistribution of wealth, and reminding mainstream feminists that reproductive rights should move beyond abortion and consider the politics of reproduction more broadly, including who can have children, how they can have children, and what conditions raising children takes place in.

One of the most notable, and personally inspiring, examples of care being integrated into women's liberation can be found in the work of a number of 1970s-era Black women's activists, who oriented much of their fight around the right to care for themselves, their families, and their communities. For them, women's liberation wasn't an escape from care but an attempt to integrate care into a life of stability and meaning.

If you were a white woman during much of the twentieth century, popular culture and government policies conspired to convince you that care and domesticity were your destiny, an irrefutable happily-ever-after. If you were a Black woman during much of the twentieth century, popular culture and government policies conspired to convince you that your caregiving and domesticity weren't worth much. Most notably, there was that time when President Franklin Delano Roosevelt signed unemployment insurance and Social Security into existence in 1935 as part of the New Deal. Excluded from the act were agricultural workers and domestic workers, many of whom were Black.

The work of Black nannies, the women caring for America's white children, just wasn't seen as worthy of support.

Black mothers caring for their own children didn't fare much better. Early twentieth-century welfare policies discriminated against Black women, who were expected to work outside the home. Even when these jobs took everything out of one, body and soul, on a daily basis, and barely paid enough to feed one's family. For these reasons and more, gender liberation looked different for Black women and their white working-class companions. Many of the women on top fought for the right to work. Many of the women on the bottom fought for the right to care.

This radical care activism appeared in leftist manifestos, like one essay titled "The Capitalist System's Family: An Analysis by Four 16-Year-Old Young Women—Overthrowing New Structures." It was published in the book *Lessons from the Damned: Class Struggle in the Black Community*, authored by "the damned," published in 1973:

> [W]e see the beginnings of a new kind of family, a family with mothers who put children first, brothers who love women like they love themselves. . . .We will be the rebirth of mothers. We are now going through a long and hard struggle that may last for many, many years. The old mothers will not give in so easily. But it is the time in history for the rebirth of mothers who are lovers, who will raise lovers, who will raise young women and men who can give without fear and without greed for self.

I've come across so many radical, utopian political texts that degrade or completely ignore family life, in favor of impersonal visions that focus on cooperation among members of society at large. But this time, a goal of economic equality is not anonymous harmony but intimate love, particularly love among mothers who can care well, and raise children who can care well, setting off a multigenerational feed-back loop of care. The harmony, these writers understand, starts with the intimate love.

Radical care also appeared in the 1960s and '70s welfare movement, which was driven by tens of thousands of mostly Black women, who wanted the means to be able to properly care for, and love, their chil-dren and their neighborhoods. Beginning in the 1970s, Ronald Reagan and others from the Left and Right made "welfare" a dirty word, ac-cusing the lazy (and by "lazy" Reagan and others meant Black moms) of trying to siphon off the state. But really, these women were just fighting to be able to do the kinds of things that white married women are often praised for doing by social conservatives: spending time with their kids, helping them with their homework, cooking a nutritious Sunday supper—family values.

Welfare activist Johnnie Tillmon was born in Scott, Arkansas. She was a sharecropper's daughter, who spent her late childhood and young adult years working in the cotton fields and washing clothes for a white man, according to historian Premilla Nadasen. In 1959, at age thirty-three, the then single mom moved to Los Angeles with her children to be with two of her brothers; most of her family in Arkansas had died. In Los Angeles she ironed shirts in a laundry and organized for better conditions as a union shop steward.

Four years later, she got sick and ended up in the hospital. A neigh-bor suggested she apply for welfare, but Tillmon resisted at first. Her reasoning: She wasn't lazy. But eventually she went through with it, out of concern for her teenage daughter who needed extra attention. Once she was in the system, Tillmon found the welfare agency's treat-ment of recipients overly intrusive and dehumanizing. Women were disqualified from welfare if they had a man in their lives or made extra income; caseworkers would make house visits and dig through all their belongings in a hunt for a sign of either man or money. She started organizing to increase benefits and make welfare a more humane process, first locally, then nationally. Plucky and charismatic, she eventually became the chairperson of the National Welfare Rights Organization, leading roughly thirty thousand women in the fight for government assistance.

"As far as I'm concerned, the ladies of NWRO are the frontline troops of women's freedom. Both because we have so few illusions and because our issues are so important to all women—the right to a living wage for women's work, the right to life itself," she wrote in her best-known piece of writing, "Welfare Is a Women's Issue," which appeared in *Ms.* magazine in 1972.

MOTHERWORK

In addition to the work of Tillmon and other Black women's advocates, sociologist Patricia Hill Collins has identified a type of activism she calls motherwork. It refers to ways in which Black women care for their communities, labor necessary for their survival. These include the tradition of Black doulas and midwives who ensure Black babies and moms get the care they need, which a racist medical industry isn't likely to provide, as well as informal collectives and coalitions aimed at making sure everyone's needs are being met. "'Motherwork' goes beyond ensuring the survival of members of one's family. This type of motherwork recognizes that individual survival, empowerment, and identity require group survival, empowerment, and identity," writes Collins in her essay "Shifting the Center: Race, Class, and Feminist Theorizing About Motherhood."

This shouldn't, Collins warns, mean caregivers have to be in charge of everything. Black mothers have a lot of cultural expectations freighted upon them, one of which is the "superstrong Black mother." But the unfair pressure to be strong doesn't discount the ways in which motherwork, or the sharing of care responsibilities among friends and families, strengthens lives and communities and inspires Black women to improve the world.

When the COVID-19 pandemic began, Melissa Barber, a Black woman, single mom, trained doctor, and resident of the South Bronx, checked in on her neighbors. She wanted to help them navigate job loss, fear, illness, or whatever else they might have been dealing with while simultaneously figuring out a system through which neighbors could help one another stay resilient and healthy. For Barber, health care, individual care, community care, and activism all blur together. Healing and change take networks, people who trust one another and work hard to understand everyone's needs.

So, in addition to her full-time job as a program director for a non-profit, and her efforts to take care of and advocate for her epileptic and autistic daughter, Barber began organizing. She distributed pain medicine, masks, and gloves and directed individuals toward testing sites and, later, vaccination sites. Also, she facilitated distributions of food for several families in her building and community, as well as a large food donation to one of the local mutual aid groups. On top of that, she conducted research by looking at how her community fared, with the intention of learning how they can best help one another in the next crisis. "For me, this is all very organic," Barber told me about her instinct to care for her community. "I can see why people might put labels on it, but for me, it's just what I do."

Five years ago, Barber and four other Black moms created Mott Haven Mamas, a group named after their neighborhood. Today they have roughly twenty members and meet every first Monday of the month, usually at a neighborhood restaurant. When they get together, the conversations cover their personal lives and also how they can best support one another and their community. "It's a mixture of activism, fun, and release," she said. Sometimes they tell funny stories. Sometimes they share stories of police brutality. Regularly, they share their needs as moms and brainstorm ways to help one another. Who is struggling with breastfeeding? Who could use a home-cooked meal they don't have to cook themselves? A few years ago, they realized that a number of neighborhood moms had childcare needs that weren't being met. Together, they created a child daycare co-op and hired one of the moms who was a care provider to babysit and educate some of the children.

In 2021, Barber had her birthday party at Maria Solá, a community garden that is stewarded by South Bronx Unite and some of the Mott Haven Mamas. "I told all the moms they had to learn a new line dance my cousin told me about. We spent the night learning that and doing the electric slide and other new line dances, having fun, having drinks, and talking," she said. "We also made sure to check in and see what COVID was doing to everybody."

This all seems so intuitive to me, and yet foreign at the same time when I think about it in the context of women's liberation as I've experienced it. For the Mott Haven Mamas, care is both a guiding ethic and an objective; care is what they want to see more of in the world, and they help bring this about through care. The answer to so many of the burdens of care is more care. Not giving up on care because care is inherently awful, or blaming caregivers who feel crushed by its demands, but caring for the caregivers who were tricked into thinking they should care on their own.

If I had been exposed to this before becoming a parent, I would have been far less nervous about care overwhelming my sense of self because I would have understood that care, especially when you go it on your own, will, undoubtedly, at some point, overwhelm your sense of self, physically, emotionally, or both. I would have realized that just as my children are dependent on me, so am I dependent on my wider networks. Gone would be the fantasy that care was something I could keep apart from the rest of my life, that it was something I would quietly do on my own while my public-facing self maintained her creative and intellectual street cred. With those glass doors down, I could admit that I, as a caregiver, needed help too. I'd see how despite all my talk about interdependence when it came to my relationship with my children, when it came to me, my life, and how I related to everyone else who wasn't my children, I was still in thrall to the myth of my own independence.

QUEER MOTHERHOOD

In her book *Of Woman Born*, poet and essayist Adrienne Rich explores the difference between the institution of motherhood and the potential of motherhood when experienced outside that institution. "To destroy the institution is not to abolish motherhood," she explains. "It is to release the creation and sustenance of life into the same realm of decision, struggle, surprise, imagination, and conscious intelligence, as any other difficult, but freely chosen work." Just one of many brilliant concepts in her feminist motherhood masterpiece, one that I wish I had read a long time ago.

This institution Rich speaks of was a largely mid-century, two-parent, two-car-garage version of domesticity conceived of with white, straight, and cisgendered women in mind. Women of color, as I've already discussed, were not included in the dominant culture's vision of motherhood, and nor were the lesbian, nonbinary, and trans parents who didn't fit into the heteronormative box. These mothers, some of whom don't necessarily call themselves mothers, had to advocate to be seen as mothers even if they didn't fit into the institution.

Acceptance required a large-scale legal and political struggle, one that took years. LGBTQ+ activists had to fight for the right to adopt children or be legally classified as parents while self-identifying as gay. The first out gay adoption took place in 1978 in New York, and from there on out it was a battle that progressed in fits and starts all the way until 2017, when the Supreme Court ruled in favor of same-sex marriage, making it so both members of gay married couples could be listed on their children's birth certificates and legally recognized as co-parents from the first day of their children's lives.

Alongside this legal fight, queer parents set off a softer revolution, which is still very much taking place. By not fitting into the institution of motherhood, as Rich put it, these male, female, trans, and nonbinary parents have had the freedom to explore the potential of parenthood without the baggage of heteronormative 1950s sitcom life and find new ways to approach it. In her book *The Queer Parent's Primer*, writer Stephanie A. Brill tells her readers that the queer community "has the opportunity to totally reinvent what family means to us, who is in our family, how we would like to go about having children, and how we would like to go about raising those children."

I've seen a freedom among LGBTQ+ parents that I haven't witnessed among my straight friends or in writing by straight parents, a willingness to approach parenthood as a wonder or process rather than a checklist, and reject the parts that don't work for them. In Maggie Nelson's book *The Argonauts*, the queer writer navigates her pregnancy and her partner's gender transition (by way of testosterone injections from female to a more masculine, butch identity), contemplating what makes any one act normal and another radical. "What about my pregnancy?" Nelson writes. "Is that inherently heteronormative? . . . How can an experience so profoundly strange and wild and transformative also symbolize or enact the ultimate conformity?" Through fragmented writing about her fragmented identity, she concludes that pregnancy is not straight but queer. Gestating a child has undone her, renewed her, broken her apart, and put her back together. This brings her a vision of caregiving and family life that not only is more forgiving of our endlessly fragmented selves but actually relies on it. These fragments are how we achieve intimacy and self-knowledge.

When she was growing up, Natalie Martinez's identity never quite made sense to her. She was raised "very liberal Catholic, educated, progressive, but still with the foundational traditions." Her biological mother had a Latinx surname. Her biological father was a mystery. Her adopted mother was white. Her adopted father was also Latinx, but he didn't like to talk about it. She came and lived with them in San Jose, California, as a nine-month-old baby, and she was raised surrounded mostly by white people, attending mostly white Catholic schools from preschool all the way through college.

Even her process of coming out, which for many is a line-in-the-sand moment identity-wise, came with its vagaries. When she told the female dean at her Catholic high school that she had feelings for girls, feelings she didn't think she should be having, the dean did not chastise her or suggest anything like conversion therapy. Instead, she looked right into Natalie's eyes and declaratively told her she wasn't alone. The innuendo wasn't subtle. Natalie immediately realized that this woman was gay, as were a number of other members of the faculty. They neither declared it nor hid it. "It was just not something we talked about," Natalie told me. For a couple of years, she followed suit.

What they did talk about at school was the Catholic tradition's rigid definition of family life, and what it means to be a self-actualized woman: "There are certain rules you must follow. You can't get away from the dogma. When you get to a certain age you must meet a boy, get married, and have little babies." But what if you don't want the boy, but you do want the baby? Which Natalie, deep in her heart, wanted, unrelated—as far as she could tell—to the pressures of the hetero-normative patriarchy. "I always knew I wanted to have kids; that felt very authentic. But I had no idea how."

She graduated from college, contemplated being a minister or an academic, decided to work in the nonprofit sector instead, fell in love with a woman at work, married her, and together they set up home in Berkeley, California. Doctors determined that her wife's body would be more capable of getting pregnant than Natalie's, so the two decided to let her be the birth mother. Having a baby as a lesbian couple is already complicated enough.

When her wife got pregnant quickly, Natalie was elated about her wife's pulsing womb all while mourning her own still one. That's not to say Natalie's body didn't also undergo a transformation to prepare for the baby. In the months leading up to their baby's due date, Natalie pumped her breasts every two hours with the hope that she and her wife would be able to co-breastfeed. Natalie ended up making just enough milk for a single feed—the first of her daughter's life.

What followed were other moments of creativity, boundary blurring not possible among heterosexual couples: "With us, there was no clear path when it came to how to be parents. It felt like nobody had talked about so much of this before." This was scary. Learning on the job is hard enough with a small child, even when you follow all of the institution of motherhood's, as Rich would put it, script. To feel like both your kid is terra incognita and you, as a mother married to another mother, are also terra incognita was rough. Sometimes Natalie and her wife fell back on stereotypes to get through the day. Natalie, the self-described more masculine partner, takes out the trash, kills the spiders, and roughhouses with her daughter—activities she sees as masculine-leaning. Her wife, the self-described more feminine partner, does the laundry, sits quietly with her daughter, and reads her books: "Some of this has to do with playing to our strengths. But, on the other hand, it doesn't matter who you sleep with; gender norms creep into your homes." Other times Natalie feels more liberated, free to experiment with the structures of family life and who she is as a partner: "Sometimes I call myself a parent. Sometimes I call myself a mother. It doesn't follow any binary construct. I can be hard and soft at the same time. If you are a man, you can get in trouble for being too soft. If you are a woman, you can get in trouble for being too hard. But I feel I can move in between, and be who my child needs at the moment." It's not possible to care for herself, her child, and the world without embracing this fluidity, Natalie and other lesbian moms understand. It's a fluidity they had to fight hard for, and one that all caregivers, no matter how we identify or who we sleep with, can gain from embracing.

"It is precisely because the lesbian *is* different that a value system bent on prescribing a limited sense of possibilities for women can neither tolerate nor affirm her. . . . The power of difference is the power of the very plenitude of creation, the exhilarating variance of nature," Rich wrote in *Of Woman Born*, published in 1976. This was the same year she published the chapbook *Twenty-One Love Poems*, through which she effectively came out as a lesbian. Her radical thoughts on motherhood appear to have coincided with her evolving queer identity, and I suspect the two were related. Her queerness allowed her to queer motherhood, and we all reaped the benefits as a result.

"No one has imagined us. We want to live like trees, / sycamores blazing through the sulfuric air, / dappled with scars, still exuberantly budding, / our animal passion rooted in the city," she writes in one of the love poems. In it, Rich is speaking of lovers, but I think it applies to mothers and caregivers too. No one imagined who we could be, how we could rise, and how we could root, if we could define our conditions, and make up the rules, ourselves.

CHAPTER THREE

A New Man

On the Rise of Male Caregivers and How Care Changes Men

DOMESTICATED

In spring 2015, a group of researchers set out to recruit roughly twelve hundred men from communities around Rwanda to participate in a domestic violence prevention program. They had to be between the ages of twenty-one and thirty-five, married or cohabitating, the father of a child under the age of five or expecting a child, and be willing to attend weekly sessions on fatherhood, parenting, and couple relations, including topics like sharing household tasks. Learn all this, the researchers predicted, and the men might be less inclined to use violence against their wives.

Interventions for reducing domestic violence generally aren't paired with teaching men how to be more active at home and do more domestic labor. Instead, the issues are often thought of as separate. First, let's stop men from hitting their wives. Then, later, we can think about getting them to sweep and change diapers. But as far as the team behind the intervention saw it, the hitting and lack of sweeping and diapering were all connected.

"These types of interventions sometimes get critiqued, with people telling us that we shouldn't focus on care and just focus on violence. Working with men on care is a nice thing to do, they say, but not the priority," Kate Doyle, a researcher and program director who worked on the project on behalf of Promundo, an organization dedicated to achieving gender equality through engagement with boys and men, told me. "But these approaches work because they do multiple things at once so men start to think about their families and gender more holistically. If you took away the care aspect, we don't think we would have had the impact we did."

The men enrolled in the program were required to take fifteen classes over the course of several months, during which they learned to take on more of the cooking and cleaning, better communicate with their partners, and care for their children. By the end of the intervention, they improved in a number of measurable ways. These men became more hands-on dads, helped more around the house, and were less violent toward their wives. At a twenty-one-month follow-up, there were significantly fewer incidences of domestic violence and sexual violence in the homes of the men who went through the program as compared to a control group of men who did not. When researchers returned five years later, they found that the effects of these classes could still be observed. The men in the program continued to do more housework and childcare and were less violent toward their female partners.

While the project was not able to determine a measurable, causal link between how much care men did and how much less likely they were to hit their wives, many of the men reported a relationship between both. Through caregiving, men learned to empathize with their wives, felt closer to their children, and had more respect for the type of labor their wives did. Over time, their violent impulses diminished.

"They got to see what it is to be more involved with their children and partners. Just spending time together," Doyle said. "Many said that they appreciated how this intervention encouraged them to go home instead of going for a beer. They appreciated that they got to be involved in home life, and that their families wanted them there. And their wives and children would often tell us how nice it was that their husbands and fathers would come home after work and say hello and want to talk. Those tiny changes are connected to the biggest changes."

What was true for these men in Rwanda is, in the broadest sense, true for others around the world, including in the United States. Men can care, and are changed, often for the better, by care. In the past few decades, they've started doing more of it than ever, and revealing themselves to be quite capable in the process. It's been a quiet and slow-moving shift, not yet large enough to achieve gender equality but radical nevertheless. When men care, they are, consciously or not, engaging in a fundamental reconsideration of what it means to be a man and how men and women relate.

Historically speaking, the "ideal" American man, more myth than reality, is strong, dispassionate, competitive, and confident. He's the Marlboro Man, James Bond, the Quarterback, or any other of the archetypes of stoic, twentieth-century masculinity. He is in control, the rational one in the room. His meticulously systemizing brain works best when ooey, gooey emotions, with all their subjectivity and impulsiveness, are kept at bay. He is also a consummate task completer with a trophy wall to prove it, and therefore unsuited for the inefficiencies and imprecise workings of care.

Or, in the more recent model, he's the jokester. He's one of the guys from MTV's *Jackass*, or the president of that one fraternity whose parties you were either heavily encouraged to attend or discouraged from attending, depending on the source. The guy who is having too much fun to take anything seriously. The one whose sense of invincibility belies his deeply rooted denial that he, too, is a human who, like all other humans, needs and bleeds. Like the macho man of his grandfather's generation, vulnerability and dependence are anathema to his vision of masculinity.

And yet not a single man I've known intimately, not my father, brothers, nor husband, cut this figure. They're nervous, sensitive, irrational, emotional, and all experience the long-standing, fundamentally human, impulse that is the desire to connect and depend on others. And all in their own different ways, with their own different particularities, tendencies, neuroses, and tics. One loves gossip and openly struggles with anxiety, another loves to cuddle and if you are under a blanket on the couch he will get right in next to you and lay his head on your shoulder, another always leads with kindness, and another feels most himself when he is in a setting that permits his deep silliness. But none of them feel allowed to express these shadow selves, their softer, more vulnerable modes of being in the world at large. At hockey practice, or in Las Vegas, or in a business meeting, or in the company of men they don't know well, they must not only conceal these parts of themselves but also perform their absence. Only in the company of loved ones do they feel free shedding the skins of societally defined masculinity, and only in caregiving for their children or their parents does this tender side feel natural and shame-free.

Male-associated toughness has its place in care, but it is not enough to live only in this mode. Caring for others demands the ability to respond to another's tenderness with tenderness, a way of being rarely tolerated from men outside of care. The men I know have embraced care for many of the obvious reasons, like loving the people they care for and wanting to see them thrive. But less expected, less discussed, is the way that being a caregiver gives them a free pass to explore and embrace these non-macho selves and find a way to connect more deeply within and without. For my father, brothers, husband, male friends, the Rwandan men, and so many more, care is the place where it becomes okay to be, and become, more fully themselves.

THE RISE OF THE MALE CAREGIVER

"If you are a woman who has to constantly fight with her husband to get him to help with the kids or do housework, I am sure it is very frustrating. But, as a historian, if you step back and look at what men were not doing and refusing to do twenty or thirty years ago and compare that to what they are doing now—from a historical perspective it is quite a turnaround," Stephanie Coontz, a family studies historian, told me. This revolution was not fueled by will. There was no point in the past fifty years when men demanded to be able to do more care like women demanded to be able to do more paid work. It's hard to blame the men; as long as care and domestic life were demeaned, work and play outside the house praised, and the definition of masculinity limited to a narrow slice of the emotional spectrum that is antithetical to caregiving, why would they be drawn to care? Care and manliness were poles apart.

Today's men do more care than men have done in centuries, and, by some measures, ever in history. "Nothing has had more of an impact on men getting more involved in caregiving than women entering the workforce in greater numbers, especially in managerial and professional positions," Brad Harrington, executive director of the Boston College Center for Work & Family, explained to me. As women gained higher-status jobs and earned more money, there was less and less of an excuse for making them the default caregivers in any single household. Even if my husband resisted caregiving entirely, which, thankfully, he doesn't, the fact that I have professional obligations and we rely on two incomes makes it so he has to take care of his children more often than my dad did.

Over the past fifty years, fathers went from being distant authority figures in the household to more hands-on caregivers. A 2016 study of parents in eleven Western nations found that twenty-first-century fathers spend more time with their kids than those in previous generations. Mothers are also spending more time with their children, but the increase is larger among dads. In 1965, mothers spent an average of 54 minutes a day on childcare and care-related activities according to this cross-national study. In 2012, that number rose to 104 minutes a day. By comparison, the time dads spend with kids has quadrupled. In 1965, dads spent an average of 16 minutes caring for their kids a day. In 2012, the average was 59 minutes. Other research has found that the number of stay-at-home dads who stay home specifically to care for their family, rather than because they are out of work or have a disability, has increased considerably. Some of these are half of a same-sex couple with kids, a type of family whose numbers have grown exponentially in recent decades, as legal barriers to gay parenthood eroded and social acceptance of gay relationships has risen.

Men are doing a lot more caring for the old, ill, and disabled as well. The number of paid male home-care workers tripled in recent years, and a 2015 survey from the AARP found that men make up 40 percent of all unpaid family caregivers—which means 16 million American males are actively caregiving. The rate is even higher among millennial men, an increase suggesting that younger men may be more open to taking on caregiving than their older counterparts, and that their doing so is more socially acceptable. There's a popular stereotype about these men that paints them as lightweights who only do things like raking the lawn or picking up medicine from the pharmacy, while women do the messier, more emotionally demanding tasks. But the AARP found that this was not the case: "Although there are some misperceptions that male family caregivers perform activities related only to managing finances and providing transportation, evidence suggests they are also performing a range of personal care activities that include helping their loved ones with eating, dressing, bathing, and toileting."

And they like it. A report from the Boston College Center for Work & Family, cowritten by Brad Harrington and colleagues, found more than two-thirds of dads said they would like to spend more time with their children, even when they were already spending a significant amount of time with them. The Pew Research Center found similar enthusiasm among dads, discovering that the majority of dads feel they "spend too little time with their kids." The COVID pandemic provided fathers with this experience and inspired many of them to rethink their work-life balance. Research from 2021 found that only 26 percent of dads "plan to continue to work as they did before the pandemic," whether by way of reduced hours or pursuing less demanding jobs. As a point of comparison, 35 percent of mothers at the time said they intended to cut back on work.

Studies also show that parenting tends to make dads feel good. Research on gay dads found that they reported greater life satisfaction after becoming a parent. This was true for both the parent who took on more childcare responsibilities as well as the one who did less. Another study of a cross section of American dads found that they are neck and neck with moms in finding parenting "extremely important to their identity" (57 percent of dads said this and 58 percent of moms), in saying that parenting is rewarding all the time (54 percent of dads and 52 percent of moms), and are more likely than moms to say they enjoy it all the time (46 percent of dads and 41 percent of moms). Those last two represent a rosy take, as no parent who is actually parenting finds parenting rewarding or enjoyable all the time—possibly the reason dads claim this more often than moms. Still, such romanticization represents an investment in the role among men. They're in love, and not just with their kids, but with themselves as parents.

Research on non-dad caregivers tells us a similar story. A 2019 study

from the University of Chicago and Better Life Lab, which aims to elevate the value of care and advance gender equity and is a program of
the think tank New America, found that 85 percent of what they call
high-intensity male caregivers say they find their work as a caregiver satisfying. This category includes "people who have ever provided ongoing
or periodic living assistance on a regular basis to an adult family member
or close friend OR parents who have ever provided care to a child under
18 with a medical, behavioral or other condition or disability." They
also asked dads who have cared for a child of any age without a medical
or behavioral condition or disability what they thought of the work of
fatherhood and 93 percent of them said they found it satisfying. Both
groups, in similar proportions, also said they felt respected inside and
outside the home for their work as caregivers.

WHY THE CARE GAP PERSISTS

Despite the increase in the care that men do, and as much as they
claim to find meaning in it, it is far from enough to close the care gap
between men and women. Remember all those men I'm related to,
the ones whom care liberates from the confines of modern masculinity? Not a single one does as much caregiving as his female partner,
daughter, or sisters. The women in my family, like women everywhere,
continue to shoulder much of the burden of care on their own, risking
their financial security and sanity in the process. Unlike the generations
before us, we're often shouldering these burdens in addition to the
burdens of our own paid work, which leads to a special flavor of burnout particular to this moment in time. Between the jobs and the caregiving, we are left with little to no time for ourselves, and the attendant
stresses, frustrations, and sadness ripple throughout our households.

According to the U.S. Bureau of Labor Statistics, employed fathers do roughly 1.1 hours of active childcare a day, while employed mothers do roughly 1.8 hours. Unemployed dads do roughly 1.5 hours of active childcare a day, while unemployed moms do around 3 hours. Things are slightly more even with housework, for which men do a little bit less than half. The total number of hours worked by men and women, when including both paid and unpaid, or household, work, tends to be fairly equal because men are more likely to work longer hours at paid jobs. However, this research fails to account for the "worry work," or cognitive labor, that women tend to do on behalf of their families. This is the mental ticker tape that pops up during exercise, in the line at the grocery store, or at four in the morning, reminding women to not forget (never forget!) all the things their parents or children need. While such labor may be hard for social scientists to quantify, please believe me and every other woman I've ever met when we tell you that it is exhausting. Women's leisure time tends to be polluted by these thoughts about all the things that need to happen for those for whom they care. And that's when it's not interrupted by actual care.

Male laziness and obliviousness are a common explanation for this gap. We have the guy who has never inquired how the condiments in his refrigerator are replenished, or his parents' doctor's appointments get scheduled, or his children's clothing transforms from dirty to clean and appears separated by categories in their dresser drawers at the end of the week. He's happy to make a market run but would never think about grabbing dinner for tomorrow night too. And not only has he no idea about what size shoes his children wear; he doesn't, despite being an otherwise intelligent human, have the instinct to go look at their current shoes and take it from there. It's hard to say where laziness begins and authentic ignorance ends with these matters, or if they are even separate categories. In my own life, with my husband, I often fail to separate one from the other, while also overlooking another factor that stands in the way of his doing more care. When it comes to what bedtime routines should look like, or the best main dish to serve along-side latkes, or how to respond to a crying child, I can be a real bully.

There are a number of external impediments stopping men from doing more care—and one of these impediments is women like myself. It's a phenomenon that sociologists call maternal gatekeeping, which refers to the way that women get in the way of men doing more do-mestic and care work by criticizing men or, in some cases, stopping them from doing something. When my husband makes soup, I analyze it with the intensity of a reality TV show judge. When he gets the kids dressed for a special event, I almost always have a comment: "That shirt?" "The socks don't match." When the kids are yelling at or hitting each other, he is almost always being too soft on them—or hard on them. I let him know.

Research shows that maternal gatekeeping can significantly de-crease how much men do in their homes. Popular culture presents it as a nagging wife railing on her bumbling husband, but in real life the dynamic is far more complex. Just as it is hard for men to take on a new task, one they were never trained for, it is hard for women to let go of something they have put so much effort into and are more likely to be judged or punished for. If the soup is off, our kids or guests won't like it. If kids look sloppy at the family event, all unimpressed eyes will be directed toward me. If the kids don't understand limits, then I, the one who spends more time with them, will pay the price.

Failures of care, small and large, the imperfect birthday cake or the wrong medicine administered, tend to be blamed on women. Some-times such blame is direct, like when a teacher emails only the mom when their child forgot something for school, or a home-care aide calls a daughter but not the son when their father runs out of weight-gain shakes. Other times it's a look, a sigh, sometimes imagined but often not, that lets women know that it is all their fault.

Another external factor that prevents men from caring more is the toll care can take on their paychecks. We've all heard about the financial setbacks women undergo when they become mothers. Sociologists call this the motherhood penalty, and it can lead to not only decreased earning potential but also stymied careers in the long run. This motherhood penalty amounts to, on average, a 3.6 percent salary decrease for each child.

Fathers, on the other hand, often experience a "fatherhood boost," which can lead to, on average, a 6 percent increase in earnings according to longitudinal research from sociologist Michelle Budig. "Fatherhood may serve as a signal to potential employers for greater maturity, commitment, or stability," Budig explained. This penalty and bonus isn't equal among all classes. The fatherhood bonus is most likely to reward wealthier, better-educated, and securely employed men; the motherhood penalty is most likely to hurt lower-income women, while the wealthiest women also experience a parenthood bonus of up to 5.4 percent.

But there's a catch. Working fathers are rewarded only if they don't bring fatherhood to work, never request flexible schedules or time off, and don't sneak out early to take their child to baseball practice. Should a dad request that his workplace accommodate any care-related demands, he's likely in no better a position than women.

"You will hear rhetoric about how when men do caregiving they are applauded for it or it is looked upon as heroic, but when women do the same they are penalized. But that is only true if care is something men do sporadically. If men do what women do they will be penalized just like women," Harrington told me. "Men have power, but they still can't make choices. If they want greater flexibility, or to cut hours, or to go part-time to do more care, they will be seen as uncommitted to their careers."

One fix to both maternal gatekeeping and the fatherhood penalty would be to offer, normalize, and maybe even celebrate paternity leave for dads. Taking a decent chunk of time off after the birth of a child can lead to closer relationships between fathers and children, and fathers being more involved in parenting, in the long run. This is a phenomenon that is well-documented in studies, and one that I experienced firsthand.

My husband, Nathaniel, only got paid paternity leave with our second son, and the difference was manifest. Each baby speaks its own nonverbal language, and it is up to a caregiver to learn that nonverbal language. When my first son, Augie, was preverbal, Nathaniel never quite understood what he wanted and so it felt easier for me to just tend to Augie by myself rather than explain to Nathaniel what to do. With our younger son, Levi, Nathaniel had eight paid weeks at home during which he and I unpacked this new baby's language together. As a result, we began our relationship with him on equal terms, and it has remained that way to this day.

Sadly, 70 percent of American fathers take fewer than ten days of leave after the birth of a child. These low, essentially inhumane, numbers are a result of the lack of availability of paid leave for men, and also workplace biases against men who take time off to care. A substantial number of men who have access to paid leave take less than they are offered because doing so is a short- and long-term financial risk. If they don't get paid leave to care for a new child or a healing partner—the vast majority of men don't—they lose wages from any time taken off. It doesn't stop there. In our current work culture, taking paternity leave also hurts a man's reputation in the professional realm for the long run and can lower his earning potential for the rest of his career.

U.S. representative Colin Allred is the first man in Congress to publicly take paternity leave. There's a chance another man before him took it, but never in history had a congressman been brave enough to announce to the world that he was taking time off from work to take care of his postpartum wife and his newborn child. This happened in 2019.

He took leave for all the common reasons fathers take time off
work following the birth of a child. He wanted to be with his child.
He wanted to help his wife. More unusually, he was making good on a
promise made by his younger self. Allred was raised by a single mom,
and didn't know his father growing up. "Because of that I was dead set
on always being involved and being present as much as possible," the
Texas congressman and former professional football player told me.

Colin's likely not the first representative to feel this way. But he's
the first who felt like he could act on it without potentially threatening
his masculinity or reputation as a man. Four years as an NFL linebacker
protects a guy from such things. "I can talk about the importance of
men taking leave, and of men being there in the early days of their
child's life and changing diapers, without there being any conversations
about my masculinity or anything like that," he said. "[Having been a
linebacker] gives me credibility with every guy I talk to . . . it gives me
a voice that people listen to."

Colin's departure from the world of aggression and domination he
found on the football field began at law school at the University of California, Berkeley, where he took classes on gender and civil rights and
met his now wife, a fellow law student. He still loves sports and has a
complicated fondness for football. Even more, he appreciates the way
having been a football player, checking off all the masculinity boxes,
allows him to challenge gender norms and get away with it.

With Colin's first son, he took off two weeks, which happened right
after he took office. It didn't feel like enough, so with his second child
he took off a month and then went on a reduced schedule for another
month. "It has been one of the harder things I have done, mentally and
physically," he said. "I am as exhausted as I ever was playing in the NFL.
It is a different fatigue. You are very tired." It's worth it, though. He
feels closer to his kids and has a deepened sensitivity to the demands
of caregiving. "It is a talent, a skill, a discipline, something that is so

important. I had respect for it before and I have so much more respect for it now."

This respect plays out in the policies he fights for, as well as his conversations with other dads in which he isn't afraid to be front and center about his obligations as a parent and why spending time with his kids is important to him. He's not alone. Among congressmen, he's seeing an increasing willingness to talk about fatherhood, along with a slower-moving acceptance of paternity leave. "I ended up being the first one to do this, but I don't think it's seen as revolutionary. The other men are partly there," he said. "I have some colleagues who are very happy for me but might think I am showing them up a bit. Their wives are starting to ask them why, if I took leave, couldn't they?"

NEW STORIES

One answer for the wives of congressmen and everyone else lies in the stories we tell ourselves about ourselves and the stories we inherit from the world around us. Men are not generally raised to think of themselves as caregivers, by their families or the wider culture. Making matters worse, we often tell them that they are incompetent at it. Hollywood and advertisers have long relied on the clueless dad for a punch line—the Homer Simpson formula is evergreen. In 2012, Huggies released a commercial in which they claimed to prove the strength of their product by subjecting them to the ne plus ultra of incompetence: dads. "We put them to the toughest test imaginable. Dads, alone with their babies, in one house, for five days," the voice-over explains. A group of competent-identifying dads got together to petition against this portrayal, and the commercial was soon removed. Still, the trope of the blockhead dad lives on.

There is an exception to the incompetent dad, and he's the dad as hero. One of the most popular Reddit threads on fatherhood is called "Dad Reflexes." On it, people post videos of themselves and other dads achieving heroic physical feats while protecting their children from bodily harm. There is the dad who is making breakfast when he sees, from the corner of his eye, his daughter falling off the counter. He grabs her, upside down, his wrist tight around one ankle, right before she's about to hit the floor headfirst. There's also the dad who, with the instincts of a wolf, manages to grab his son off a bicycle right before the boy would have run into a parked truck.

While these videos can be entertaining, they do little to broaden our ideas about what it means to be a man who cares. Here caregiving takes the form of one-off physical acts of heroism. Important, but they only represent a sliver of the ways in which we rescue each other through care. The majority of the time, protection is a much subtler, quieter act: "Did you take your pills?" "Come here; I need to put sunscreen on your face." "Have some fruit." There's also all the care that doesn't involve protection, the listening, sharing, nurturing, and daily doing-doing-doing that tend to resist easy hero narratives. The dads of "Dad Reflexes" don't talk about this much.

The problem with these limiting, and limited, stories about men caring for others is that they narrow our imaginations for how we raise our sons, and what grown men can imagine for themselves. "Women are generally assigned the responsibility of family caregiving in homes, and those skills easily translate to their roles as caregivers. But then I think of my male friends and some of them don't even know how to make a meal. There's just a basic skill set that men aren't given, and it's because historically men aren't expected to care," Robert Espinoza, an expert on aging and long-term care, told me. As a result, men suffer from a lack of confidence when it comes to care. Male caregivers to old, disabled, and ill individuals often report insecurities about their fitness for the role. They're particularly nervous about the personal care side of care, including eating, dressing, and bathing, as they tend to have little experience with these activities. Many dads feel the same. A Pew Research Center poll from 2015 found that 39 percent of fathers thought they were doing a "very good job" raising their kids, compared to 51 percent of mothers.

Attempts to recruit men into paid caregiving work often focus on branding. They try to make caregiving seem tough, the kind of thing a guy's guy could really get into. But potentially more important than changing the optics around care is boosting men's confidence that they can care, Espinoza said. "Bringing more men into this work requires a different level of training and teaching them new skill sets. It's not just better ads." The same goes for bringing more men into unpaid care. We don't need to sell men on care by turning it into a tough activity for tough dudes. We just need to help them feel that they can do it, and well.

A small but growing number of men have begun to reject these clichés and seek support through conversation, embracing a fuller, deeper, and, with that, more conflicted relationship with caregiving. They come together, virtually and in person, through support groups, Instagram pages, and online publications. They exchange small-scale tips on how to manage as well as large-scale thoughts about how they are process-ing their new identities as caregivers.

"The dads who join our communities have a lack of confidence, or this block that makes them think they can't be a great dad," said Brian Anderson, executive director and cofounder of Fathering To-gether, an organization that educates dads on parenting, builds com-munity through online and in-person gatherings, and mobilizes dads to change the political and cultural landscape to better support fathers. On a good day, and despite the political, religious, cultural, and eco-nomic differences of the dads in his group most days are good days, the community members are there to "remind dads they have what they need. They just need to uncover it a little bit."

Men want to talk about the struggle to transition to caregiving for the first time. About the pain of being underestimated as caregivers. About learning to express vulnerability. About moving past "father knows best" and instead trying to be more receptive and give their kids what they need. They want to talk about the hard parts of care, and are unafraid to admit that their Mr. Fix-It tendencies are no match for the loneliness and exhaustion of early parenthood. They want to say how deeply they feel for, and with, the recipients of their care. How uncomfortable it is to really feel. Together, this conversation represents a shift away from men viewing care as a checklist experience, or one that involves discrete tasks with a clear beginning and end. In its place sit the infinitude, fragility, and intimacy that have long challenged and enriched women in care. This shift is often signaled by a newfound willingness to identify, directly, unequivocally, as a caregiver.

Sian-Pierre Regis says it took him years of caring for his mom before he came around to calling himself a caregiver. "I decided to own the word 'caregiver,' even though I am not doing the work society thinks of as a caregiver. I am not giving her pills and wiping her butt. But it is a word I chose to use because what I do is care," Sian-Pierre, a filmmaker in New York City, told me.

In 2016, Sian-Pierre received a call from his mom, Rebecca. He was thirty-two. She was seventy-five. She had just been fired from her job at a hotel in Boston, where she had worked for twelve years as a housekeeper and, later, manager of household services—they felt it was a case of age discrimination. A single mom, she had raised two kids on her own and had little opportunity to save over the years. Sian-Pierre's brother is schizophrenic and still relied on her support financially. Most of what was left over from helping him out went to paying for her subsidized apartment, where she had lived for forty years. Now she was jobless and feeling prospectless, with $600 to her name.

Sian-Pierre quickly got on a train. No particular plan in mind, only the impulse to be there and do something. He spent the next few months shuttling back and forth between the two cities, helping her navigate online job listings and insisting that she was never going to have to deal with this on her own: "I remember sending money, sending cake. Whatever I could to provide emotional care from afar."

Then he had a film idea. What if his mom made a bucket list and pursued it instead of finding work? What if he turned this into a documentary, a meditation on ageism, care, and joy?

Following a successful Kickstarter campaign through which he raised $57,823, Sian-Pierre and his mom began creating and working their way through her bucket list over the course of three and a half years. It included the expected (skydiving in Hawaii), the unusual (milking a cow), and the particular: Sian-Pierre and Rebecca traveled to England, where she was born, to spend time with Rebecca's oldest child, Joanne. Shortly after Joanne was born, Rebecca became extremely ill and sent Joanne to be raised by her sister back in the United Kingdom.

While the bucket list was the pretext for the documentary, *Duty Free*, the film's emotional heft comes from the shifting dynamic between son and mother. The balance of care had been tipped, with more flowing from him to her than ever before. This shift continued during the editing process and subsequent completion of the film when a whole new experiment began, far more challenging than anything on the bucket list. In 2020, Rebecca moved in with Sian-Pierre and his partner in a three-bedroom apartment in Chelsea.

"It can get frustrating: there are no boundaries. And the care dynamic is changing at a faster clip because there are so many things she wants to do or is curious about that she can't do by herself. Still, I have a deep sense that I wouldn't want anything in my life to change," he said. "We used to have roommates, and every time a roommate was shuffled in and out, I would joke that it was like a different episode of *Friends*. This is my favorite episode. As a multigenerational household, we get to rely on each other and learn from each other in different ways." The inversion in his relationship with his mom not only provided him with inspiration for the film but also made him feel like making a film of his own, a lifelong dream, was possible for the first time. "It's built this confidence in me. I've never stood so firm in my strength and my power, and it's because I live with these two people who believe in me."

Sian-Pierre and Rebecca's multigenerational living arrangement is becoming increasingly common. The Pew Research Center found that the percentage of parents living with kids has doubled in the past twenty years, and experts predict this will rise as our savings are no match for the rising cost of living. Still, when Sian-Pierre travels around to talk about his movie, which was released in 2020, he finds many men who hesitate to identify themselves as caregivers or dig into their experiences of care despite the fact that they now live with their parents and care for them.

"When I speak to men about caregiving they're conflicted. At first, it's sort of like: 'My dad just moved in and it's tough.' And that's it." But then they get talking, and the men loosen up. They're afraid, confused, and often feel alone. "The more I talk about this with men, the more open they become to feeling this is like something they can do. It's not that they don't want to. They're more just afraid of failing. Because at no point in this journey were we taught how to care."

MASCULINITY IS FLUID

You might think I am pushing too hard, asking for too much. Men are, by nature, independent, adventurous, aggressive, competitive, and stoic. Who are we to demand that they go against evolution, DNA, and any other predetermining factors and add nurturing to this list? But this thinking is time-sensitive, as today's definition of masculinity has little in common with the many masculinities of the past.

Sometime around 1517, Sir Thomas More, Catholic social philosopher and author of the book *Utopia*, wrote one of many affectionate letters to one of his children:

> It is not so strange that I love you with my whole heart, for being a father is not a tie which can be ignored. Nature in her wisdom has attached the parent to the child and bound them spiritually together with a Herculean knot. . . . This tie is the reason why I regularly fed you cake and gave you ripe apples and fancy pears. This tie is the reason why I used to dress you in silken garments and why I could never endure to hear you cry.

There were many men like More who not only loved their kids but also spoke often of this love and the vulnerability that came along with it. Today's parents often describe parenthood as having your heart walk outside your body, a metaphor whose surface sweetness belies the violence underneath. Parenthood disembodies, implodes previously understood boundaries of body and soul, denies us agency over our emotional well-being, and yet, weirdly, we mostly like it. It seems likely these dads of the past would have readily agreed.

This tenderness wasn't limited to their children. Over history, men have been far more physically and emotionally affectionate with one another than is acceptable today. During the nineteenth century, men, straight and rugged American men, addressed each other as "my lovely boy" and other terms of endearment, and it wasn't uncommon for them to sit on each other's laps or hold hands in a photograph. This didn't necessarily mean they treated women with this affection, or funneled their affection into a critique of racial, heteronormative, and gendered power structures. Still, they showed love to one another freely and without much apparent internal conflict.

They also were far more hands-on with their kids than most twentieth-century dads. "As recently as two to three hundred years ago, men and women shared the idea that both are responsible for providing the necessities of life, and both are responsible for tending to emotional and caregiving relationships with others," Coontz, the family studies historian, told me. Women did the bulk of infant care, though rarely on their own. Servants were common across classes and often took on a significant amount of the responsibility for young children. Following these infant and toddler years, men played a hands-on, active role in their children's lives, and were seen as responsible for teaching them knowledge and skills as well as providing them with a moral foundation. If kids were unruly, it was seen as Dad's fault. Men also helped out with caring for the old and disabled. Their greater physical strength compared to that of women made them better candidates to bathe Grandpa, or another sick adult. "When the farm was the center of production, the wife was seen as co-provider. There was not a notion that men made a living and women stayed home with the kids," Coontz said. "There was some division of labor, but it wasn't half as rigid as it would eventually become."

The shift away from this is not, exclusively, a product of the patriarchy. Men didn't suddenly get more power and collectively think, Phew, let's get out of the home. In *The Wonderbox: Curious Histories of How to Live*, philosopher Roman Krznaric looks at how the men's traditional, home-based work was hit harder by the Industrial Revolution than women's. "As men entered the paid workforce, the old household craft skills that they once passed on to their sons were lost, just as their previous role in looking after children became a distant memory," Krznaric writes. Traditional male tasks like gathering wood, making tools, shoes, and furniture, were suddenly taken over by manufacturing. Education, previously the man's domain, also became something that took place outside the home. But as much as appliance companies and Silicon Valley start-ups have tried, traditionally women's work, the work of cleaning, cooking, and child minding, has remained somewhat immune to technological advances.

History is not the only example of the fluidity of masculinity. Men's brains tell us the same. Their brains, like all human brains, are plastic. They adapt to new experiences and respond with new channels and habits and patterns that make them more tuned in to these experiences. Despite the claims that women are the most nurturing gender, that it is written, indelibly, into female DNA, it is not the case that men are somehow less able to care. "Research in this area as a whole converges on the idea that there is a global neural caregiving system and it is basically the same in males and females and across all animals. What differs is how readily that circuitry gets engaged," James Rilling, an anthropologist and neuroscientist at Emory University, told me.

In 2008, Rilling was building a curriculum for a course about human social neuroscience. He planned on unpacking love, attachment, and parenting for undergraduates, helping them understand what binds us to one another. While compiling texts and studies to include, he noticed a big gap in the research. Nearly everything we knew about parenthood was based on studies of mothers. What about the dads? They were doing more care than they had in a long time, and there was plenty of research about how they were good for their kids, but little about what the experience of care was like for them.

Rilling decided to focus on the biology of fatherhood. For his first study, he looked at the hormone levels and brain function of fathers of children ages one through three. He found that fathers had lower levels of testosterone and higher levels of oxytocin, the bonding hormone, compared to non-fathers. Others made similar discoveries. A team of biological anthropologists from Northwestern University tested the testosterone levels of young Filipino men with a four-and-a-half-year interval. The ones who had kids during that time had larger decreases in testosterone than those who did not. The team also found that the more involved dads were in caregiving, the lower their levels were.

Another team of researchers found that both mothers and fathers experience an oxytocin boost from skin-to-skin contact with infants and both experience an activation in the same care-related parts of their brains in response to stimuli from their children. Fathers who were the primary caregiver showed more activity in this region than those who were not.

In addition, Rilling and his team have found that among dads brain systems involved with pleasure and motivational systems are related to the amount of contact with their children. The more involved a dad was, the more these systems were activated. "There is a positive correlation between how involved fathers are in caregiving and how strongly the parts of his brain involved with reward and motivation activate when viewing his child's picture," Rilling said. "There is still the question of direction or causality. Could it be that some fathers inherently find their child more rewarding at the outset, and then those fathers become more involved as caregivers? Or that as fathers become more involved as caregivers, they form a stronger bond with their child and start to respond more?" Either way, it's clear that caregiving is not that different for moms versus dads.

For everyone, parenthood is a learning process. Few of us know instantly what to do or say to put our babies at ease. Moms, on the one hand, tend to soldier through, because the world has already decided they should be good at this. Dads, on the other hand, may be more likely to give up, their lack of intuition a sign they are unfit for the job. This myth of instant connection "is damaging to mothers, because they feel like bad mothers if they don't instantly bond," Darby Saxbe, an associate professor of psychology and director of the Center for the Changing Family at the University of Southern California, told me. She continued, "But it's even more damaging to fathers, as it gives them permission to ascribe this instinct to one sex and not the other. Dads stay away, thinking, 'She knows what to do; she has this instinct, this ability to nurture and understand the baby.'" Saxbe is attempting to prove otherwise. Her research uncovers the vast array of new skills a new parent has to learn, skills that no one has going in, because so much depends on tending to that one-and-only person to whom we give our care. The development of empathy, the learning of their babies' cues and investment in relieving their pain and stress, is always, for everyone, a work in progress. "That plasticity comes online with experience," she said.

While I couldn't find any biological or neuroscience studies on nonparental male caregivers, anecdotal research suggests that these men experience something similar to new fathers. The act of care, they claim, turned them into caregivers, nurturing, empathic, and sensitive to rewards of tending to another. "Men who had experience providing care were much more likely than men in the general population group to say that men, not just women, have a natural instinct to care, that providing care is a skill that can be learned, and that society's expectations and workplace structures are often what keep men from giving care," explains a report by Brigid Schulte from the Better Life Lab.

REIMAGINING MASCULINITY THROUGH CARE

In 2018, the American Psychological Association released "APA Guidelines for Psychological Practice with Boys and Men." Created over the course of thirteen years and drawing on more than forty years of research, the organization had come to the conclusion that "traditional masculinity is psychologically harmful and that socializing boys to suppress their emotions causes damage that echoes both inwardly and outwardly." The announcement on the APA website acknowledged the subtle irony of these recommendations in the second graph. Psychology, like all other areas of medicine, had treated men, mostly white men, as the default humans since its creation. How is it that they are only now seeing the problem with men?

But being the default humans comes with drawbacks, which men are increasingly starting to realize. As long as "men" is synonymous with "humans," then the particularities of masculinity are not taken into consideration. Unlike women, who have been questioning and challenging the boundaries of femininity since the dawn of the patriarchy, men have been relatively complacent about what exactly goes into the making of a "man." What does it mean to be a man? When and how does that definition help men? And when and how does it hurt them?

Often enough. The patriarchy has rewarded men, but those rewards do not come for free. Men commit 90 percent of homicides, make up 77 percent of homicide victims, are 3.5 times more likely to die by suicide as compared to women, and have a life expectancy that is 4.9 years shorter than women. "The main thrust of the subsequent research is that traditional masculinity—marked by stoicism, competitiveness, dominance and aggression—is, on the whole, harmful. Men socialized in this way are less likely to engage in healthy behaviors," the APA writes in their report.

Being macho has a negative correlation with men's physical health, as manly men avoid vegetables and doctors and embrace smoking and drinking. Being macho can also hurt your feelings. A meta-analysis of seventy-four studies found that the more a man conforms to traditional masculinity norms, the more likely he is to have mental health problems, including depression and stress. He's also less likely to experience life satisfaction, good self-esteem, or psychological well-being. The belief in self-reliance is one of three traits that are particularly damaging to men.

Most men don't really want to be this way, explained Matt Engar-Carlson, the director of the Center for Boys and Men at California State University, Fullerton, who worked on the APA guidelines. Few actually are. Research shows that the majority of men consider themselves moderately masculine and most say they are not masculine enough. All the men I've had close relationships with fit this description. Aware of what is expected of them, and the embarrassing gulf between those expectations and who they are. Quietly, internally, they are familiar with the power of nurture, dependency, cooperation, and care, but they are reluctant to reveal this to others. Pursuing those sides of themselves is a social risk. "Most clinicians know that shame is where it is at for men," Engar-Carlson told me. "Many men experience a shame cycle for not being tough enough that is so brutal. Culture shames them, and unfortunately a lot of women shame them, too, though it may be inadvertent. Men hear that they can't be who they are."

Caregiving has some overlap with some of the traditional, and healthy, ideas about masculinity like being responsible, competent, and protective and, when the moment demands it, stoic. But it's far more likely that care will challenge, rather than endorse, traditional masculinity. There are just too many open-ended questions, moments of weakness, and repetitive tasks to leave machoness untouched. Engar-Carlson sees this as a positive, and one of the many reasons why men should seek out caregiving.

"When we put men in caregiving roles, whether they chose to be in it or are forced into it, it gives men a chance to reach inside and embody parts of themselves that are already there, but often not widely shown nor reinforced by greater society. It helps men feel part of something greater around them. That can feel really good," he said. "Caregiving gives men an opportunity to combat the shame associated with not being tough enough, which is often a cause of the internal conflict men often experience when they are in non–traditionally male roles. It can also give men an opportunity to feel helpful, worthwhile, and like something matters."

He pointed to the large body of research that shows how men need connection and relationships and are "at their worst when alone." Social isolation raises their chances of dying early, being depressed and anxious, and killing themselves. Beginning in the early 2000s, the number of middle-aged men who took their own lives began to rise, a trend that experts struggled to unpack and address. Many suspected that unemployment was the main cause, believing that the despair was mainly the result of a loss of professional and social status. Few considered whether their roles at home with their families mattered too.

Silvia Sara Canetto, a psychology professor, is an exception. Since the 1990s, she has written and theorized about how men's lack of involvement with unpaid care work, combined with their heavy involvement with paid work, may be connected to their higher rates of suicide. In 2021, she partnered with researchers around the world to study this hypothesis in twenty countries and discovered she was right. The more unpaid care work men do, whether for children or dependent adults, the lower their suicide mortality rate is. "An especially promising finding is that in countries where men reported more care work, higher unemployment rates were not associated with higher suicide rates in men," Canetto told me, explaining that care work gives men other avenues of finding purpose and connection and more reasons for living. "If all of your life is invested in a single pursuit, whether paid work or unpaid family work, and that comes to an end for some reason, then you may be left without sources of meaning and purpose, and without important relationships to contribute to, and rely on," she told me. "A large body of research indeed shows that, for women as for men, doing both family care work and paid work is associated with better health and well-being than doing only one or the other."

HE CARES

As a child, David Bullman felt like he couldn't get anything right. What was a small act of mischief in his eyes was seen as a grave breach of conduct by his parents. The local culture probably had something to do with it. As did his dad's job.

He grew up on Fort Carson, a U.S. army post in sunny Colorado Springs, raised by a career military dad and a mom who didn't question the rigidity, stoicism, and perfectionism that was expected of their only son. "If I asked for help for a problem, I was wrong," he told me. He felt as though his sister rarely got in trouble, no matter what she did, while he often got in trouble, even if he had good intentions. Sometimes his dad could be heavy-handed when it came time for punishment. The subsequent shame, untreated and unquestioned, metabolized into rebellion. "If I was going to do something wrong anyway, I was going to make it worth my while."

David got in trouble. And then in more trouble, and more trouble, and as he grew ordinary trouble wasn't satisfying enough, so he moved on to serious trouble. At age eleven, he started taking hard drugs. A few years later, he got involved with guns and violence. "I was an addict from eleven to twenty-seven, addicted to heroin, cocaine, methamphetamine. Anything that could fit a needle."

He was a tough guy's tough guy, living a life built by and for toughness and the thrills such a hard exterior enabled. By age twenty-two, this toughness landed him in prison, where he stayed nearly a decade.

There were a few chances to get out for good, but the drugs and guns were too easy, too appealing. He violated his parole, and back to prison and rehab he went. The cycle continued until one day the prison sent a former addict to talk to him: "If you think of a personification of an old-time convict, this is what this guy looked like. Bald and tattooed. He told me his story and it just clicked and made sense," David said about Ralph.

Ralph didn't tell David what to do, but he did tell David how he got off drugs. One day, Ralph realized that he had a choice in life. He could either drive the bus or be driven by the bus. This metaphor clicked. David felt like he was ready to drive, and his first big trip was reconnecting with a woman he knew since he was two and who had lived across the street throughout his childhood. They got together, and Andrea was the one who picked him up from prison on the day he got out. Home they went, to her house, now their house, where she lived with her four children.

Two years later, in 2011, she gave birth to their baby, a girl. Six days later she was in the hospital with a collapsed lung, an injury from her labor. David hadn't just become a father; he became a primary care-giver. "Here I am, scared to death of this baby. You can put me in any kind of war zone, you could put me in anything, but when the baby came along I was terrified of her. I thought I was going to break her. One of the nurses taught me how to give her a bath, to do all these things with her that I have never done. The nurse took my hand and said, 'You are not going to break this baby.'"

This was bigger than ordinary first-time-dad jitters. For most of his life, he had never wanted kids. And even if he did, he had little confidence that he would make a good dad. "I am an old-school biker, been like that all my life. Having kids was just like, whoa. My stepdaughters would tease me before my daughter was born and tell me everything was going to change. I called bullshit, because I was this, and I was that. But when my daughter was about six months old, I had to look at them and say, 'Wow, you guys are right. Sorry.' My whole world had changed. I'm not the hard-ass I used to be. I had to learn how to have feelings and have emotions and how to be human and not a robot. Because with the kids you can't just turn it all off. I had to learn to ask for help, because for a long time I would try to keep that in, and think I got to learn this on my own and do this on my own. But it got to the point where I couldn't, where I had to ask for help, and doing that was the hardest thing I ever did. It got easier and easier as time went on, and the emotion came into it. I went from being a stone-cold asshole to being the complete opposite. I had to change everything about me."

David and his daughter are close. He brings her to bike shows, where his biker friends spoil her. She knows how to work all his power tools, and he predicts that one day her husband will be making the sandwiches while she fixes stuff in the garage. He also served as her main playmate for two years following a stroke, during which he was bedridden: "She had a bazillion toys and would bring toys up to my room in these tote bags and say, 'Daddy play.' She was about two and she was playing like my bed was her race car and I said, 'Are you ready to play?' And then she said, 'I can't; my car is broke. Damn thing ran out of gas, so I lit it on fire.' I thought, Damn, you really are my kid!"

David has always loved to talk, but now talking comes woven through with expressions of his emotional state. Before he used to share his life story as though he were "reading from a book." Now, when he shares, it's personal, with feeling. He can share his trauma, and speak to family and friends about his PTSD and night terrors. He's also comfortable sharing his anger, his regrets, even his joys: "That is the biggest one. Men don't like to show joy and excitement. Now I know it is okay to sit down and be happy."

Today David is active on Fathering Together, Brian Anderson's social network for fathers, where he leads a group for dads in recovery.

David learned about the group through an ad during the Super Bowl and realized how alone he felt as a parent. Turning to one's own parents would be many people's first step, but this wasn't an option for him, as there is a big gap between the way he is raising his kids and the way he was raised by his parents. The community has proven to him that question asking, about parenting or anything else really, is not a weakness.

In recent years, David's been doing more caregiving than he'd ever anticipated and, on most days, he's sure he can handle. His wife tragically passed away in 2021, making David a single dad who struggles to pay his bills and take adequate care of his daughter. There are far more resources for single moms than single dads in Colorado, something David would like to try to change if he only had the time or energy. For now, he takes some solace in the support he gets from other single-dad members of Fathering Together.

On top of that, David is caring for his parents. His mom has slow-moving cancer; his dad had a stroke. They both need help getting to and from doctor's appointments, as well as managing meals and their home. "I don't have a choice; my sister walked out and walked away. It was me or nobody. Even though me and my mom don't get along, it is still my mom, I had to step in there and say, 'Okay, I got you.' With my dad I don't have a choice; 'I got you.'

"I will sit with my dad and tell him I understand how he feels and what is going on in his head. I have been there," David, who has had three strokes, explained. "He doesn't really say much, but you see the wheels turning. I don't think he understood how to reply because he has always been a certain way. The look on his face was: What am I supposed to say? So I gave him a hug and said, 'We got this; we will get through this together.' Then I told him it's okay to be broken."

CHAPTER FOUR

———

Love and Money

The Economic and Social Might of Care

THE HOUSEWIFE

What to call a woman who spends her days, unpaid, tending to her home and family?

During the early part of the twentieth century, she was known as a housewife. This was her primary label, the role that allowed her to be identified and categorized, by others and herself. First and foremost, as per the order of the phrase, she was in charge of the house. Secondarily, she was a wife, attached to another whose status as an employed man, presumably, elevated her own. Toward the middle of the century, the emphasis turned away from her marital state and toward the work she did at home. She became a "homemaker," a more active phrase than "housewife," one that honors the labor that goes into the position. A homemaker is dynamic, strategic, and requires some smarts. A homemaker can teach you a thing or two. One can make a home with or without a man.

By the end of the twentieth century, she changed names again, this time to "stay-at-home mom." The home is still there, but now it is a location, a container even; the "stay" suggests inertia but also service—a sacrifice. Who is it all for? The answer is found in the last word: "mom." Whereas she was once defined by her relationship with her husband, and then by her home, her purpose is now bound up with her children.

There is, among many women, a strong desire to come up with a new, better, phrase. One that, like "maker," highlights the active nature of tending to the home and family. Ideally, it would ditch the passive "stay" and honor, more directly, the contributions that this person, almost always a woman, gives to her loved ones and the world around them. But what? Imperfect options include "full-time mom," which succeeds in using the language of paid work to elevate motherhood but ultimately fails because it implies that she is only, ever, a mom. Also, what does that make moms who work? Part-time moms? One is always a mom, employed or not.

"Work-from-home parent" succeeds for its gender neutrality but leaves one guessing as to whether the work consists of paid labor or care and domestic tasks or both. "Primary caregiver" or "lead parent" is pithy but doesn't do much to separate those who care full-time from those who have full-time jobs and paid help. A good many moms, with forty-hour-a-week, salaried jobs, are also the primary caregivers or lead parents. "Not employed outside the home" avoids some of these issues, but it's sad. These women are being defined by what they are not, rather than what they are doing. And they are doing so, so much.

I struggle with this language often. When I meet other parents, or caregivers to old, ill, or disabled individuals, there is often an awkward moment when I or someone else asks them what they do and they stumble to respond. Maybe one or two, as far as I can remember, told me directly, without hesitation, that they spend their days caring. The rest mentioned their caregiving amid a long list of qualifiers, regrets, and apologies. They were "taking time off" to care, the "off" implying that the care is secondary, the accident or hiccup, to the work they think will impress you. Or they present care as a sign that they are lost, as if they are waiting for inspiration to find out what they really want to do and in the meantime will care for a parent or their children. Sometimes they seem certain they want to dedicate themselves to caregiving but are also certain that I, a working parent, will judge them for it or fail to understand it. I want to tell them I understand, that I value what they are doing, that there are many paid jobs that are far less interesting than caring for a loved one, that what they are contributing to the world is tangible and admirable. But I, too, stumble. They have no idea how to evince confidence in their choice to spend their days caregiving, and I have no idea how to respond in a way that lets them know that I believe that caring for others has a value that extends far beyond any single dependent person's life.

This struggle to give caregivers a job title that befits their important role and talk about care itself isn't just a name game. The roots of this ambivalence and confusion run deep, and are impossible to separate from the history of our financial and political systems and their long-standing resistance to defining and valuing the work that takes place at home. We don't classify care as work because it's generally something that women do and most male economists have focused solely on defining and measuring the historically male-dominated world outside the home.

Adam Smith, the eighteenth-century father of modern capitalism, wrote about how rational self-interest motivates financial exchanges. We buy and sell goods and services to benefit ourselves. Left out of this equation was the care Smith's mom gave him her entire life, well into adulthood. Smith's father died before he was born, making her a single mom from day one; Smith never got married. All the attention and energy she devoted to him, not out of self-interest but out of, presumably, love and duty, did not factor into his theories on what makes economies tick, theories that still color our understanding of the economy to this day. And yet how productive could Smith have been if he didn't have her support? And why shouldn't her support be considered an investment in his output?

The most straightforward, though nevertheless deceiving, explanation as to why nonprofessional caregiving is not considered work is because it is done for free. Economists have long thought of work as something that is attached to a wage, and that wage is attached to the market. The value of an hour of a dentist's time is clear because the community the dentist lives in has decided it is worth a certain amount. The value of an hour of a family caregiver is undefined, or nil, because it is not remunerated by a wage. Ergo, economists have reasoned, care is not work and has no economic value.

There are other, more emotional explanations for why care hasn't been defined as work. It's possible these male economists did see care as a type of labor but knew that labeling it as such was a risk. Call care and housekeeping work and it becomes much harder to ignore the great amount of sacrifice, financial, emotional, and otherwise, care demands of caregivers. Deny it, on the other hand, and they would have a much easier time avoiding doing their fair share, or creating and supporting systems that offset that burden of care.

Alongside this denial, in equal parts paradox and harmony, sits reverence. We are uncomfortable mucking up something often fueled by feeling with the bone-dry language of economics. Both caregivers and non-caregivers have an aversion to talking about care in terms of monetary value and productivity because care is supposed to be love and when it's not love it's human survival. In this worldview, care is bigger, purer even, than money and anyone who speaks about it in financial terms is missing the point and demeaning care in the process. Even paid caregivers are expected not to complain about wages because their work often comes with a deep sense of purpose.

But is it not possible to hold this all at once? What if, in one hand, we honor the love and purpose and all the other ways care is bigger than money? And in the other, we acknowledge the way caregivers contribute to our economy and society at large and deserve to have their work valued in financial terms? This won't corrupt care. I promise. Instead, it allows us to get a fuller sense of care's worth and, with this knowledge, better support caregivers.

"We need to inoculate ourselves against this idea that we shouldn't put a monetary value on care. Virtue is not always its own reward, and paying or supporting people who provide care is not going to undermine the moral and cultural value of care," Nancy Folbre, a prominent economist who has long fought for a place for care in the world of economics, told me. Folbre has written a number of books on the subject and received a MacArthur "genius grant" for her work. By avoiding discussing the economic worth of care, she wisely pointed out, we are, in effect, defining its economic worth: "We already put a monetary value on care and that value is zero. Zero is a number, and it's what sets into motion the disadvantages of providing care."

Over the past hundred years, economists like Folbre have made an attempt to assess the value of care in economic terms. It should surprise no one that once we begin tabulating and calculating all the hours that go into caregiving, we discover it's worth quite a lot. So much, in fact, that it's ridiculous that it is not regularly considered in national economic accounting measures, like the gross domestic product (GDP), or worthy of national investment.

Care is an essential piece of the economic puzzle. It is its own form of productivity, one through which we invest our time in the well-being of our society and its members. It's also how we show respect to and maximize social engagement for all members of that society. Those homemakers, housewives, lead parents, whatever we call them, are the ones who turn sticky-fingered toddlers into voting, law-abiding citizens and ensure dignity for all during our weaker moments.

Evaluating the monetary equivalent of caregivers' contributions to the economy and the value of their labor is trickier than doing the same for dentistry, but, despite the claims of many mainstream economists, it is not impossible. We can count the number of hours spent on caring and consider what the value of that work would be in the marketplace. Sometimes this is done by counting what the caregiver could be making in their line of work. If a lawyer takes time off to care, we would figure out how much she would have made per hour as a lawyer and place that value on an hour of her time caregiving. Alternately, we can look at what an hour of care would cost in the marketplace. If the lawyer takes off two months to care for her bedridden mother, we would figure out how much a local professional home health-care worker would get an hour and then place that value on an hour of the lawyer's time caring for her mother. In the first scenario, in strict number-crunching terms, her time caregiving is worth more than it is in the second scenario, as lawyers generally earn more than paid caregivers.

We can also count the ways care fuels other forms of productivity, and the financial impact that care has on both the givers of care and the receivers of it. One version of this is to calculate the number of hours of care done by women, men, the rich and the poor, country by country, and see how that time impacts an individual's financial well-being, a group's financial well-being, and collective growth. Or compare countries that support caregivers and allow them to blend care with other paid labor with those that don't, and see the effect care support has on the economy. None of these on their own perfectly captures the economic and social might of care, but together they bring us closer to the truth.

"Unpaid care and domestic work produces and reproduces the labour force on a day-to-day basis and over generations for the market, but conventional analyses of employment and labour markets tend to ignore it altogether," explains a 2015 report from UN Women. What the authors want people to understand is that counting care is not a feel-good attempt to make up for misogyny or give caregivers an official pat on the back for a job well-done. Simply put, without care there are no employees, in the present or the future. A father can't go to work if his wife isn't watching the children, or vice versa, or if there are no daycares or teachers. Children will not grow up to be functional employees without care, whether from a parent or a paid caregiver.

NUMBERS

Globally, unpaid care work is worth $11 trillion, or 9 percent of the global GDP, if every hour spent on care was paid for at the local minimum wage, according to a 2018 report from the International Labour Organization titled *Care Work and Care Jobs: For the Future of Decent Work*. In the United States the ILO found that unpaid care work would represent 14.7 percent of the GDP, or roughly $2.5 trillion, if it were counted. This is nearly as much as the entire retail industry contributes. In Argentina, the value of time spent on unpaid domestic work and care would be worth 10 percent of the GDP if counted. In India it's 39 percent and in South Africa it's 15 percent, as a point of comparison.

The total value of the 34 billion hours of unpaid care given to an adult with limitations in the United States every year is $470 billion according to a report published in 2019 by the AARP, based on data from 2017. Unpaid care is a huge piece of our health-care puzzle and, by some economic measures, of greater value than the $366 billion spent annually on paid care.

Another way of putting a monetary value on care is looking at the way in which our lack of support for caregivers hurts our economy. The

lack of available and high-quality childcare in the United States costs
our economy $57 billion, in terms of lost earnings, productivity, and
revenue, according to research from the Council for a Strong America,
a bipartisan nonprofit, and the business-advocacy group ReadyNation.

If caregivers over the age of fifty could both work and care, the
U.S. GDP could grow by $1.7 trillion by 2030, and by $4.1 trillion by
2050, according to analysis from the AARP in 2021. Increased individual productivity would be made possible by "flexible hours, telework
options, paid time off and family medical leave, affordable backup care
and referrals to community resources."

These figures, all the product of a select group of future-thinking
economists' hard work, are important advocacy tools. Policy makers
and politicians often veto programs to support caregivers because of
the price tag. But their calculations rarely take in the full picture of how
an investment in care would work, and pay off in the long run. "The
first thing that people ask when you propose a policy is 'How much is
it going to cost?' And you have to be able to say, yes, it costs 'X,' but the
benefits are much greater; they are 'Y.' If you don't measure the benefits
that are 'Y,' then you can't make the argument that it is a cost-effective
choice," Folbre said. These care-focused calculations show that support
for caregivers isn't an act of charity or luxury for individual caregivers,
but a sound economic investment for broader society.

"It helps us see the payoff," she continued. "I'm not saying it is easy
to do, and I am not saying I have completely figured out what the payoff is, but I am looking for more people to try to answer that question
and pay attention to it."

On top of shifting the policy debate, these figures help caregivers
feel seen and appreciated. In a capitalist system, where self-worth and
financial worth can be hard to separate, there's dignity in discovering
that what you do is worth something. When a single family caregiver
learns that their unpaid care of a parent is part of an overall effort that

is worth $470 billion, it calls attention to the caregiver's efforts in a direct and universally understood way. They suddenly matter in one of the most widely acknowledged ways a person can matter at this point in history. Their time, their effort, are worth something that can be expressed in money.

None of these figures is perfect, but the art of counting is always imperfect. Economics, like so many of our attempts to understand the world, is an act of translation, a flawed but essential process. These figures help us see how any one caregiver matters for our collective financial existence, and how financial support from the collective can improve the experience of care for any one caregiver and the recipient of their care. Research on programs that offer no-strings-attached cash transfers to parents of young children suggests that this cash can boost the well-being of the child in the long run. Parents who have received money are better able to supervise their children, fight less with their children and spouses, and are less likely to seek mental health treatment, and their children find time with their parents more enjoyable.

Brain scans show that the stress from poverty is, unsurprisingly, bad for parents. Infant cries are harder to take for those who are already overwhelmed, and from there it's a ripple effect. Children of parents who report poor mental health are more likely to have poor general health and/or a mental, emotional, or developmental disability—all issues that will cost society a lot of money in the long run. Cheaper, and better, in so many cases, to invest in the well-being of parents up front whether through a universal basic income or a tax credit. One analysis found a $100 billion annual investment in a childcare tax credit would be worth close to $800 billion to society, a figure generated from the predicted gains made in children's health, education, and future earnings.

Before the COVID-era expanded child tax credits, which the U.S. government gave to parents in 2021, dad Kevin Crawford was driving for DoorDash every night just to make ends meet. Based in

Grand Forks, North Dakota, the father of seven children, ages three to twenty-three, two of whom came from what he and his wife refer to as adopted embryos, took on the gig because his day job as a programmer wasn't making him enough money. "It's actually a decent-paying job, but because of a large family and the completely bananas rental market, it just hasn't been enough. Going by our budget, we need about six hundred to one thousand dollars more per month," he told me. Kevin went into parenthood thinking, and understandably so, that his master's degree, hard work ethic, and relatively humble lifestyle aspirations would make it possible for him to provide for his family. When they didn't, he turned to driving for DoorDash, which proved to be a decent solution. He could cover his budget gap and remain flexible in case a kid was sick or needed extra help prepping for a test.

The costs of time, however, were brutal. Kevin was working from eight in the morning until eleven at night most weekdays, as well as all day Saturdays. Sundays were the only days he'd see some of his younger kids, which was "painful for a father." Then the monthly child tax credit expanded and Kevin and his family received a check for $1,000 every month.

"I got to be home with my family at night. I got to make them dinner and sit around the table together. I got to let my wife sleep in on Saturdays. I got to help with their schooling. I got to pray with them each night. We got to watch TV, or YouTube actually, together as a family. We got to play games. We got to go on evening walks. We homeschool, so I could work through it with them and help with the areas they had trouble in. Of course, it didn't solve every problem, but I felt like they had a dad again, instead of just a stranger who pays the bills and maybe kisses them good night. No, we weren't floating in cash. We didn't get to throw the money away on entertainment or splurge spending or vacations; we got to be a family. That's all I want," Kevin said.

In January 2022, the COVID-era expanded child tax credit ended, the $1,000-a-month checks ended, and Kevin went back to Door-Dashing. He laments the effect this will have on his relationship with his kids nearly as much as the effect it will have on his ability to raise good people who will one day go out and do good in the wider world. "Having healthy and mentally strong children is good for our society as a whole. The advance payments mean I can invest that time into developing my kids into good citizens, rather than scrambling just to keep food on the table," he said. "All I want is the chance to provide for my family on a standard forty-hour week and to do what I can to support our nation as a whole. All we need is a little help."

THE LONG AND WINDING HISTORY
OF COUNTING CARE

This need to consider the economic and social value of Kevin's and other caregivers' care work isn't something we only recently realized. Economists have been making this case for over a century, a clumsy and circuitous, two-steps-forward-one-step-back struggle even in the best of times. Someone notices that the productivity (caregiving) of a large segment of workers (caregivers) has been left out of economic discussions and they fight for it to be included. Peers listen to them, but never enough to lead to lasting change.

In 1915, the United States created the office that would become the Bureau of Home Economics, the first serious attempt to count care at a national level. One of its primary goals was to help women efficiently manage their housekeeping and caregiving duties, and ensure that dinner tables featured healthy food despite food shortages caused by World War I. This wasn't an act of charity, or some lightweight offering for the ladies, as the architects of this program well understood that the goings-on of our households affect life outside them. The better a child eats, the healthier this child will be, the less costly health care will be for the child, and the more the child will be able to contribute to the economy and support communal efforts down the line.

Helping out in the effort was the long-forgotten Aunt Sammy, Uncle Sam's "wife" who had a weekly radio show for twenty years called *Housekeeper's Chat*. She was a character created by the Bureau of Home Economics who gave advice on cooking, chores, and parenting—always voiced by local actresses with regional accents and dialects. This was service journalism with a women's empowerment agenda, as Aunt Sammy's creators were hoping to help listeners understand that domestic work is a serious science and encourage those who did it to embrace radio and other new time-saving technologies for the home. Millions tuned in.

The Home Economics movement, of which Sammy was a part, didn't just want to help homemakers; it also wanted to better understand, and document, the depth of their work. The tool for this was a Time Use survey that asked homemakers to keep track of all the time it took to care, clean, cook, and more. It was a quiet revolution, a seemingly simple act born of a radical vision. By counting domestic work, the home economists had the data they needed to identify such work as labor and connect the dots between the unpaid labor in the home and the paid labor outside the home.

"The notion is generally held, especially by the masculine half of the population, that the housewife is a lady of leisure. So many household chores are supposed to have vanished from the home that the housewife has theoretically nothing to do but put on her best bib and tucker and listen to the radio or go to a bridge party. But certainly for millions of homemakers this is all too far from the truth, and especially of the mother of small children it is not *often* true," explained Hildegarde Kneeland, a Brooklyn-born economist and sociologist who helped lead the effort to gather time-use research for domestic work, in a nationally broadcast 1931 radio talk titled "How Much Time to Care for Small Children." The whole thing is filled with observations and arguments that, sadly, still scan as highly relevant today.

"*Her* schedule is full to overflowing," Kneeland continued. "The usual household tasks—the cooking, dishwashing, cleaning, and laundering—simply have to be accomplished along with the care of children. This double duty brings the mother's working hours to a total far beyond what would be considered reasonable in any of the occupations listed by the census. In industry we have long had the standard eight-hour day, with one day off in seven, and in many industries we are now getting the forty-four- and even the forty-hour week. For the housewife with small children, such working hours would seem like a real vacation. To her, a working week of seventy hours is nothing out of the ordinary—a schedule of ten hours of work a day for the seven days of the week is taken for granted," she explained, referring to data collected by the Bureau. These women made up a third of the labor force, as she described it, and yet were unpaid—"employed 'without gain' . . . a fact we are curiously prone to ignore."

Society did not consider being a housewife an occupation. Her work, hard and important, was not classified as work and therefore was considered "unworthy of the attention of those concerned with economic matters," Kneeland later wrote. If you are sensing that Kneeland was really pissed off about this, I think you're right. She believed domestic work must be counted, for social, emotional, and financial reasons. We live in a world where money ascribes cultural and social value, and, by virtue of being unpaid, housework and care are not ascribed any value. Making matters worse, a homemaker well might internalize this attitude, which "undermines her own interest in her work, and the efficiency and satisfaction with which she tackles it." Only those with an extremely strong, and therefore probably unhealthy, sense of self are able to value work that nobody else much cares about. The rest of us, social and therefore a bit needy, prefer to see our efforts acknowledged and praised by our wider communities. When this doesn't happen, we feel bad.

Though far worse than the harm done to her self-image is, in Kneeland's reckoning, the simple fact that she isn't paid. "More important than either of these disadvantages under which the housewife labors is her lack of economic independence." Care has long been, and continues to be, a major financial liability. Give it to others and you risk, like many women in my family, financial precarity for much of your life. Both of my grandmothers far outlived my grandfathers, and spent the last thirty years of their lives without enough money. They had no careers, no sizable savings, because they had spent most of their adulthood caring for their family. Worse, this didn't strike me as a deep injustice until I became a parent and had to consider that spending too much time on care may lead to my own potential future financial precarity. Ours is a society in which doing what is vital, what is human, can make you broke and nobody in power seems to notice.

THE PROBLEM WITH THE GDP

A decade after Kneeland attempted to quantify and value homemakers' labor in the United States, a young British economic historian named Phyllis Deane took up a similar endeavor across the ocean. In 1941, at age twenty-three, Deane traveled to British colonies in Central Africa to test out a new national income accounting system that two English economists were working on. As in many countries in the years following the Great Depression, economists in the United Kingdom were eager to have a standardized way to measure their economy. They wanted to know what their country was worth, and to have a

neat and easy measure to determine when that worth expanded and
when it shrunk.

In Africa, Deane, then a recent graduate of the University of
Glasgow, noticed that there was a lot of work happening around her
that wasn't being acknowledged by this new income accounting system. This included all the million tasks it takes to keep a household
going in a nonindustrialized society. The hauling of wood for the
stove, the arduous collecting of water, the production of daily meals.
She also noticed that most of this hard and yet unacknowledged work
was being done by women. "At present it seems illogical to exclude
the value of women's services in collecting firewood, preparing and
cooking food, and so on, yet include their work on the land," she wrote
in her recommendation report, based on her experience. "Most of the
labour for the basic unit of production, the family, is supplied by
the woman. She does most of the recurrent agricultural work, most
of the planting, the weeding, the fetching and carrying, the routine
harvest work and the preparation of food." Deane was ignored, and
the British economists went ahead with their vision of a standardized
measure for economic growth.

There were similar concerns in the United States. Simon Kuznets
was an American economist and one of the main contributors to the
concept of national accounting measures. He helped conceive of what
is now the GDP, which measures the total value of all finished goods
and services within a country's border over a specific time period.
Shortly after the Nobel Prize–winning economist shared his system for
measuring national economic growth with the world, Kuznets ques-
tioned his creation. "The welfare of a nation can, therefore, scarcely
be inferred from a measurement of national income as defined above,"
he wrote in a 1934 report to Congress, explaining that it couldn't
adequately capture so much of what we value, including caregiving.

Others have been making the same point ever since, pointing to what the GDP ignores and how those blind spots make for a less complete picture of the economy than many realize.

When record numbers of American women entered the paid workforce in the 1970s, the GDP, or total value of the goods and services produced over the course of a year, began to rise. And it made perfect sense: More women are working; we are more productive; our economy is growing. But some economists question this premise. When women work outside the home, there is less productivity in the home. Except nobody had ever measured the productivity of the home in economic terms, so nobody knew, for certain, how much productivity had now been lost. All that cooking, cleaning, and care that women had replaced with paid work had vanished, but nobody took note. Perhaps, they wonder, if it had been measured in the first place then the GDP would not have risen when women went to work outside the home. Perhaps it actually shrunk.

Some economists saw the omittance of the domestic space from economic thinking as a source of curiosity or befuddlement. Others, like Nobel Prize–winning economist Gary Becker, considered it a major oversight. "Parental altruism or 'love' toward children provides a powerful framework for the analysis of both the quantity and so-called quality of children," Becker told a roomful of prominent and likely skeptical economists in 1987, explaining how the allegedly irrational realm of love and care actually had direct implications on the allegedly rational world of economics. They were gathered in Chicago for the one hundredth meeting of the American Economic Association and Becker, the president, was delivering his presidential address. A few years later, Becker would go on to win the Nobel Prize in economics in part for this work of extending the field of economics to the world beyond markets and into the family home. Becker saw the family as the cornerstone of economic well-being.

"The family is such an important institution that progress in understanding how it behaves is justification enough for any discipline. But most economists, including the audience here, are not particularly concerned about family behavior. Your interest must be stimulated through a demonstration that its study helps in the analysis of other problems," he opened the speech, attempting to convince his predominantly male peers that the conditions in which we raise children are intricately bound up with the functioning of our economy and society overall. "Families have large effects on the economy, and the evolution of the economy greatly changes the structure and decisions of families," he said in concluding remarks. Upshot: Families are, to use an economist's favorite term, productive.

Becker had the right ideas about valuing labor in the home, and the economic models to prove it. Unfortunately, they came with rather fixed, and unrealistic, ideas about the gendered division of this labor. His hypothetical family often had Dad as the wage earner and benevolent head of household and Mom as the homemaker and caregiver, living in perfect, economically advantageous harmony. Except, as Marianne A. Ferber and other like-minded feminist economists pointed out, sometimes Mom wants to or has to work, sometimes Dad isn't kind, and sometimes Mom and Dad get divorced, leaving Mom no one to depend on.

For Marilyn Waring, feminist, politician, and scholar, the absence of domestic labor from economics is a source of rage. In 1988, the New Zealander published *Counting for Nothing: What Men Value and What Women Are Worth*, a critique of how mainstream economics excludes domestic labor and the way women contribute to the economy. Her main target is the United Nations System of National Accounts, which was created in 1953 to standardize the way individual countries measure their economies and GDPs. Waring questions why, in their formula, women and unpaid caregivers are classified as "nonproducers" and therefore not considered part of the market and can't expect to benefit from it. International standards for GDP measures were revised in 1968, 1993, and 2008, but the thinking on caregivers didn't change.

"Now, how about the women who have been pregnant and who have had children? Yes. Now, I really hate to tell you this, because it might well have been hard labor, but at that moment, you were unproductive," Waring told her audience at a 2019 TEDx talk in Christchurch, New Zealand. "And some of you may have breastfed your infant. Now, in the New Zealand national accounts—that's what the figures are called; that's where we get the GDP—in the New Zealand national accounts, the milk of buffalo, goats, sheep, and cows is of value but not human breast milk. It is the very best food on the planet. It is the very best investment that we can make in the future health and education of that child. It doesn't count at all."

Things are no different in the United States. Breastfeed and it's not part of the GDP. Formula feed and, bam, you've just contributed to economic growth, according to our measurement systems. If a man hires a nanny, the GDP rises. If the man marries the nanny, after which she still watches the children but presumably no longer receives a wage, the GDP falls. Did productivity, or the ratio between the value of something that is produced (a safe and healthy child) and the work it took to produce it (caring for this child), really drop?

Even more stinging: National economic measures classify the money parents and caregivers spend on children as consumption, not investment. As if raising children is something that only happens in the present tense, like eating a piece of chocolate cake or fixing a broken water heater. There's no acknowledgment that for all parents, consciously or not, the day-to-day of parenting is connected to who these people will be in the future: In what ways will they contribute to society? In what ways will they burden it?

SLOW CHANGE

Toward the end of the twentieth century, the fight to find new ways to count unpaid labor and reform the GDP took on a new urgency. This was the result of a growing understanding that getting women to work would not, on its own, lead us to gender equality. A revolution in the workplace had to be matched by a revolution in the home, and this wouldn't happen if we didn't figure out how to economically value housework and care.

At the Fourth World Conference on Women in Beijing—a 1995 gathering of NGOs, government delegates, civil servants, and the media, where Hillary Clinton gave her "human rights are women's rights" speech—conference organizers presented the invisibility of caregiving in economics as a major global problem. The "platform for action" that came from the conference demanded that the world do better at counting unpaid, invisible labor. They called for more data, expanding measures of work and the economy to include care and household labor "with a view to recognizing the economic contribution of women and making visible the unequal distribution of remunerated and unremunerated work between men and women."

In the early twenty-first century, these arguments began to prompt some concrete action. In 2000, the United States' Bureau of Economic Analysis created a Household Production satellite account, or a department that specializes in one area of the economy. It is dedicated to the research of invisible labor. The BEA took another step in the right direction when, in 2003, it began conducting an annual survey on how Americans use their time. This was the most comprehensive attempt to capture how Americans spend their time in the country's history as well as the history of the world.

Research from these time-use surveys helped economists from the Bureau learn that time Americans spend on household labor, which includes cooking, cleaning, and care, was worth $3.8 trillion in 2010. If included in the GDP, it would have raised it by 26 percent. In recent years, largely because of a push by feminist economists, other countries have begun gathering time-use data and creating household production satellite accounts as well—all in an attempt to get a better picture of the economic value of this unpaid labor and the demands it places on caregivers.

The work isn't easy, says Benjamin Bridgman, an assistant chief economist at the BEA who works on household production and did not speak on behalf of his agency. Large-scale time-use surveys are not comprehensive and are fairly new, which makes historical comparisons difficult. They only ask one member of the household. There isn't a lot of international data to compare them to. Also, there is no easy way for economists to understand the relationship between data on time use and data on consumption. "This has been something that has percolated in the BEA for a long time, and there has been a lot of interest in the economics community going way back," Bridgman said, alluding to the work done by the Home Economics movement back in the 1930s.

Today federal economists are increasingly aware of the risks of ignoring unpaid labor. "If there is one household where somebody is engaged in a lot of childcare, and then they switch and put that child in daycare, it may look like consumption has gone up, but it's not true," he told me. "We are thinking a lot about how to capture that, and there are a lot of challenges, but part of my job is to push through those challenges and do the best we can do." Recently, he and his colleagues found that the rise in household production increased significantly during the COVID pandemic and that this increase helped us avoid a recession. Unsurprisingly, I don't remember anyone thanking caregivers and homemakers for helping save the economy.

* * *

While I find big numbers impressive, I struggle to emotionally connect with them. Perhaps this is a monetary version of the saying "One death is a tragedy. One million is a statistic." One undervalued caregiver infuriates. One million undervalued caregivers is just women's collective and sad fate. To regain my fury, it helps me to do some imprecise math and figure out what these numbers mean in homes like mine. When I take what I've learned about the economic value of care nationally and attempt to convert that to the total value of my husband's and my labor, I find that I "make" much closer to the same amount of money, if not the same amount of money, as he does. It is so deeply ingrained in me that the care I give is a labor of love and not of economic worth that I can't even imagine what it would feel like to view us as true economic equals. To his credit, I don't think he would respect me more, and we already share most financial decisions. But my self-worth would get a boost, as would my anger on behalf of my grandmothers and all the other women past and present who made great contributions to the U.S. economy and the economies of their homes but were never recognized. My grandfathers, like many people's grandfathers, didn't include the women in their lives in financial planning, and their jobs' retirement plans didn't much take wives and mothers into account. Generations of women's caregiving was, ledger-wise, worthless. I don't want to be rendered the same.

Thankfully, during the twenty-first century more and more prominent voices are piping up to question why care is left out of economic measures and what it would take to correct that. A 2009 report written by top economists, commissioned by the president of France, critiqued the way the global economy is measured. This "can lead to misleading indicators about how well-off people are and entail the wrong policy decisions." A few years later, the Organisation for Economic Co-operation and Development, an intergovernmental economic organization based in Paris, called for better data on care work, and the International Conference of Labour Statisticians, an international group that sets standards for labor statisticians, said their field needs to create more sophisticated ways to measure and value caregiving. The World Bank too. They don't like how human capital, including care, is left out of the GDP, and think we need to do more to capture a country's "wealth," which includes both natural resources as well as unpaid labor. These changes can feel far away, the stuff of 650-page, heavily footnoted reports and international conferences. But the action that comes out of them can lead to substantial differences in the lives of caregivers who would be, at last, taken seriously in big conversations about money.

"I'm feeling positive," Elissa Braunstein, a professor of economics and editor of the academic journal *Feminist Economics*, told me. "There has been important, substantive progress though we do need to keep pushing." Braunstein said she doesn't have one particular goal in mind as to how care is best accounted for through economics. The point is to keep trying to assess the value of caregivers' time and care relationships for society at large. Some argue for the inclusion of household labor in the GDP, but she's not sure that's the right fix. Instead, her work focuses on trying to connect the dots between the time spent on household labor and the impact that has on the state of economics overall.

If Braunstein could wave a magic wand she'd create "a completely different metric of well-being [from the GDP] that takes into account non-market production and time. We would do a better job of seeing what it takes to produce human beings during the entire span of one's life, including childhood, elderly, and disability. A full-life-course perspective."

HUMAN CAPITAL

In the 1970s, philosopher and economist Amartya Sen proposed an alternative to the GDP and other economic measures. He thought that instead of measuring just what people do, we should also be looking at what kind of people they are able to be. Focusing on "beings," as well as "doings," as he conceived of it, was central to a humane way to measure a society's growth.

Over time this thinking developed into the Capability Approach, which encourages us to judge the moral fitness of a society based on whether individual humans have the capability to do or become whatever they are capable of. This isn't about just freedom to do something but also the opportunity to do it as well. Sen encouraged us to consider how a wheelchair user may have the freedom to work. But do workplaces make their space accessible? Do employers acknowledge that public transit for the physically disabled is more limited and therefore their disabled employee might not be on time? Does that person really have the opportunity to succeed in that job?

Or a poor child may have the "freedom" to go to a high-quality preschool and a poor parent may have the "freedom" to send her child to that preschool, as nobody is stopping them. But did that child have the opportunity to go to that preschool? Did the child have the opportunity to be surrounded by enough quality care, from both the school and a less exhausted parent when the child returned home, to thrive?

Sen's work as an economist and philosopher was inspired by the inequities and prejudice he saw in his native India. As a child, he lived through a famine during which only the poor went hungry. He also saw his father help a wounded Muslim day laborer who, out of economic necessity, went to work during riots only to be knifed by "Hindu thugs" and later die. What was being lost in both of these scenarios could not be adequately captured in the GDP. These experiences led Sen to see that there are other, often more subtle, ways of accounting for human value that don't involve money or the economy.

Wealth alone does not fuel a society. We also need to be in a place where our capabilities are developed, encouraged, and nourished, so that we can develop into the best version of ourselves and then bring that best self into our contributions to society. This isn't the everyone-gets-a-trophy variety of best, but one in which people have the ability to achieve a satisfying, fulfilling, and materially comfortable life and, from that place of emotional and material security, find ways to give back to the world around them.

Everything from wage laws and workplace protections to education and a just criminal justice system helps make this possible. So does the ability to give and receive care. Good care gives children the confidence and opportunity to be curious about themselves. Are they shy or social? Interested in putting stuff together, strategizing with a team, or imagining new worlds? What kind of work, should they have a choice in work, do they imagine themselves doing as adults?

Care also helps children understand their relationship to others. Did they learn about building community? Soccer games? Church? Sunday potlucks? Did their parents and caregivers model open-mindedness, empathy, and cooperation? (Did their parents even live in a society that afforded them the bandwidth to model such attributes?) Do children feel taken seriously? That they matter? And more straightforwardly, did their parents explain to them the power of citizenship, volunteering, voting, and activism?

A large body of research confirms what my mom, not a social scientist, has long known in her heart. Quality caregiving, paid and unpaid, from the family and others, has a positive influence on children and their future ability to engage with the world. Parents and other caregivers affect children's sense of connection to their communities and societies and their ability to flourish in them. They teach them the cultural norms and expectations required to function in the wider world, as well as the importance of altruism and putting others' needs before their own. Home is where citizens begin, where future caregivers are made.

Many economists who think about care this way want us to stop exclusively viewing children as one half of a private relationship and start seeing them as a public good as well. Parents, with all the lunch making, bedtime story reading, and soccer game cheering, not to mention all the time and time and time and money and money and money they devote to their children, are investors in the future. Their children are our future taxpayers, caregivers, and contributors to our current safety net for the old. Social Security, our guaranteed income after the age of sixty-two, requires younger people to pay into it so that there are funds for older people who are receiving money.

Investments made in early life, whether it be through supporting parents to provide better care or high-quality childcare for small children, pay off economically and socially in the long run. Neuroscience tells us how early this shaping and forming begins. Brain synapses that develop in a child's first one thousand days create the groundwork for their cognitive and emotional functioning for the rest of their life. In order for this development to happen in a healthy manner, children require health, nutrition, and responsive caregiving. The better the care children receive in their first few years of life, the better they do in school, the higher their earning potential, and the less likely they are to commit crimes in the long run. This all makes it unfathomable, not to mention unconscionable, the way the United States offers little in the way of support for parent caregiving or supplemental caregiving for young children. We spend less money—or a smaller percentage of our GDP—on early-childhood education than the majority of other developed countries.

"We don't choose the families we emerge into, but the parents we have can dictate the type of people we become based on the care and concern and empathy we receive," Diann Cameron Kelly, a social worker and higher education administrator who has studied the connection between our home lives and civic lives, told me. "When you are talking about parenting, you are talking about being under someone's tutelage for at least eighteen years. That is a very long time."

Kelly's own childhood inspired her academic interest in the relationship between civic engagement and care. Voting and volunteering were big values for her parents, and she began her first volunteer job at her local hospital at age fifteen. She was what was known as a "candy striper," a name inspired by the red-and-white-striped pinafore these volunteers wore, and brought books, magazines, and the occasional glass of ice water to patients. "I grew up in the Bronx and Harlem. There was always stuff for me to do in the community," she said.

Roughly two decades later she explored this dynamic in her research. She wanted to better understand how learning to be altruistic, self-reflective, and to care for others as children helps shape us as "socioeconomic beings." Her work looks at the relationship between parents' and children's attitudes toward voting and volunteering; the more parents discussed such things with their kids, and the more kids witnessed this civic engagement in what she calls an "altruism-rich" environment, the more likely kids were to be civically engaged themselves and vote as young adults, she found. "The choice to engage in civic duty is not intrinsic to human nature but rather is situational," she wrote in her 2006 paper on the subject. She went on to explain how, without parenting, democracy as we know it wouldn't exist. She stands by this still and yet wouldn't want anyone to get the wrong impression. Parents matter a whole lot, but they can't create citizens alone. Good early-childhood education, good teachers, good neighbors, and good friends are all necessary for the formation of future citizens.

Perhaps as we understand the collective social and economic

benefits of caring well for our children, we will begin to do the same for the care of old, disabled, and ill individuals. We all benefit when the people in these groups are given what they need to thrive and contribute to the best of their individual abilities.

The better a society treats older adults and the more positively it views aging, the better older adults do, Becca Levy, a psychologist at Yale, told me. She has spent decades researching the costs, physical, psychological, and even economic, of being an age-phobic society that doesn't offer adequate care and support for its older population. When we treat our older adults and the care they require like a burden, they internalize these beliefs and suffer for it. Levy has found that people with negative age beliefs are more likely to get dementia compared to those with positive age beliefs, even when adjusting for those who are genetically predisposed to it. Meanwhile, positive age beliefs among the old can lead to higher cognitive functioning, boosts in psychological health, recovery from disability, and better overall health and a higher life expectancy, according to her research.

Together, this tells us that Americans' bad attitude toward aging has a considerable and negative effect on the well-being of older adults, one that is also quite costly. Health care for this group represents a substantial chunk of overall health-care spending, and, in the course of a single life, half the money we spend on health care will be, on average, spent when we are a senior. Levy estimates that a shift in attitude toward older adults could lower these costs by $63 billion a year. That's a lot of money that could be saved if we only accepted what is abundantly self-evident and incontrovertible. Aging is a natural part of the human life span. There is nothing wrong with being dependent. There is nothing wrong with needing more care. There is nothing wrong with expecting more care. We can care more for older adults as a society, by doing things like making stoplights last long enough for slow movers to make it across the street, and making more television and movies that represent them as people navigating a rich and complicated time of their lives. Then there's the more direct ways, which might include more financial investment in paid care, as well as making sure that family caregivers are able to care for older adults properly while still being able to hold on to a job. It's hard to not feel like a burden on your adult children when the reason they are so stressed out and broke is that they're caring for you. In addition, good care is one way to combat the extremely high loneliness rate among people over the age of sixty-five and give older adults the practical and emotional support to contribute to the wider world in whatever way they can. A national survey led by a team of researchers from Stanford found that the majority of older adults in the United States have pro-social values and are looking to give back. Perhaps an old person can't drive, but they can cook. What if a family member or friend drove them to a homeless shelter or a house of worship where they could prepare food for the community? Or maybe with care they can get help navigating online job searches and find a job that helps them earn money and gain a sense of purpose. Or watch a grandchild on a Sunday afternoon. One need not be in perfect physical or cognitive shape to participate in society.

Ageism doesn't just hurt the way older adults feel about receiving care, or the way our society fails to care for them; it also impacts the way the individual caregiver experiences the act of caring for this population. "Ageism and negative age beliefs can make someone feel that caregiving is only a burden and the person that they are caring for has little value," Levy said. Whereas "someone who has positive age beliefs may have a better sense of the value of giving care to another person. Both in that they would see the range and diversity of skills that person has, and also the ways the person has accomplished different things at different points in their life. They would likely see a more dynamic person and the value that they gain from spending time together."

* * *

Another group that is penalized for their vulnerability and dependencies, and would benefit from a more caring society, is disabled people. There is huge variability among the people who live with disabilities, a demographic that includes one in four Americans and ranges from those who have challenges with mobility, cognition, vision, and/or hearing to those who are neurodiverse. In all these cases, a more caring society can be the difference between this group's ability to develop their capabilities and engage in the world and this group being limited by their disabilities. Such a society would do things like making sure public institutions, such as schools, hospitals, and transportation, would accommodate everyone, and that any assistance that a person with disabilities requires would be manageable and affordable, or free.

When it comes to the individual needs of disabled people, the concept of care is more complicated. For some, the idea of needing care feels paternalistic, and suggests a diminishment of agency and autonomy. "Assistant" or "attendant" may more accurately capture the relationship between a disabled person and their aide, if they have one. "As soon as it became my responsibility to make sure that everything I needed to get done got done, I was no longer being taken care of. It is an important distinction, because the notion of being cared for comes with diminishment of agency," Matan Koch, a disability activist and consultant who was born with cerebral palsy and is a wheelchair user, told me. He relies on assistance for a number of self-care tasks, which he sees as helping him take care of himself—and not being cared for. "The old joke is that you know you have an assistant and not a caretaker if you want to do something stupid and they will not stop you from doing it."

This distinction matters because many people still see disabled people as weak, childlike, and incompetent, and these biases are a major reason why this group still experiences large employment and earnings disadvantages. Koch, a graduate of Yale and Harvard, said he is over-looked or ignored because of his wheelchair, in professional environ-ments as well as casual ones. "I cannot tell you how often I'm in a restaurant with someone and the waiter will ask the non–visibly dis-abled person next to me what I want to order."

There are two different yet ultimately complementary sides to combating the ableism and discrimination Koch experiences. One is, as he prescribes, viewing disabled people as competent, strong, and capable of independence. The other, as other disability rights activists advocate, is placing less emphasis on independence as a measure of a person and replacing it with an embrace of interdependence. That goes not just for the people with disabilities, or those who assist disabled people, but everyone. Maybe, one day, if we all accept the inevitability of dependency in our own lives, we will be less likely to make any as-sumptions based on another's visible dependency.

At age forty-six, Denise Lance, who also has cerebral palsy, left her research job at Kansas University and moved back to her hometown in Missouri. The hope was that she would be able to afford assistance and could even offer someone a private apartment free of charge in exchange. But help was hard to find. Friends and family did what they could but couldn't do everything, and she can't afford to pay for all the help she needs; Medicare doesn't come close to covering it.

"I was feeling stressed about needing so much help and frustrated that the 'experts' on independent living (most of whom did not have disabilities) made it sound so easy to just get the right supports. Then I started reading Brené Brown's books and realized that needing help was not a flaw, or need for shame; it was part of my humanity," she explained to me. For a long time, she felt like she, as a disabled person, was paradoxically being held to a higher standard of independence than others. "Is anyone really independent? Why should I be held to a higher standard?"

A year after moving home she presented some of these ideas in a
2016 TEDx talk called "The Independence Myth: People with Disabilities Are Interdependent Too." In it, she explains: "The more I try to live
independently, the more I question the concept of true independence. We
humans are gloriously interdependent, but we fight too hard against it. I
have four college degrees including a master's and PhD in special education, and a second master's in English. So, I'm overeducated, but guess
what? I still can't tie my shoes, drive, or feed myself with a spoon. Proud as
I am of my academic accomplishments and the tasks I can do alone, there
remains a nagging voice inside me saying, 'You need too much help. You
are a helpless child, and always will be.' Society's emphasis on independence hammers me with shame. . . .What I struggle with most is asking
for help . . . The more I think of it, though, the real problem is that I was
convinced early on that needing help is a sign of weakness."

Today she wishes to see more of this thinking in the disability rights
movement. "I wish we were teaching young children that it's great to
do as much as you can for yourself, but asking for help shouldn't be a
source of shame."

Embedded in this lesson is something else she wishes she heard
more of as a child, which is to imagine herself as someone who doesn't
just need assistance but can provide it to others as well. She wants to
depend, and be depended on.

AND THAT WHICH IS PRICELESS

Then there are those instances of care in which money or nurturing
capabilities are not the point. Maybe because the dependent is too ill,
old, or disabled to be able to give much back, or just because the act of
giving care itself is valuable enough. Sometimes we care in the present
tense, for care's sake alone, with no future or potential for growth in

sight. We care because we agree there is a value to life, and we demonstrate this value by showing life, one life at a time, respect.

Dignity is an old concept but relatively new as a political imperative. The U.S. Constitution, for example, makes no mention of dignity, nor do many other founding documents of democracy. But in the past fifty years dignity, as a right, expectation, and value, has taken off. This is largely thanks to the also relatively new concept of human rights, which argues that dignity is one of the fundamentals of life to which all humans are entitled. What this means exactly in legal terms is hotly debated among international policy types, though for those of us who aren't drafting law our intuitive sense of the word is probably as good a definition as any.

To be treated with dignity is to be valued and respected, a treatment that used only to be a sure thing for the elite but is now increasingly seen as applicable to all humans, even animals. We all want dignity for ourselves and our loved ones in life and even in death. We also, in our more generous moments, want dignity for those outside our intimate circles. Dignity is the minimum we can offer one another to communicate that a person's particular life is worth something. And care, particularly intimate care, is one of the most reliable currencies of dignity. It's a demonstrable way for one human to let another know they matter. The measure of a life.

Joseph Varisco moved to Chicago in 2005 in pursuit of liberation. "I realized I was ready to fly, and was ready for a relationship," he told me.

Before that, he had spent all of his twenty years in Bensenville, Illinois, a suburb just west of O'Hare Airport. His childhood wasn't the smoothest. Two of his siblings were developmentally challenged, and his mom is what might now be described as neurodivergent, though nobody ever used that term while he was growing up. And there's also the fact that he's gay. Coming out went over okay in his Italian,

Catholic working-class household, but it garnered the predictable bullying and humiliation from his peers. When Joseph was eighteen, his
father sent him to live with his uncle, where he spent a couple years
helping to take care of his grandfather, a grumpy old man who was
dying from prostate cancer, while also attending college.

Shortly after Joseph's move to Chicago, an acquaintance from
home invited him to join a gay men's spiritual retreat. "I thought
it would be this Dionysian thing, just an excuse to gather and fuck.
But that is not what it was at all. Instead, there were many older
gay men finding kinship through sometimes problematic shamanistic
practices," he said. It was there that Joseph met Rich, who was in his
midsixties at the time.

In the LGBTQ+ community there is a tradition known as "family of
choice" or "chosen family." These relationships often replace biological
families for those who feel rejected by, or alienated from, parents and
siblings because of their gender or sexual identity or other reasons.
Rich and Joseph stayed in touch, but they didn't become a chosen
family until three years after their initial meeting. At the time, Joseph
was in a bad way. He was going through a breakup and had just finished
a master's degree only to land in a job market ruined by a recession:
"Every drop of savings was gone." Rich, who had long struggled with
depression and isolation as an unhealthy, older gay man, asked Joseph
if he would be willing to help him declutter his home for pay.

"His place was pretty bad, but I said, 'All right, let's do it.' I moved
in there and completely transformed it," Joseph said. Rich was "deeply
moved, and very grateful. He said he wanted to help me, to give me
financial support until a job does show up." The two grew close, each
a cure for the other's loneliness. "He just wanted to be able to share
affection, and have someone to talk to who cared about what he said.
He wanted to be seen, and to be valued," Joseph said. "His own family
had disowned him for his identity."

Eventually, Joseph found a job and moved out, but he still came over a few times a month to stop Rich's books and religious iconography collection from overtaking his apartment. It was, on its face, a cleaning job. But more than that, it was a way for two people to take care of each other: "We had this lovely ritual. I would get there before he wakes up and make him coffee, and he would wake up and we would sit down and talk, and share updates on one another's life. Connecting with another gay man, in an intimate but not sexual way, meant so much to him."

In 2012, Joseph learned that he was HIV positive. Rich was one of the first people he told, the day he got his diagnosis. First Joseph texted, just after midnight. Rich, awake, texted right back. They quickly decided to move the conversation to a phone call. "I was sitting on the bottom step of my building's front porch. It was cold and raining, no snow yet. Everyone else was asleep. My car window was backlit by twinkling multicolor holiday lights," Joseph remembered. "It felt like I was telling someone else's story. Reading from a script."

It was on this call that Rich shared, for the first time, that he, too, was HIV positive. Vulnerability begat vulnerability. Rich went deeper, sharing how recently he was scammed online by people who feigned romantic interest but really just wanted his money. He had little left.

The mixture of Rich's honesty and painful shame convinced Joseph to be open with his diagnosis to his wider community. Knowing he was okay in one person's eyes opened up the possibility that others might feel the same. Initially, Joseph shared his diagnosis casually, and then, more formally and publicly. He began curating performances and art shows about being HIV positive, and Rich came to every single one. With time, the arts and LGBTQ+ communities rallied around Joseph, and he secured enough funding to turn this work into a legitimate, rent-paying job. Fates swapped, Joseph was now the one with money. He still regularly paid visits to Rich's to help declutter and catch up.

In 2019, Rich got gangrene. It happened fast. First, he had his leg amputated, to above the knee. He was in and out of lucidity, in and out of the hospital and recovery centers, until he finally got the green light to go home. Joseph went to his apartment with him, where he cleaned and cleaned and re-bandaged and re-bandaged the wound. Nevertheless, the infection spread, from bad to worse, bone and muscle tissue in plain sight. Joseph kept cleaning it. There was no one else to do it.

On day three, Rich fell out of a soiled bed. He had no idea where he was: "I lifted him into the wheelchair, got him into a shower, and he was a bigger guy, and I called his doctor. I took him to the hospital and waited for six hours. I then called the family and told them that I am going to leave now because they are not going to let me in because I am not a blood relative. I go back and clean the house and grab my gear, and then head out to my neighborhood and try to get my head to an okay place."

Rich's health stabilized and was relatively okay for a year. Then came the COVID-19 pandemic; it became difficult for Joseph to visit as often. He didn't want to get Rich sick. They made a few exceptions for Thanksgiving, Christmas, and birthdays, following all the protocols to ensure safety.

February 2021 arrived and there was a new president, vaccines were available, and it felt like maybe, just maybe, there would be a reprieve. A day or two before Joseph was supposed to visit Rich, Joseph received a call from Rich's niece. They didn't know why or how it happened, but Rich froze to death in his car two nights before.

When Joseph inquired about a funeral, or memorial service, anything, Rich's family told him they had no plans. Joseph took it on, emptying out his 401(k) to cover the costs of the ambulance, coroner's report, and cremation. Rich wanted his ashes to be scattered in two monastery locations, one in Scotland and one in Kentucky. Joseph has permission but hasn't been able to make it to either place yet.

For now, Rich's ashes sit in Joseph's home along with Rich's collection of religious iconography. Rich wasn't a religious man in a strict sense, but he constantly sought connection to something larger than himself, something larger than all of us. To, as Joseph put it, the source of kindness. "I guess maybe I thought of him as my brother. I would call him Uncle, because of our age difference, but the way I spoke to him was brotherly.

"Our relationship never felt like an obligation, but sometimes it was frustrating. He could be picky about certain things. In the end it came down to the fact that he deserved dignity because he was human, and because he was there, and because who else would do it. And of course because I loved him. And that is what you do for people you love; you take care of them. And that concept is so intuitive and natural to me, and it shocks me that it is not part of some larger, intuitive, natural experience for all of humanity. That I find difficult to understand."

PART TWO

Looking Within

CHAPTER FIVE

Survival of the Most Sympathetic

*Rediscovering Charles Darwin
and Our Instinct to Care*

LIZARD-BRAIN PARENTING

Nobody wants to wake up to feed the baby. Not me, still walking like a cowboy three weeks after birth and experiencing a shade of exhaustion I would have previously thought fatal. Not my husband, who received zero days of paid paternity leave and was expected to write articles about Wall Street during the day only to come home to dirty bottles, dirty dishes, dirty onesies, and a conversation-deprived wife every night. But Augie is crying, and I go, traveling the roughly twenty steps from my bedroom to the kitchen counter where we mix purified water with formula powder, and then ten steps back to his room, where I hold him on a new IKEA POÄNG chair and give him what he needs.

And then I feel good. Not in a self-conscious way, as though I was doing what a good mother does, fulfilling some narrative etched into my subconscious from network television. My 4:00 a.m. sleep-deprived, postpartum mind lacked the ability to process my actions through the filter of external expectations and cultural tropes. This wasn't a story

I was telling myself. Deep in my lizard brain, the only bit of brain left at that hour, there was only impulse and subsequent feeling, and the feeling was a positive one.

"How is Augie?" "How is motherhood?" "How are you doing?" Sometimes these questions came couched in enthusiasm, an attempt to remind me of the miracle of life. Sometimes these questions came couched in sympathy, an effort to tell me that the pain of early parenthood was not mine alone. Either way, I had no words to describe how I felt. I'm garrulous, a lifelong oversharer, a girl whose most consistent note on report cards in grades K–12 was "talks too much," and who ended up unsurprisingly an opinion writer and personal essayist. I always had something to say, except this one time, this one very important time, when I answered anyone who asked that I had nothing to say and that that was the most interesting thing I had to say. I felt preverbal, like an animal, like I finally really belonged in one of those evolution charts a few bodies over from the ape. *Homo sapiens.*

For me, the pleasures of new motherhood, challenged as it was by everything that is hard about new babies combined with everything that is hard about having new babies in the United States, were not the pleasures of an advanced thinker. Not the pleasure of listening to a perfect symphony, or reading a perfect sentence, or meeting a new person and feeling seen. In fact, the advanced thinker in me didn't like new motherhood much at all, and instead felt physically and emotionally depleted by the perforated nights and the monotonous days centered around this small human's caloric absorption and hydration. I had a little notebook dedicated to this very subject in which I recorded each bottle, each pee, and each poo, including their duration and consistency, the dullest writing assignment of my life. This pleasure was different, elsewhere, found in small, contained moments of raw instinct when I knew that I could and should so I did, and then something warm and soft pulsed through me to make me want to do it again.

This animal brain took me by surprise. It's not that I didn't understand that parents love and care for their kids; I felt that deeply and authentically from my parents throughout my childhood. But I thought, fundamentally speaking, that care was a conscious mechanism—and not an impulse that fired off on its own, yielding a pop of good feeling in return. What was going on?

The path to valuing caregiving will require more than changing our social, political, and economic systems. We must go deeper, to the roots, and consider the way our collective story about humanity's fundamental nature ignores and mispresents care. My understanding of this nature, and perhaps yours too, can be boiled to down to a single pithy phrase used by everyone from science teachers, to political theorists, to Wall Street bankers, to obnoxious youth soccer coaches, to describe the one-and-true secret to any person's or species' success: survival of the fittest. Most of us associate this phrase with Charles Darwin and his theories about evolution.

In popular culture, Darwin is synonymous with competition, our alleged perpetual, instinctual, thirsty race to the top. Darwinism, as we understand it, both explains and fuels our every-man-for-himself culture of independence, a culture that seeps into all aspects of our lives, coloring our relationships with people we know and don't. But few of us know that Darwin didn't come up with this phrase that is endlessly credited to him, nor does it accurately capture what he had to say. Even fewer know that he, and many of the neuroscientists and evolutionary biologists who followed him, didn't exactly see things this way. My animal brain was no anomaly. Humans, Darwin argued, are as cooperative and caring as they are competitive. He even had a moving care experience of his own that inspired his thinking on this very subject.

CHARLES DARWIN WAS A GOOD DAD

Charles Darwin was a good guy. This is not in relative terms, a comparison to the many other great men in history who were, by most interpersonal measures, terrible. Leo Tolstoy was a cruel and selfish husband and father; Charles Dickens, the same; Pablo Picasso, an incessant and often indifferent womanizer; Einstein, not as bad but a serial cheater nevertheless; and Gandhi, who had asked his young grandniece and regular companion Manu to sleep in his bed with him to, in her words, "test, or further test, his conquest of sexual desire."

No, Darwin was a good guy even by normal guy measures. He was a family man, kind, thoughtful, and attentive to his wife and children. He doubted much of Christianity, and yet was always careful not to offend his wife for her more traditional Christian beliefs in a divine maker. In fact, some historians believe he put off publishing his big ideas about evolution for decades in part because he didn't want to undermine his wife's faith and all the comfort it brought her. Even if it's not true, the fact that it could be true says a lot about the kind of guy he was.

He showed equal sensitivity to his children, who delighted him and inspired his work. Darwin had, in his own words, "a fine degree of paternal fervour," and was the kind of dad who insisted his children sleep on the couch in his study when they were sick. His daughter Etty remembered her father as "the most delightful play-fellow," the source of a number of her and her siblings' favorite childhood games. One was called Taglioni, in which he would dance with children while standing on his knees. In another, Darwin turned into a growling bear.

He was also humble. And not humble as in a synonym for "weak" or "uncertain." Darwin possessed a steely confidence, with just enough nerve to question millennia of answers to one of the most profound and difficult questions to ever possess human beings: Where did human life come from? It was more of a Mr. Rogers variety of humility: an ability to listen, to ask questions, to speak slowly and thoughtfully on what he did know, and to step back when the conversation turned toward the unfamiliar. One of the reasons Darwin got his spot on the HMS *Beagle* at age twenty-two, for the trip around South America that seeded his ideas about evolution, was his reputation of being well-mannered.

Time and fame did not change him. Novelist Henry James visited Darwin when the latter was sixty and reported: "Darwin is the sweetest, simplest, gentlest old Englishman you ever saw. . . . He said nothing wonderful and was wonderful in no way but in not being so."

Goodness and connection weren't just traits Darwin valued in his personal life; they were also intellectual preoccupations. He was a careful observer of "the dependence of one being on another," as he wrote in *On the Origin of Species*, and was wary of any interpretation of his work that privileged our capacity for competition over our capacity for cooperation. We aren't bloodthirsty, single-minded strivers, he wanted everyone to understand, but a species whose survival depends on both protecting ourselves and others.

Darwin's sympathy was, as he himself argued, likely woven into him through the slow march of time. But his fixation on it, intellectually and personally, was in part a response to a devastating family tragedy. In 1849, Darwin's eight-year-old daughter, Anne, fell ill. She was coughing and achy with a fever, and though her symptoms improved briefly, she soon took a turn for the worse. This was the age when doctors knew sadly little about the human body, and even less how to heal it. Charles, having exhausted limited options, decided to travel with his sick daughter three hours by train to a spa, located at the foot of the widely admired Malvern Hills. There Anne would receive the "water cure," a new treatment created by a doctor named James Manby Gully. This was a form of hydrotherapy that involved being "packed" in damp towels and sheets to help stimulate circulation, taking hand and foot baths, and sitting under hot lamps. None of it worked. In April 1851, Anne died of what is now thought to be tuberculosis at the age of ten. Losing a child was a common occurrence back then, but statistics don't go very far in dulling pain. Anne was Darwin's favorite child.

In his memorial of Anne, penned shortly after her death, Darwin wrote intimately about who she was and the relationship he and Anne shared. She loved to play with her father's hair, "making it beautiful," as she described it. She was tender with young children, he recalled, and kind to all members of the household, servants included. "I quite thank you" were the last words Darwin remembered her saying to him, after he gave her a cup of water. It was this, all of this, Anne's finely tuned social instinct, the joy she took in caring for and connecting with others, that drew Darwin to Anne and made her absence that much harder. With time, Darwin found ways to conceal the wound, but it never healed.

In *Darwin, His Daughter & Human Evolution*, Randal Keynes, the great-great-grandson of Charles Darwin, writes about the impact fatherhood, including the loss of Anne, had on his great-great-grandfather's work. Darwin had spent the early part of his career focused on understanding the physical evolution of animals and plants. But his relationship with his children, and the loss of his favorite, heightened his curiosity in the development of humans. In particular, he wanted to better understand where goodness came from. Why, exactly, was Anne so caring?

Over time, Darwin arrived at the conclusion that we are born with a moral sense. He was convinced by his observations of animals, who showed concern for one another. He was also influenced by the writings of philosopher David Hume, who believed that "natural virtues" were innate, rather than something arrived at by way of abstract reasoning. Then there was everything Darwin learned at home. He carefully observed his children, beginning at a young age, and had a journal filled with notes on the development of their facial expressions, emotions, ideas, and, eventually, sense of right and wrong—unbidden. "About this time was fond of pretending to be angry & giving me a slap. with a scold, & then insisting upon giving me a kiss as reconciliation," he wrote of his son William at age one. Over 150 years later, psychologists performed rigorous studies on the presence of moral principles in young children and came to similar conclusions. We come into this world primed to cooperate and connect.

Darwin was making progress, but there was still one thing he couldn't understand in terms of evolution. Why did he still feel so much love for Anne, and why were memories of her still so vibrant, nearly two decades after her death? Why did it still hurt so, so much? How did this pain, this longing to care for his long-deceased daughter, help the species survive? He thought, and thought, and thought, until, eventually, he came up with a possible answer: "Parental and filial affections . . . lie at the base of the social instincts," he wrote in *The Descent of Man*, published in 1871. Our inclination to be good is, evolutionarily speaking, a product of our inclination to love and care for our children.

Darwin believed sympathy, or what today we might think of as empathy, altruism, or compassion, is the "all-important emotion," part of the pulsing origin of the social instinct. We can't take good care of our children without sympathy, and without it our children wouldn't survive. Therefore, "communities which included the greatest number of the most sympathetic members, would flourish best, and rear the greatest number of offspring."

"Survival of the fittest," or what Darwin himself originally called "natural selection" in reference to the fact that living beings who are better adapted to their environment are more likely to survive, is a fair, one-liner summary of his work. But only when coupled with "survival of the most sympathetic." Unfortunately, only the former concept, with its focus on competition and selfishness, rose to prominence in popular culture. "Survival of the fittest" had the advantage of appealing to those with power, giving those who say it with a straight face a chance to defend their greed and dominance as a product of a higher order: It's not their fault; it's nature's fault! Nature wants the strong to thrive and the weak to just go away because that is how species improve and survive. Far be it from them to mess with nature. "Survival of the most sympathetic," meanwhile, never gained as much traction. "While cooperation wasn't completely ignored, it was not taken up by main authoritative scientific figures," historian Ian Hesketh told me. "Sympathy," and its squishy associations with sentimentality, femininity, and care, held little currency in Darwin's age, and even less in much of the century that followed.

What popular culture, and, often, scientific culture, wanted from Darwin was an excuse to defend social and racial hierarchies, alpha behavior, and independence. The struggle for survival became less about genes and more about one human versus another—mano a mano, you against me, every man for himself. In this equation, independence is more valuable than dependence, because only the independent, and not those caring for dependents or who themselves were dependent, had the capacity to defend themselves. Such ideas were ubiquitous during my 1980s childhood, in which representations of man as an essentially solitary, selfish, and competitive being seemed to be everywhere. "The point is, ladies and gentlemen, that greed—for lack of a better word—is good. Greed is right. Greed works," fictional businessman Gordon Gekko explains in one of the better-known speeches in film history, from the 1987 movie *Wall Street*. Fans of the movie knew that, yes, this Gekko guy is off, the world he inhabits is off, and yes, these are the rules of the game.

I now know there were other people we could have listened to, other scientists and thinkers from the near and distant past, who looked at the world and saw sympathy as central to the human story, rather than an aberration or a manifestation of our essential selfishness—or the idea that being good is *really* only about helping. "There is a long history of scientists, people who have studied the nature of human nature, who found it to be fundamentally cooperative, the thing that makes human society possible," historian Erika Lorraine Milam told me. "There was, then and now, no single way of interpreting Darwinian ethics." Arabella Buckley, a contemporary of Darwin during the Victorian era, was one of the first people to reject the savage "red in tooth and claw" interpretation of *On the Origin of Species*. Instead, she focused on Darwin's insights into mutualism and cooperation, weaving in spirituality and a sense of maternal obligation. "Life" is a mother, in Buckley's cosmology. Living beings are her "children." The "struggle for existence" ends in "tender love for every being, since it recognizes that mutual help and sympathy are among the most powerful weapons . . . which can be employed in fighting the battle of life."

Peter Kropotkin, a Russian prince turned anarcho-communist, contemporary of Darwin, and fellow naturalist, published a book called *Mutual Aid: A Factor of Evolution* at the turn of the twentieth century. He, too, saw cooperation, not competition, as the primary engine of human survival. "The mutual-aid tendency in man has so remote an origin, and is so deeply interwoven with all the past evolution of the human race, that it has been maintained by mankind up to the present time," he writes in the book. During the years that followed, a number of scientists followed Buckley's and Kropotkin's leads, applying similar ideas about cooperation to field research on animals and discovering, largely, that they were right. Togetherness isn't some nice and tidy story to tell ourselves about our origins, a nursery-rhyme gloss on humanity, but a fundamental, and often complicated, feature of our existence.

Unfortunately, much of this and other like-minded writing can only be found in the "forgotten books" corner of the internet, where, with luck, you might discover PDFs of yellowed pages microfiched by some anonymous librarian long ago. These ideas are no easier to stumble upon in the classroom. In 1990, a science educator published an academic paper documenting the ways in which competition had won out over cooperation in American education. The paper is titled "Mutualism: The Forgotten Concept in Teaching Science."

THE EVOLUTION OF CARE

Today there is scientific consensus that we are products of both competition and cooperation and they both play out in complex and compelling ways on the individual and group level. With this curiosity about cooperation has come a deeper understanding of caregiving's central role in our ability to not only get along but also just plain exist.

A very, very long time ago there was a nonhuman caregiver who had an unusual for the time, genetically driven instinct to provide extra protection and care for her offspring. As a result, these offspring fared better than those whose caregivers didn't provide the extra care, and thus the children were more likely to survive and go on to care well for their offspring, as well as pass these care genes on to the next generation. As for humans specifically, our propensity for caregiving is likely one of the main reasons we succeeded as a species. Human babies require a lot of caregiving, and, over time, our brains and bodies adapted to ensure we could carry out the necessary tasks. We developed neurological wiring for these tasks, the same wiring that allows us to develop bonds with other people and our communities more broadly. For example, species with longer childhoods tend to be more empathetic overall, which, scientists hypothesize, is connected to caregiving. Longer childhoods means longer periods of parenting, which means a greater demand for empathy from parents. The less empathetic, on the one hand, wouldn't be up to the task, and thus their kids wouldn't do well. The more empathetic, on the other hand, would be better parents and, as a result, raise children with a better chance of survival.

From the gene's perspective, this might all be about self-advancement. When we care for our kin, whether it be our children or close relatives, we are helping our genes live on. This theory, known as kin selection, was popularized by evolutionary biologist William Donald Hamilton in the 1960s. There's plenty of research demonstrating the ways in which we are more likely to care for our kin, emotionally and materially, than nonkin. Sometimes even our care for nonkin can be a function of kin selection, which happens when our brains fail to differentiate between who is a relative and who is not. "[The] recognition of kin among humans depends on environmental cues that other humans can manipulate. Thus people are also altruistic toward their adoptive relatives, and toward a variety of fictive kin such as brothers in arms, fraternities and sororities, occupational and religious brotherhoods, crime families, fatherlands, and mother countries," writes cognitive scientist Steven Pinker. Another explanation for why we care for non-biological relatives is Robert Trivers's theory of reciprocal altruism. This is the idea that when I help others, even when that helping comes with a cost to me, there is conscious or subconscious hope that that person or group will help me in the immediate or distant future. That future help offers your genes a better chance of carrying on.

Many have succumbed to the temptation of believing that our genes are our ids, the drivers of our psychological motivations. If our genes are selfish, and only concerned with replication, then we must be too. But our feelings or cognitions are not a mirage, while our genes represent truth. Humans have layers and layers of intention and expression that extend far beyond what their genes want and those layers are all just as important. When it comes to care, we do it for genetic survival reasons, as well as so many psychological, cultural, and personal reasons, all of which shouldn't be discounted. Eldercare, for example, has no tidy evolutionary explanation at this point, and yet it is common across cultures and time.

Processes like kin selection don't explain "what is going on in the mind of an individual," Rachna Reddy, a biological anthropologist and primatologist, told me when I asked about how evolutionary theories play out in the community of chimpanzees she studies in Uganda. "I think the motivation is rooted in their personal history, the history of their relationships, and their memories. Feelings seem to be what drive them, feelings that may be rooted in kin selection, but that isn't how they experience it."

Through her research on primates, she has seen how the instinct to care can take many forms and arise in all different types of individuals— including adult male chimps who adopt orphans who are not their close genetic relatives. Even among chimpanzee mothers with biological children, there are a lot of different approaches to care. Reddy has seen a wide variety of relationships among chimpanzee mothers and their children, with moms and kids having different temperaments and different needs in terms of how much time they spend together. All these different types of parenting happen side by side, as chimpanzee moms tend to do much of their parenting in social settings. This gives the young a chance to engage with and learn from a large number of other kids and nonparent adults—all with their own care styles.

As a human mom, I can't help but feel envy. Our culture expects us to mother with extreme independence and in a cookie-cutter style— calm, attentive, and mindful. For those who don't follow the prescription, for moms like me who force their kids' shoes on their tiny feet in the morning instead of gently nurturing their kids' internal motivation to put these shoes on themselves, shame awaits. The idea of a bunch of mothers hanging out with one another, all parenting differently, and not a single one feeling bad about herself for it brings me great joy, even if these mothers are chimps. They intuitively understand what we humans consistently struggle to wrap our heads around: The instinct to care can be expressed in many forms.

When we move beyond trying to understand the initial motivation of why we care as individuals, and start to consider how we care as a group, we get an even better sense of how caregiving influenced the human story. In the late twentieth century, Sarah Blaffer Hrdy was one of the rare mothers working in the field of primatology and anthropology and, as a result, asked different questions from her male predecessors and colleagues. Based on her research, she argued that humans' success depended on not only quality caregiving but also collective quality caregiving, which eventually leads to better social bonds overall. Our babies are born needing a great deal of care in order to survive, too much for one person to give. As a result, our survival as individuals, and ultimately as a species, depends on what Hrdy refers to as alloparents, a group of non-mom parent figures, including fathers and relatives, who share in the responsibility of caring for our young. Over time, this need for collective caregiving led to deeper connections with our families and communities, as our need to trust others with our babies helped humans learn how to trust and cooperate with one another overall. This means that care isn't just a manifestation of our capacity for societal cooperation, but one of the reasons we have this capacity in the first place. We didn't just learn to work together to better compete for goods. We also learned to work together to be able to care.

THE NEUROSCIENCE OF CARE

Chances are, the sight of a puppy or kitten softens your mind and brow. There's a rush of good feeling, and a longing to hold this big-eyed and soft creature and give it what it needs. Or maybe you're one of the growing number of people who find comfort in caring for an adorable, needy robot like the furry little Purrble or Paro, a baby seal. What's happening there is that the animals, real or battery operated, are tapping into our caregiving system, a network of neurochemicals and pathways that fire up when we are called to care. Caregiving systems can be found, to varying degrees, in nearly all of us, save for psychopaths and people with a few other severe psychological disorders. This same response to a being in need of care can be seen in creatures who have been on the planet a very long time, as well as in their more complex descendants, mammals.

For much of modern science, the act of caregiving was overshadowed by research on attachment, or what it is like to be cared *for*, and altruism, or why people are good to one another. Care, or what it is like to care for someone in an ongoing dependent relationship and how that changes us, has only just begun to be investigated and theorized about by researchers in the past couple of decades. Among their findings is the discovery that caring for another can lead to surges of feel-good hormones in our brains. One of these is oxytocin, sometimes known as the "togetherness" or "love" hormone, even if it's hardly a fairy dust that makes all caregiving moments sparkle. The oxytocin-related urge I felt with my newborns did not inspire me with the same variety of love and togetherness as a lazy Sunday picnic with a new crush. But it was magic enough to make me feel attached to my tiny sons and, despite the hostile conditions, want to keep caring, which seems to be the point.

Numerous animal and human studies have established a link between oxytocin and a desire to care. Scientists have conducted experiments where they injected animals with oxytocin; the result was a spike in the animals' interest in caregiving. When scientists did the opposite, blocking the uptake of oxytocin along with other complementary hormones, they observed a sharp decline in the animals' interest in caregiving. Observers of humans have noticed the same thing: High levels of oxytocin correlate to more caregiving, and more caregiving correlates with higher levels of oxytocin in kids. The more we

experience these feel-good hormones in response to caring for a particular person, the more the bond to the recipient of our care is cemented
in our brains. We don't care because we love, but we love because we
care. The lizard-brain care comes first.

Neuroscience research on the plasticity of the brain during intense
moments of caregiving supports this idea. Being a species predisposed
to care doesn't mean that each and every one of us is born with perfectly calibrated caregiving systems fired up and ready to go. Our motivational systems, as scientists put it, often need external outputs to
trigger them. We do the care, repeatedly, over and over, and, with time,
we actually become more sensitive to care's rewards.

New mothers' motivational systems are turned on by a cascade of
hormones triggered during pregnancy. But, fortunately, for both the
sake of gender equality as well as men's and non–biological parents'
capacity to care, one does not have to give birth to connect with a
child. Shifts in care-related hormones have been observed in all types
of caregivers of small children, whether they gestated the baby or not.
Neuroscientist Ruth Feldman conducted an experiment for which
she studied the brains of three different groups: straight mothers who
were the primary caregivers, straight fathers who were the secondary caregivers, and gay fathers who were the primary caregivers. Her
team filmed these parents interacting with their children, measuring
their oxytocin levels before and after the interaction. Later the parents
would watch a video of this interaction while receiving a brain scan.
They learned that primary caregiver moms experienced heightened
activity in their emotional processing centers compared to secondary
caregiver dads; secondary caregiver dads experienced heightened activity in their mentalizing centers, or the part of the brain that allows
us to understand the mental state of oneself or others, compared to
primary caregiver moms; and gay primary caregiver dads experienced
both in equally high amounts. Feldman's takeaway is that the human

brain, when in contact with someone who needs care, is primed to find a way to provide it. Our predisposition to care may have arisen from the biological parent-child relationship, but it is not limited to parents and children, or those who share genetic material.

"Our findings show, in my opinion, not the superiority but rather the plasticity of the parental brain," she says. "Until 1850, one out of three mothers died in childbirth. Who raised the children? Neighbors and aunts; women who hadn't given birth took in the children. Suddenly, the entire network responsible for attachment in their brains started to activate. This network is very flexible because it is critical for survival," she told the Israeli newspaper *Haaretz* in 2018.

Other researchers have documented similar effects on the brains of caregivers through brain imaging and hormonal analysis. The brains of new mothers are radically reshaped in the first year of parenting. Fathers too. Caregiving can heighten our sensitivity and empathy to the ones we are caring for, making us more attuned to the other. These changes can be triggered by our biological relatives, or total strangers.

Though for all caregivers, biological parents and everyone else, this is never a sure thing. Our caregiving drive is highly individualized and subject to malfunction. Not every person is affected by oxytocin in the same way, meaning some of us are more responsive to the caregiver's high than others. Overall, negative feelings like stress can impact these feel-good responses. Sometimes, even in the most relatively stress-free situations, our caregiving networks fail to properly fire up. This is best documented in postpartum mood disorders, when, due to a combination of hormones, biology, and circumstances, the arrival of a new baby brings depression, anxiety, and/or psychosis. Failures of care in these circumstances are not the result of insufficient will or a lack of compassion on the mother's part, but of a medical condition that demands medical attention.

Even with these challenges, the pull of care remains deeply woven into our collective consciousness. In the early 2000s, social psychologist Jonathan Haidt and colleagues began exploring something they called "moral foundations theory." This was the idea that while some elements of morality are relative, there are also select moral instincts that are universal and pre-wired into us. Such thinking went against other prominent theories of morality, which argue that our ideas about right and wrong have been developed over time.

Haidt and others studied people from around the world, searching for any and all overlapping values. After a series of cross-cultural studies, they determined that care is one of the foundations of human morality, in addition to fairness, loyalty, respect for authority, sanctity, or the idea that some things are sacred and others are contaminated or profane, and liberty. Research on children, including infants, supports this idea. Care, that adhesive feeling Darwin had for his children and they had for others, is universal.

THE MYSTERY

In 1869, Darwin read an essay by Alfred Russel Wallace, another British naturalist who had also discovered the theory of natural selection, and it shocked him. Like Darwin, Wallace had spent years trying to understand goodness in light of their theory about competitive genes, struggling to understand exactly how our capacity to care and feel compassion could be explained in exclusively evolutionary terms. Wallace was baffled until he discovered his answer in the most unexpected of places for a well-regarded man of science. One evening he attended a séance, a popular pastime in Victorian England, and the conjuring of spirits had opened him up to once-foreign possibilities, a realm of existence beyond comprehension.

The essay contained Wallace's spirit-inspired answer: The human mind is too wondrous and expansive to have evolved on its own. We must, he wrote, "admit the possibility that in the development of the human race, a Higher Intelligence has guided the same laws for nobler ends." Something else, something bigger than nature, had placed within our neurons and cortexes and synapses a special sauce, the source of goodness and love. This about-face away from what could be measured and observed and toward what can only be felt was a shock to Darwin, who soon let Wallace know of his great disappointment. "I hope," he replied, "you have not murdered too completely your own and my child."

Like most of us, Darwin had an easier time pointing to what he didn't believe than to what he did believe. He knew we couldn't live without care. "It is surprising how soon a want of care, or care wrongly directed, leads to the degeneration of a domestic race," he wrote in *The Descent of Man*. But he didn't know where it came from. God was not the reason for our complex, sublime capacity to care, love, and empathize; he was mostly certain of it. But where did we get this capacity from? How does it work? We still don't have one tidy, universally accepted explanation. The origin and function of that lizard-brain feeling of warmth and purpose I got from feeding Augie remains a subject of debate among evolutionary biologists, anthropologists, psychologists, game theorists, and theologists, and I like it that way. It leaves room for a mystery, one that haunted Charles Darwin, and one that I, too, have an urge to explore.

I imagine we will likely never be able to explain, with absolute certainty or one grand unifying theory, the origins of care; why it feels right when I feed my children, nurse their wounds, hush their sobs, and share their triumphs and their despairs, a flicker that sometimes glows and sometimes burns, a destructive and productive kindling. But we are, the subject of the next four chapters, beginning to understand how care transforms us as bodies, minds, and souls. A transformation that Darwin, father of ten, could never fully explain, but nor could he deny.

CHAPTER SIX

The Feeling Is Mutual

How Caring for Others Can Better
Our Minds and Bodies

SOMETHING LIKE HAPPINESS

Eric Gardner and his wife, Gretchen, conceived their first child on an army base in Afghanistan in 2005. It was Christmastime, and they were both on R and R, or a rest and recuperation break. Neither of them felt up to traveling home, so they, with permission, spent the holidays in the VIP section of a largely unoccupied military base.

As in all families, the impending arrival of a baby called for some practical and emotional accounting. Who would care for this new and vulnerable being while her parent was, or parents were, working? Feed her? Bathe her? Soothe her? Add to this the additional weight of being a dual-military couple during the height of the War on Terror. The odds that one, or both, of them would be deployed in the first year of being new parents were extremely high. The odds that one, or both, of them could be wounded and killed in battle were not something anyone really wanted to think about.

Gretchen, they reasoned, was more eloquent and polished, and therefore more likely to rise in the ranks. Eric, though successful so far, couldn't envision a long-term career within the service. Nearly a decade of active duty hadn't given him much time, space, or motivation to think about change, or new beginnings. But then Gretchen got pregnant, and he found himself excited about the prospect of doing something different, something slower and quieter. At the age of thirty, Eric moved on, honorably discharged from service and now free to be the primary caregiver to his daughter.

Their decision was met with shock, surprise, and, as expected, a little scorn. Eric wasn't surprised by the ribbing, but he also didn't really get it: "I was getting out to make sure that the family that I was raising would be taken care of." If this sounds surprisingly tender for a fourth-generation military man and former company commander, Eric has his mom to credit. He learned the value of caring for another through, yes, her love, but also from the times she passed him books on child development and asked what he thought about them. She was an early-childhood development expert who helped run childcare centers on military bases, when not taking care of her own children, and the mechanisms and mysteries of childhood were often on her mind. When Eric became a father he felt scared but not altogether unprepared.

His first daughter was born in 2006. Eric used his commando gear to stash the wipes, pacifiers, and pouches he needed during the days alone with his daughter, days that were longer and harder than he had thought they would be. He was tired, lonely, and felt the rancor all exhausted new parents feel when someone tells them to sleep when the baby sleeps. And please don't call him Mr. Mom—though he did have his moments. "In the army, I could go tell one hundred and twenty guys to get up that hill with people shooting down on them, but I couldn't get this girl to sit down so I could get her diaper on with anything close to ease," he told me.

What helped him get through the day was the knowledge that by caring for his daughter, and then a few years later daughters, he would do the important work of nurturing them and shaping them. What he didn't anticipate was how caring for his daughters would shape *him* for the better. He, like me and so many others, had conceived of caregiving as a single current, a unidirectional flow of energy, support, and insights that is generated by the caregiver and received by the dependent. But the charge flows both ways.

Like roughly one out of three veterans who fought in the War on Terror, Eric experiences post-traumatic stress disorder. Some of his buddies cope with PTSD through medication issued by the local VA hospital. Others stay in the military, where they can easily avoid dealing with it: "If I was still in the service, I would not have to worry about it, because aggression, reactive decision-making, and always moving forward is part of the culture. If you are an infantryman you have to move toward the sound of gunfire, taking cover only when you can. But this is not what you do when you are raising kids. You have to slow down. I had to articulate to myself what I was feeling. You can't just sit there and shut off the world and expect positive things to happen if you are angry."

For a long time, he felt ashamed about his mental illness, and the vulnerability that comes along with it. It's not, he understands, ever likely to go away and the treatment options are limited. Many of his veteran buddies rely on opioids for help, but he's never been comfortable mixing drugs with caring for his daughters. Therapy's been helpful, as has his Alpha-Stim, a device that allows him to self-administer micro-electrical currents that help reduce his stress and anxiety. Though most helpful is his ability to listen to himself, a skill he sharpened and perfected through caring for his daughters: "Being with my daughters made me realize that I had to understand myself."

The day-to-day act of caring for them, predicting their needs, tending to their feelings, and forgiving their imperfections was an education in the art of listening. Not the issuing and following orders type of listening

that he did plenty of in the army, but a deeper variety of paying attention that was necessary for effective caregiving. First, he worked on this
listening with his daughters, and then, over time, he was able to direct
this increased capacity to listen inward. There they were, his needs, his
feelings, and his vulnerabilities. He began to sort through the debris of
his painful and violent past and come to better understand his PTSD
triggers, which include noisy airports and hot days. The better he got to
know his daughters, the better he got to know himself, understanding
what he can cope with, what he can't cope with, and when listening
matters more than making a plan or figuring something out.

"In the service you are competitive, aggressive, and out there to
solve problems," he explained. "When I engaged with people before
I had kids, I would just tell them the answer to whatever they asked.
Now I know how to stop and really listen."

Around the time I had Augie in 2012, the narrative that caregivers
hate caregiving went mainstream. "Exhausted," "burdened," "unhappy,"
"overwhelmed" competed for the most commonly used adjectives to
describe caregivers to children and adults in essays, books, blog posts,
and research papers. One commonly cited study on the unhappiness of
parents claimed that parents find being with their children less enjoyable than making food or watching television, which on its face sounds
pretty depressing, until you read the fine print: "Positive affect and enjoyment are strongly influenced by aspects of temperament and character (e.g., depression and sleep quality) and by features of the current
situation." In other words, there is no deeply concealed truth that parenting is a universal nightmare, only highly variable, inconsistent humans stumbling through their highly variable, inconsistent existences.
But that's not a very catchy headline.

I understand the need for the caregivers-are-miserable narrative for
political purposes. The world should understand how hard the majority

of caregivers have it in a country that offers them no support or, for the paid ones, a living wage. At the same time, it felt like we were losing something here. When the primary word we associate with care is "burden," we demean the experience. Care is not a fairy tale, as it used to be presented when idealized and sentimentalized by a world that didn't allow women their own desires or emotional complexity. But neither is care a horror story, one in which caregivers will inevitably lose themselves to a dark oppressive force, which is how many books and movies often present it today. Instead, it is a process, a complex psychological experience that can challenge, complicate, and enlighten, often all at once.

Like Eric, I have psychologically benefited from care. Being Augie and Levi's mom has made me emotionally stronger in a way that transcends the fairy tale versus horror story paradigm. The point isn't my resultant happiness or my misery, but the way in which care led me to have a more honest relationship with myself, drawing my attention to old traumas and emotional tics that I long ignored.

When I was sixteen, my parents announced they were splitting up. They told my three siblings and me at the same time, everyone gathered on the couch in our living room in our Southern California tract home. Brand-new at the time of purchase, it had five bedrooms, two stories, a curved staircase, wainscoting, a swimming pool—the third on the right of a pink-stucco-house-lined cul-de-sac. The house was a dream come true for my parents, grandchildren of impoverished Jewish immigrants, and children of parents who worked long, hard hours to achieve a middle-class existence. It was a way to say we made it, we belong, without anyone else's history or decor choices getting in the way. They couldn't exactly afford it, but maybe, they believed, if they got in there they would have become the kind of people who could, the kind of people who belonged, as if simply living in the house would bestow upon them the kind of confidence, clarity, and control that would manifest in both the quality of their marriage and the size of their bank accounts. California is filled with people for whom this kind of magical thinking works—but this time it didn't. Neither my parents' unhappiness nor their financial stresses could be relieved by the pristine granite countertops or custom woodwork. They had met so young and couldn't shake off the idea of something, someone, else.

Separation is courtship in reverse, and can be a long, complicated process of untangling assets, worlds, and feelings. My parents took around twelve years to let go, which included an initial separation, move to another house, five-year reunion, move to yet another house, second separation, heated divorce, moves to a variety of sad apartments, and then slow rebuilding of their lives outside the context of a thirty-plus-year relationship. I was the closest confidant to both of them throughout most of it, engaging in long phone calls, going to upscale department stores to browse sale racks and get a salad with my mom, and waking up early on Sunday mornings to hike with my dad.

Over a decade later, long after they both remarried and I got married and became a parent, I came across, mostly by chance, a pop psychology essay on "parentification." I had heard the term in passing before, but it sounded too clinical and overly prescriptive to be applicable to my mostly stable emotional life, and so I didn't think much about it. This time, however, there I was.

There are two types of parentification. The first is instrumental, when a child is responsible for tasks like bill paying or food shopping that are generally done by adults. This was not me. The second is emotional, and it's when children are expected to "gauge and respond to the emotional needs of the parent, serve as confidante and an unwavering source of support, and provide crisis intervention during times of psychological distress" as one paper put it. Check, yes, wow, check. Parentification is common during a divorce, when parents are in need of emotional support but can no longer turn to their longtime partners, and is most likely to happen to bright, sensitive, and empathetic kids. Parentification can turn one into a compulsive caregiver for life, always looking for ways to help others, even when nobody asked.

During the very long death of my parents' marriage, I took to this role with a myopic ease. While my parents and siblings were always loving and supportive, I had played a leadership and nurturing role in my family from an early age. My parents will tell you that I wanted it, that I was a wise-beyond-my-years type of kid, one with a strong internal compass, precocious competency, and inborn empathy for others. I believe this is absolutely true, while also believing that there are other potential truths that could never flourish in my particular house, with our particular constellation of personalities and life stories, and that's just how it goes. Their version of the story is indeed the one we lived and the one that led to me, following their separation, believing that their well-being and that of our family was mine to worry about.

The practical part of being parentified came easily to me. I'm a decent task manager and creative problem solver; organizing family trips or holiday dinners takes little effort for me. The psychological part had its benefits, too, as family intimacy has always been important to me, and so I found easy meaning and satisfaction in keeping mine close. "They fuck you up, your mum and dad. / They may not mean to, but they do," wrote British poet Philip Larkin, arguably his most famous two lines of verse. True, and yet sometimes in that fucking up you gain a few powers too. Research shows that parentified children can grow into adults with strong interpersonal skills, having spent their formative years sharpening their ability to empathize, connect, and communicate. They're also more likely to value and maintain deep family bonds and, at the same time, be more autonomous and self-reliant than their peers. Larkin, by the way, had a very close relationship with his mom. The two of them wrote to each other twice a week for thirty years discussing everything from relationships and books to the mundane details of their daily lives.

Underneath all this good from my years as my parents' best friend, good that makes me feel like me and good that I still celebrate, sat a more troubled layer of my emotional life that, before kids, rarely saw the light. Here was the belief, not always conscious, that the internal and external emotional problems of those around me were mine to fix. I've never pursued an outwardly perfect life, but I did believe that something should be done about every problem for everyone, and while one may not succeed, one can at least try.

Except people, and life, can't always be fixed. Levi tick-tocks between fragility and fire at a dizzying clip when he's upset. Augie retreats within, often behind the scrim of a book, his features drained of vitality. Over the years, I've learned what works to ease the spell of sadness or anger. With Levi, it's a gentle presence, patience, and an occasional aggressive hug. With Augie, directness and humor. But fixing them or their problem? Making it all better? I no longer feel as though that is entirely up to me. Sometimes when I can't help myself, sometimes when I try anyway, Augie will say to me, "I think it just sucks, Mom."

He's right, of course. Life, other people, even oneself, can surprise us for the worst, and when that happens it's possible to both show up and just let it be. This seems like the kind of lesson that should have come from my more equal relationships with people who didn't depend on me for food, shelter, socialization, and love. The ones who would be fine enough without me. Yet I never found myself there with my adult family, husband, or friends. It wasn't until I had kids and experienced the deep up-closeness one gets of another person, another life, through caregiving that I found my way to this truth.

To care well for my sons, I had to get to know them better than I've ever known anyone else. Viewing the world through their eyes, those glorious little walking ids, I saw how inevitable pain and disappointment are in the big, bad, imperfect world. I felt their suffering, their weaknesses, their vanities, and I came to understand how ridiculous it is to believe I could, or should, fix everything. I am able, finally, to see the ways my parents' divorce and subsequent parentification of me negatively affected me, and, bit by bit, undo this damage.

There's no neat end to this story. My ability to distinguish things we can control from things we can't remains far from accurate. But, thanks to Augie and Levi, thanks to every day I juggle care, I've learned to relinquish, to depend more on others, and to allow the struggles of others to exist outside the context of me potentially fixing them. Sometimes. More often than before. Believing there is a fix for everything might just be my forever weakness, the stickiest of vanities, but now it is one I can see, one that I can accept is a little outside my control.

THE INVISIBLE CAREGIVER

One of the reasons we don't think about care as an important psychological journey is because the research on it remains scant. Caregiving is not, historically, something male scientists did a lot of, and, therefore, they didn't feel it was worthy of study. When they finally came around to studying care, their limited experience led them to have an equally limited view of their subject. "It's a primary, important behavior for humans that scientists forgot about for a long time," Tristen Inagaki, an assistant professor of psychology, explained to me, pointing to the long legacy of white and male scientists overlooking caregiving. She said that when she began studying the science of social connection in the 2010s she was surprised by how absent her experience as a woman and as a Japanese person, a culture that "highly values caregiving," was from the research.

The first scientific attempts to better understand care took place in the mid-twentieth century, when psychologists began to formally study the psychological impact mothers have on their children. At the time, this was considered controversial and groundbreaking. Parents, the thinking until then went, were there to ensure the survival of their children. Psychological bonding was possible—ancient literature is filled with parental love, like when Odysseus's mother dies of grief over him—but it wasn't the main objective, not when childhood death was such a likely outcome. For most of history up until the twentieth century, roughly one-quarter of infants died before turning one and roughly half of all children died before finishing puberty. Even up until the late 1900s, experts encouraged parents to prioritize their children's physical health and independence over bonding.

The specter of death combined with the fact that, for many families, children's most important role was economic made parenthood far less emotionally grounded than it is today. Experts and everyone else seldom discussed how adults deeply shape their kin; almost no one considered how raising kin may shape the adults. As recent as the 1950s, it was still commonplace for parents to believe that babies cried just to get attention.

Donald Winnicott and John Bowlby, two British psychologists who took an unprecedentedly close look at the parent-child relationship, helped change this. Their work, which might seem obvious to us today, was considered a breakthrough at the time. Winnicott was one of the first to observe that a healthy relationship between mother and child is essential to the child's development. "I once said: 'there is no such thing as an infant' meaning, of course, that wherever one finds an infant one finds maternal care, and without maternal care there would be no infant," Winnicott wrote. He would later go on to develop his still-respected theory of the "good enough mother." This is the idea that a "mother" (he didn't think it needed to be the biological mother) should be warm, empathetic, and sensitive to a child, but not always, or perfectly so. The "enough" part refers to the fact that the mother should fail the child at times, which benefits the child in the long run. It's how they learn resilience. "The good enough mother, as I have stated, starts off with an almost complete adaptation to her infant's needs, and as time proceeds she adapts less and less completely, gradually, according to the infant's growing ability to deal with her failure," he wrote.

Bowlby is best known for his work on attachment theory, much of which he developed alongside psychologist Mary Ainsworth. This is the idea that feeling securely attached to a caregiver at a young age is crucial for one's emotional and social development. The World Health Organization commissioned Bowlby to write a report looking at the mental health effects of maternal deprivation among children in the years following World War II, and his main conclusion was that "the infant and young child should experience a warm, intimate, and continuous relationship with his mother (or permanent mother-substitute) in which both find satisfaction and enjoyment." A child should feel connected to a caregiver, and both the child and caregiver emotionally benefit from the relationship. This connection is, Bowlby argued, essential for the child's future well-being.

Bowlby's theories, along with those of like-minded colleagues, were an important break from those of Sigmund Freud. When Freud read Darwin, he saw it as evidence that humans, descended from animals as we are, have selfish animal instincts that must be socialized out of them. Bowlby read Darwin and saw evidence of our instinct to attach to others, an adaptive skill without which we wouldn't survive.

Unfortunately, Bowlby's curiosity about caregiving didn't much extend to the caregiver. In 1988, decades after his first insights into attachment, he wrote: "The occurrence of altruistic care of young is readily understood since it serves to promote the survival of the offspring." "Readily understood," in this case, meant that a parent's instinct to care for their child was so obvious that it didn't merit a more thorough investigation. The big and interesting transformations, Bowlby and others assumed, were taking place in the kids, not their caregivers.

"The field of developmental psychology emerged in the late nineteenth and early twentieth centuries to study how children learned to walk, talk, think, and feel as psychologists sought to understand how children's minds were shaped by early experiences at home and school," Darby Saxbe, professor of psychology at the University of Southern California, told me. "But despite burgeoning interest in how parenting affects children, many of these foundational researchers were fairly incurious about how parenting affects parents." At NEST: The NeuroEndocrinology of Social Ties, her lab at USC, Saxbe and her team are working on what is now considered an exciting new frontier: the developmental psychology of parents. They want to fill the gaps left by Bowlby and colleagues and better understand how caring for children "can rewire our brains, bodies, identities, and relationships."

Historically, researchers afforded even less curiosity to caregivers to the old, sick, and disabled than caregivers to children. Scientists didn't begin publishing research on the experience of these caregivers until recent decades, and even then, it lacked nuance. Instead of focusing on the full spectrum of feelings experienced by caregivers, the researchers homed in on the bad side. Caregivers, they thought, were an ideal opportunity to study human misery, and so misery they sought out.

MORE THAN A BURDEN

David Roth knows caregiving can be good for you. The epidemiologist and biostatistician has been studying the physical and emotional state of caregivers to dependent adults for decades, carefully documenting the potential positive outcomes of caring for another. But when he writes grant proposals, he usually leaves all that "half-full" stuff out. "I don't think I have ever applied for a big grant to study the benefits of caregiving," he told me. "You don't get a grant from the federal government to prove that things are going great; you get one to solve a problem."

Scientific research, generally speaking, isn't particularly interested in exposing what's working well in the world. This isn't a product of cynicism so much as an optimistic pragmatism. We aren't content learning how things are going right when there is a problem to solve. We're Americans. We're doers. There's always a problem to solve. It's an imperfect system made further imperfect by the fact that identifying a problem is far from a science. Despite their commitment to test and measure and collate and experiment and observe, scientists are people and people have biases and these biases appear in their work. Homosexuality, for example, was long pathologized by scientists as something that needed a cure. So was women's anger.

"The caregiving research in psychology and the social sciences got started as a natural experiment of stress," said Roth, again referring to caregiving for dependent adults. It's not ethical for scientists to conduct experiments in which they randomly assign one group of people to a stressful situation and another to a less demanding situation and see how each group fares. So they focus on something they perceive as stressful, like caregiving, and examine it through this lens, in order to better understand the mechanisms of stress.

It should come as little surprise that the findings from most of the early caregiving researchers are depressing; they were, for the most part, built on the assumption that to care is to suffer and they only reinforce it. Care for another and you are more likely to be miserable, sick, and die earlier than you would have if you never worried about or tended to anyone besides yourself. "Clinical observation and early empirical research showed that assuming a caregiving role can be stressful and burdensome. Caregiving has all the features of a chronic stress experience," begins one study on caregiving for the old and disabled. You can find echoes of this in a large number of studies, news articles, and even caregiver support materials for both parents and caregivers.

I know I have said this already, but it merits repeating. Caregiving *is* a burden. It's physically and emotionally hard on everyone who does it, particularly those who care for old, sick, and disabled people, and especially so for older caregivers who take care of a difficult partner, relative, or friend. The problem with the research isn't the way it presents caregiving as a burden, but how it presents it only as a burden, with little curiosity on what makes it a burden, and even less on what makes it an opportunity. "If you look closely at the caregiving studies, you will notice that very few actually measure helping behavior. So, it could be that negative reactions to helping are due to the pain of watching a loved one suffer, and not to helping them," Stephanie Brown, an evolutionary psychologist who has written about the overly negative lens placed on care, told me.

One problem with a lot of the research on adult-to-adult caregiving is that it only looks at caregivers who have reached out for help in some way, either in clinical settings or by seeking out services or programs, and not those who haven't requested assistance. It's like using the patients of a hand doctor to learn how everyone's hands are doing. Another problem is that the definition of caregiver in these studies sometimes includes only those who are doing it in the most intense of conditions; around the clock, on their own, for years.

In any instance, it can be hard to separate the good that one experiences through the act of caregiving from the pain one experiences from the stress caused by the reason you need to care in the first place. Hard but not impossible. Once caregiving researchers began looking for the benefits of care, they found them, often to their surprise.

THE PHYSICAL AND PSYCHOLOGICAL BENEFITS OF ADULT CAREGIVING

Few things in this life are all bad, or all good, in all circumstances. This tends to be especially true for those efforts and struggles and moments that bring us the most satisfaction, the ones that give shape to our days and allow us to say, "*This*, yes, *this*, is my life." Hiking a tall mountain, building a business, and being a firefighter are a few of the many human pursuits that we understand can be sometimes difficult, sometimes stressful, but still overall positive. A stressful situation doesn't always mean regrets. Some of our greatest sources of pride come from stress. It's also generally understood that in each of these situations there is such a thing as too much. We can climb mountains too high in the literal and metaphoric sense, and this will ruin the climbing for us. The stress will outweigh the benefits.

Things are no different in human relationships. For most of us, maintaining an ongoing, intimate connection with another person, be it your mom, best friend, partner, or sibling, isn't effortless. We don't expect constant harmony, and we know that the well-being of the connection is affected by the circumstances in which it takes place. In these types of relationships, we've learned to have realistic expectations and that it is okay to sometimes need a break. Care is no different. It's also a human relationship and, therefore, a mixed bag. There's plenty of stress and sacrifice and struggle to be documented, especially when the care is given in societies that don't support caregivers. But, as scientists have only just begun to acknowledge, there is plenty of good too.

Connecting to other people is good for our minds and bodies.

Friendship and community matter as much as adequate sleep, diet, and abstaining from smoking in terms of longevity. Helping someone, or even just being kind to them, fires up the pleasure centers in our brain. Scientists call this a helper's high and it is particularly pronounced when our giving is voluntary and effective. Meanwhile, loneliness is connected to cognitive decline and increased mortality. All of this translates to care.

Anyone who has ever cared for another is familiar with exhaustion. Unable to shower exhaustion. Too tired to talk exhaustion. Can't think exhaustion. Siphoning our vitality, teaspoon by teaspoon, until there is nothing left exhaustion. Yet longevity studies suggest that, for many, the opposite is happening. It's possible that we are extending our lives through the act of care. Researchers have found that both parents and caregivers to old and disabled people tend to live longer than their non-caregiving counterparts.

When Lisa Fredman first found a longevity boost among caregivers to adults, she was surprised. "I thought, what on earth is going on here? . . . I blamed myself. I thought something was wrong with my data," she told the *New York Times* in 2011. At the time she explained the difference in mortality rates as evidence of self-selection. Healthier, more emotionally stable people tend to become caregivers because they're the ones with the physical and psychological bandwidth, which in itself was good news. The narrative surrounding caregiving was so bleak that to learn that it didn't inevitably deplete caregivers and hasten their untimely deaths was an unexpected, positive twist.

As Fredman continued to study the health effects of caregiving over the course of the decade, she discovered that there was more than self-selection at play. A 2019 study that she and her colleagues published in the *Gerontologist* found that older women who are high-intensity caregivers—those who "assisted a person with dressing, transferring, bathing, or toileting" according to the study—have a lower mortality rate than their peers who do less caregiving or no caregiving at all. This was still the case even after they controlled for how healthy the caregivers were to start with. The proposed explanation was twofold. One, caregiving keeps them physically and cognitively active, which helps keep their bodies and minds in good shape. Caregivers to old, disabled, and sick individuals have, according to some research, better memories and think faster than their non-caregiver counterparts. Two, the nature of the activity, the act of care, likely played a role in their better health outcomes, a hypothesis supported by the fact that caregivers, despite doing stressful work, don't have higher levels of inflammation than their non-caregiving peers. Research on parents, including adoptive parents, suggests that something similar is going on with them as well. Grandparents, too, though not when they are the primary caregivers. There's a link between caring for children and living a longer life, one likely connected in part to the psychological benefits of care.

A number of polls have asked caregivers who are over the age of forty and care for the sick how they felt about care, and the vast majority considered it a positive, worthwhile, rewarding experience that was as stressful as it was fulfilling. Other studies have found that caregivers believe caring for another makes them a better person or more resilient. They feel gratitude for the chance to care for a loved one, a sense of accomplishment for being able to care and learn new skills, and believe it strengthened their relationship and added meaning to their lives. Complex humans that they are, they often even feel the good and bad at once.

Another big theme in the research on care, one that holds true for all types of caregivers, is that it is not the making the soup or feeding the soup that is horrible; it's the inability to work a job and have time to make the soup, or the fact that one never gets a break from making the soup and therefore has no time to rest, exercise, or take a restorative break—like eating the soup, alone, in a quiet room. So often, it's the bills we can't pay because we are caring that ruin our lives. The more people feel supported in their care by government policies and still feel as though they are in control of their own life, the happier they are as caregivers.

Paid caregivers have similarly positive, albeit complex, feelings about care. They are underpaid and yet, according to one large-scale study that defined caregivers broadly, including doctors and professors as well as nannies and home health-care workers, have greater job satisfaction than those working comparable jobs in terms of factors like money, hours worked, education, and more. This was the case even when researchers controlled for income, education, and gender. The ability to help others and connect emotionally at work can yield "psychic income" that these caregivers appreciate even if the work is hard.

"It surprised me," Naomi Lightman, sociologist and first author of the study, told me. Her hypothesis going into the research was that caregivers would have lower job satisfaction because of the burnout from the emotional demands of their work. "We all, intuitively, in our daily lives as caregivers, experience both sides of the coin," she added. "We have days when we are resentful and days when we are grateful to care, whether it is for pay or not for pay." But for the paid caregivers in this study and in others, the grateful days outweighed the resentful ones.

A survey of American home health-care workers and certified nurse assistants, or health-care aides who work in nursing homes rather than individual homes, yielded similar findings: Over 80 percent said they were very or somewhat satisfied with their job and many said they want to keep their jobs because of "their desire to care for others and feeling good about doing so." They are, however, less enthusiastic about their salaries and benefits. Only 60 percent found their compensation fair.

Medical sociologist Clare L. Stacey, who studied home health-care aides, has come to a similar conclusion. "Watching aides interact with elderly or disabled clients opened my eyes to the stresses associated with care, and also convinced me that caregiving—especially when carried out in the right conditions—can affirm social ties and give lives meaning, whether we are on the giving or receiving end," she writes in her book *The Caring Self*. Sadly, too few caregivers experience these right conditions, as a large number are subject to abuse and injuries on the job, onerous workloads, poverty wages, and the inability to afford their own health insurance.

THE NOT-SO-MISERABLE PARENT

Parents aren't that different. There are plenty of studies showing that becoming a parent makes one happier, while others show the exact opposite. But what interests me more is what the research tells us about why parenting makes us unhappy. Is it that the person-to-person act of caring for a child is overall misery-inducing? Or is it the stress that comes along with parenting, like feeling there is never enough money or time, that ruins the experience?

Two large studies, and a handful of smaller ones, found that it's most often the latter. In 2019, economists David Blanchflower and Andrew Clark published a study for which they examined life-satisfaction data collected from over 1 million people over the course of ten years in thirty-five European countries. They discovered a broad happiness dip among parents but then quickly determined that this was the result of the parents not feeling like they had enough money. "The negative effect of children comes from their effect on financial difficulties," they write in the paper. When economic struggles were taken out of the equation, children raised the happiness of parents in the vast majority of cases. Parental income and education also played a role, as well as the country's overall income and the level of social support.

Sociologist Jennifer Glass came to a complementary conclusion after reviewing data on parenthood and happiness from nineteen European countries plus New Zealand, Australia, and the United States. In Russia, France, Finland, Sweden, Norway, Spain, Hungary, and Portugal she found that parents range from being "slightly happier than nonparents (increases in happiness of about 1 percent compared to nonparents for Russia and France) to significantly happier than nonparents (increases of up to 8 percent from the baseline level of nonparents)."

There is a clear and obvious link between the availability of family-friendly government policies in a country and the level of happiness of the parents, with paid-leave and childcare subsidies mattering the most. Considering the United States offers very little in the way of support to parents and is the only industrialized nation in the world without a universal paid-leave policy, it's unsurprising that American parents ranked as the least happy, by a long shot.

"If you ask parents, 'Is it parenting that's making you unhappy?' they're not going to tell you it is. They're going to say they love their children. They adore their children. It's the best thing they've ever done. I say all those sappy things, and my kids would never in a million years think that it was a bad idea to have children," Glass told me. "But when you ask them to rate their happiness overall, that's where you see the happiness dip. It's not that they're unhappy that they are parents. They're unhappy that they're being forced to parent in a society that provides virtually no support."

The ability to share the burden of care matters a lot too. One study that considered parental burnout in forty-two countries found that the more individualistic a society is, the more likely the parents in it are to feel burned out. This was even the case when comparing wealthier countries to poorer countries: The overall wealth of a place mattered less than whether or not parents were supposed to handle everything on their own. Another found that the less parents feel supported by their partner and share caregiving duties equally, the less happy they are.

Still, I hate to focus too much on happiness, because I don't think the kind of day-to-day footloose and carefree cheerfulness that researchers measure is the key ingredient to the psychological well-being that can come from care. The "good" is something more complicated than happiness, deeper, richer, and longer lasting, a broad and jagged-edged brushstroke to happiness's straight and simple line. It's what happened to Eric and me, the way care elicited a more honest relationship with our lives and our feelings, disrupting the stories we tell ourselves about ourselves and pushing us to write new, more accurate ones. I know caregivers for whom care helped them see how productivity-obsessed they were, or how much they oriented their life around their public image and not what they really wanted. For others, care helped them see that they were better at intimacy than they thought, opening up their ability to connect with their adult family and friends. Sometimes this being face-to-face with another's vulnerability on a daily basis, combined with the vulnerability one feels as a result of the stresses of care, allowed them to reveal, maybe even for the first time, that they don't have it all together. They, too, are incomplete. It's okay.

Like any reasonable woman, a pregnant Kimmi Berlin felt a wave of panic when people told her how special her love for her child would be. They meant well; she knew it. But what if this was just another one of those things they say to women, another one of those external scripts dictating what women should look like and act like and feel like that only made her feel bad about herself in the end? A love like no other felt like it demanded something from her that she might not have, an intensity of emotion, or purity of thought. A museum oil painting type of mom, settled firmly on her chair while a soft-cheeked baby squirmed in her lap. This was not a love she knew she had, or was necessarily prepared to give.

Growing up, Kimmi had two versions of love in her head. One was the uncomplicated kind, the stuff of SEO-optimized listicles and fairy tales that she never experienced. The other was the complicated kind, which, in her formula, led to great personal sacrifice and unhappiness. The latter described her parents. As Kimmi saw it, her mom was overwhelmed with being the perfect New Jersey housewife—high heels, curled eyelashes, and perfect place settings—a gig she never felt comfortable with. Dad was a hardworking breadwinner who was never home. "Auerbach residence, Kimberlee speaking," Kimmi's parents instructed her to answer the phone. Kimmi also saw herself as an example of complicated, sacrificial love. As a child, she was convinced that to love her parents was to protect them from their own blind spots and harmful emotional tics and the best way to issue this protection was being the perfect daughter: "Both seemed deeply unhappy and not present in so many ways. Because of that, I felt like I had to take care of them."

She felt there was no room for error: "To me, it felt like I grew up in a household where, if you make a mistake or fuck up, you are dead."

She carried this love map into her romantic relationships. Her fear of messiness, the notion that imperfection is the enemy of affection and she would never be perfect enough, made connection hard: "So many of the relationships I had felt very performative, on my behalf. It was like 'Like me! Like me! Like me! Please accept me!' But when you are focused on that you can't also be focused on caring for someone or showing up the way they need you." Or, she learned, caring for herself. That imperfect Kimmi who could love imperfectly and was worthy of imperfect love remained elusive, until she had kids.

Kimmi and her now ex-husband have two children, ages seven

and nine. The kids deal with anxiety issues, bullying, and physical insecurities and have meltdowns. They are not, in other words, "perfect." And yet she still loves them. Of course she knew she would love them in some baseline mother way. But it's more than that. It's an honest love, one tolerant of friction and imperfections, free of the feelings of sacrifice and unhappiness she associated with love as a child: "I had this fantasy of perfect love. Like one day someone will fully love you and you will fully love them," and there would be no complicating factors. But in that formula, she realized, there is no room for flaws. For the parts we don't like about other people, or what we don't like about ourselves. Before motherhood, the idea that love could persist, despite the flaws, even when it's complicated, was unthinkable.

"They annoy the shit out of me sometimes. Sometimes I am so bored, or pissed, or angry, or agitated. I remember going on an airplane while being pregnant with my younger one, and the older one would just not stop kicking the seat in front of us. There are so many hard moments," she said.

"And yet, I have never loved anyone as much as I love my kids. I have never felt so fiercely a desire to protect or care. There is this imperfection, this human messiness, it's not all positive, and it's not all good, and still, all of those things are there and it can still be love."

She felt this for a few years for her kids until, through the process of self-discovery that came along with separating from her husband, she realized this might also be true about herself. "It was like, *Oh!!!* If I can still love them, even if I am annoyed with them, even if I am really mad at them, even when they change, then someone could do the same for me. I am worthy of love, I am worthy of all that." A mistake or imperfection doesn't disqualify one from love. She can be, she is, she will be loved.

THE MEANING

Perhaps the psychological benefits of care would be easier to see if we moved away from happiness and focused on meaning. There is plenty of convincing research making this point about caregivers to old, ill, and disabled individuals, as well as parents who report finding parenting more meaningful than their work or leisure time. One study found that the more time people spent taking care of their children, the more meaningful they found their lives. But they weren't necessarily happier.

"Satisfying one's needs and wants increased happiness but was largely irrelevant to meaningfulness. Happiness was largely present oriented, whereas meaningfulness involves integrating past, present, and future . . . ," the authors write. "Happiness was linked to being a taker rather than a giver, whereas meaningfulness went with being a giver rather than a taker. Higher levels of worry, stress, and anxiety were linked to higher meaningfulness but lower happiness. Concerns with personal identity and expressing the self contributed to meaning but not happiness."

Happiness demands ease, which is not a characteristic of care, while meaning demands friction and growth. We get meaning from the things that matter to us, that push us to see ourselves more clearly, and, on good days, grow. Meaning, like, not coincidentally, care, takes time. Care is not a happy or healthy quick scheme, even in the best of circumstances. We must return, again and again, to the person and situation that wants something from us and explore our place, our meaning, in the arc of that singular, ever-shifting relationship.

Still, happiness and meaning need not be a zero-sum game, and some research suggests that parents rate themselves as happier when asked about meaningfulness alongside happiness. The mere mention of "meaning" helped them see the present moment in a better light. Our perceptions of our lives can be dramatically shaped by the context we see ourselves in. Are we merely buying groceries? Or are we going to buy food that will nurture the people who depend on us and will grow stronger from this food? While there is little chance I will be repeating that second line to myself each and every time I wander around the market trying to figure out what I will make for dinner this week, I'd benefit from keeping this in mind more often, and so would most caregivers.

A LOVE STORY

If Robert Semenza was enlisted in a caregiver study and asked about his stress levels caring for his wife, Marie, with Parkinson's disease over decades, then stress he would report. But to speak only of his stress is to miss a big part of his story, especially the part of his story he holds most dear.

Bob, as he calls himself, is a romantic. He met Marie at age seventeen in 1950, and was so smitten that he attempted to court her despite the fact that she was dating his best friend. It took several months of competition, during which Robert was punched by her boyfriend, before he won the endorsement of her mother. Bob and Marie went steady until, per his mother's orders, he graduated from college and was permitted to get married.

He and Marie would go on to enjoy much of the promise and prosperity of mid-century American life. They purchased a new-construction house in a Stamford, Connecticut, suburb, not far from a favorite ice-skating spot. Bob worked as an accountant and commuted to New York City for much of his career. Marie stayed home, where she, with joy, took care of everyone. Neighborhood kids recall the infinite, Strega Nona–like quantities of spaghetti she cooked, and how she "actually liked speaking to us," unlike other neighborhood parents. One son, two daughters, winters skiing, and summers along Long Island Sound and hosting community-wide "Olympics" in their backyard. If Marie were still around she would likely appreciate a brief mention of her floors, which she kept spotless. The mopping, dusting, and scrubbing required to keep a house up to her standards was the only kind of "exercise," as she called it, that she enjoyed. This, as Bob and Marie and their first-generation Italian immigrant parents understood it, was the plan. A home, a spouse, a family. Ordinary pursuits, sure. But for the Semenzas, along with many in their generation, this was a dream come true.

Robert and his family couldn't understand why Marie got Parkinson's disease, scientifically, metaphysically, or emotionally, when she was diagnosed in 1982 at age forty-eight. All they felt was shock and sadness, the kind of pain that hurts the most in the future tense. We will dance, we will travel, we will cuddle, to the very end. Predictions, sure, but for a guy like Bob they felt close to inevitable. This was his love story; Marie was his love. He was energetic, a doer. Marie, warmhearted and easygoing. How else could it possibly unfold?

It was a loss. "When I see an elderly couple enjoying some mundane activity—simply walking or dining together—it fills me, at times, with a jealous longing for what they have . . . and for what we missed. I often wonder if they truly appreciate the gift they've been given," he said. But even with all the emergency room visits, long nights, adult diapers, and impossible decisions that marked three-plus decades of life post-diagnosis, Bob feels that he, in an unexpected plot twist, still got his love story.

An entry from his diary, written shortly after she passed:

On February 25, 2014, as I was driving to Saratoga to spend a few days, I was listening to some songs I had burned onto a CD. . . . And then I started to think about my love for her.

Would it have been as deep if we had just lived out a "normal" life . . . without Parkinson's? I remembered reading Michael J. Fox's book on his struggles with the disease, and how he considered himself to be a "lucky man" because of it. He reasoned that if he had not been so stricken, his life would have taken a different path . . . a more shallow and perilous one. While I could never consider, even for a moment, that she was "lucky," I do believe that the tribulations we had to endure fostered in us a stronger love and devotion which we would not have otherwise experienced.

A common goal of romantic love is, once the initial passion settles, balance. We hope to give and receive and support and be supported and if someone kept score over the years it would, if the relationship is a success, be close to a tie. Introduce caregiving to the mix and this longed-for equilibrium becomes impossible. Bob would be giving and supporting a lot more than he would receive and be supported.

At first, he didn't think he was up for it: "One of the biggest 'good' surprises early on was my total acceptance of the caregiver role, without any feeling of resentment for the hand I had been dealt," he said. There was, he quickly and intuitively understood, another way to give love to and receive love from Marie. Care gave Bob a deep sense of purpose, a place and role in the world that was uniquely his.

He did as much as he could do with her, and to the very end. In the years following her diagnosis, they traveled to Europe, went to the movies, and often drove down to New York City and the Bronx to eat authentic Italian food. He would take her someplace almost every day, even when she was living in a nursing home. There were a number of difficult moments, especially when dealing in public with her incontinence or her oxygen needs—our world remains inhospitable to all who are old, young, and disabled, collateral damage from our fear of dependency—but also a number of moments when strangers and friends gave him praise. Bob was called a hero by many who said they would lack the courage or strength to do the same. In his own subtle way, this made Bob an informal activist, demanding that the world remain open to Marie even as she dealt with disability and dementia.

The love persisted. Marie had a loyal mate, someone who reveled in her charms. And Bob had his love, doing as best as she could be doing largely because of his efforts. "My joys were made of moments," he said. "When her eyes were open, when she smiled, when she could speak in more than just a shallow whisper, and, best of all . . . when she laughed." He attempted to capture their caregiving romance in a song he composed and had recorded in honor of their fiftieth anniversary, a commitment to always be "near to you":

Near to you
All my life I'll be near to you
All my days I'll be here for you
Never far from your love

Care for you
Day and night I will care for you
My life's purpose fulfilled by you
And renewed by your smile

Bob's not sure he would ever use the word "happy" about the effect caring for Marie had on him, but the psychological benefits were clear. It felt good to be needed, and it felt even better to know he was giving the woman he loved what she needed. Is pride a type of happiness? What about satisfaction from knowing you stuck with it and gave it your all? How do you describe the glow from the moments of joy and humor that the disease couldn't take away? Or the spiritual revelations found in the three fundamentals, as he came to see it, of caregiving: commitment, loss, and renewal?

The physical benefits are less complicated to articulate. Bob was always an active guy, but once he went headlong into caregiving he knew he had to take good care of himself. Now two people depended on the strength of his body: The healthier he stayed, physically and mentally, the healthier Marie would stay. So he made time for skiing and biking, and mental health breaks—more than he believes he would have otherwise. Today, knock on wood, he continues to enjoy long bike rides, especially around New York City.

He's able to enjoy the free time Marie's passing has given him, but only because it is not a choice. "I have all the freedom in the world and I can go anyplace I want and do anything I want, but I'd give it all up to take care of her again," he said.

CHAPTER SEVEN

———————

A Philosophy of Care

Through Caregiving, We Can Encounter
Big Questions, and Big Answers

WHEN MOTHERHOOD AND
PHILOSOPHY DON'T MIX

Fifty years ago, Eva Feder Kittay learned that her daughter had severe genetic disabilities. She was only six months old when a doctor brusquely explained that she was "profoundly retarded—at best severely retarded" after examining baby Sesha for a matter of minutes. Eva spent that night in predictable agony. Her sweet, glossy-haired baby, born on a quiet December day, would never be capable of solving a math problem, dancing at a wedding, or singing along to a Beatles song. A litany of losses ran through Eva's head, though chief among them was, perhaps, the loss of conversation. Sesha would never share in what was Eva and her husband Jeffrey's greatest joy: the life of the mind.

Eva was twenty-three at the time, and considering pursuing a PhD in philosophy. She was drawn to philosophy as a response to having lost relatives in the Holocaust. Could people be good in an evil world? Now graduate school held an additional and more personal promise—it was a place apart; from her daughter, the mess of bodies and caregiving. Eva knew Adrienne Rich thought of her poetry as a place where she was nobody's mother. For Eva, philosophy would be the same. "I too needed to be someplace where I was no one's mother, where hard intellectual work would distract me from the pain of my growing understanding of all that Sesha's life could not be," she writes in her 2019 book, *Learning from My Daughter*. She began graduate school the following fall, when her daughter was around ten months old.

Early on in her career, Eva dedicated herself to better understanding how language defines us, all the while continuing to care for her daughter, who never spoke a word. Reason was another of Eva's philosophical preoccupations—the ability to reason well was, she believed, a key ingredient to a well-lived life: "I very much viewed myself as a rationalist. My favorite philosopher was Spinoza, a rationalist. For him, reason is the way to order your thoughts," she told me. "It's an idea that goes back to the Stoics, and I loved that vision of the world." Sesha could not reason.

Further separating Eva's experience with Sesha from her intellectual life was philosophy's obsession with independence. Even if Eva herself wasn't as enthralled by the notion of autonomy and self-determination as many of the white male thinkers who dominated her field were, she was still living in a world largely defined by it. Again, Sesha didn't fit into that framework. Sesha would never be independent; nor, Eva slowly came to realize, would she. When someone is dependent on you, then you yourself are not independent as long as that other person is relying on you. So much of the philosophy she bought into was based on the premise that we are all independent beings finding ways to do right by other independent beings. But care, and in this case care that would last a lifetime, changed all that.

For close to a decade following the birth of Sesha, Eva maintained a professional firewall between her work and her personal life. Publicly, the philosophy world knew her for her writing on metaphors. Privately, she was caring for her daughter and her son, an intellectually and physically healthy boy born five years after Sesha. Never did Eva's experience as a mother make it into her academic papers or lectures.

Still, even though she wasn't actively working on care, the tension between the accepted beliefs in the philosophy world and her experience with Sesha weighed on her. What did it mean that Sesha could not speak, reason, or ever be independent? And what did it mean for Eva, tethered to a dependent in perpetuity, herself? Her long-held understanding of the world had begun to fray. "To think this baby of mine could never grow up to have a life of the mind was very difficult. But she was first of all my baby," she said. "I learned that there was something prior to the life of the mind. Something prior to the importance I placed on being a person who could reason their way through things."

She began putting together questions and observations and storing them away under a mental file she labeled "Future Philosophical Project: Sesha." Where in philosophy, she asked, was a recognition of our dependency on others? An acknowledgment of relationships, relationships that define us and shape us, morally, intellectually, physically, and emotionally? And what about feelings, the surge in her heart she felt for Sesha, and the surge in Sesha's heart that she felt for her mom, that couldn't easily be defined by reason? Philosophy, she realized, had a massive blind spot toward care.

"There was a picture of the world in philosophy that I didn't belong in, and my daughter didn't belong in, and it purported to be all of humanity," she said. "What they presented as the universal condition of being human is not the universal condition at all."

I met Eva for the first time at a wedding, three years after my first son was born. She's a distant great-cousin, or something like that, and we sat at the same table surrounded by other relatives I've rarely seen. We didn't get much of a chance to talk, but I did walk away with a few phrases that stuck with me: "Ethic of care." "I look at dependency." "Something more than reason." I had little context for what any of this meant, as philosophy was largely foreign to me at the time. My education on the subject consisted of three weeks in an introduction to philosophy course, which I signed up for and then, shortly after, dropped out of during my sophomore year in college. Instead of conversations about big questions about how to be a good person or live a good life, the class was focused on, much to my disappointment, out-there theoreticals that we would have to solve with logic. When I was nineteen, these thought experiments brought to mind the Walt Whitman poem in which an astronomer's "proofs, the figures . . . ranged in columns . . . the charts and diagrams, to add, divide, and measure them," made our poet "tired and sick," the remedy for which was looking "up in perfect silence at the stars." Philosophy, or at least the kind of analytical, academic philosophy I had a very small taste of, felt like a noisy diversion from all those indelible truths I found instead in poetry, prose, intuition, and Whitman's stars.

Still, Eva's words stayed with me. The wedding coincided with the early stages of an internal philosophical battle that had been set off by caring for my first son. After decades of feeling pretty good about who I was, pretty confident in my moral compass, I had begun to realize that the dreamy, Whitmanesque logic that worked for me at age twenty was not up to the task of answering the big questions that were now running through my head. How I thought I should be, how I thought a person should be, was rapidly being exposed and punctured by care.

I DON'T KNOW

By nearly all measures, my first son was an easy kid. Whereas most young children are walking, raging ids, Augie was sweet, composed, and strategic. He didn't have tantrums, and put little effort into asserting power just for power's sake. Instead, he was prone to careful, deliberate calculations, a pragmatist in Velcro shoes. No battles over wearing the fire-truck T-shirt instead of the police-car one; no tears if the cookie broke in two. He was still getting to eat a cookie, after all.

In the late 1960s, a Stanford psychologist developed a test to gauge children's ability to delay gratification and resist temptation. Researchers gave children the choice between eating one special snack—in the most famous version it's a marshmallow—immediately and eating two if they were willing to wait for fifteen minutes. If Augie took the test, he would have not only been willing to wait the fifteen minutes but also inquired to see whether the offer would have expanded should he wait thirty minutes or even an hour. He'd wait as much as they'd let him, and then take deep satisfaction in his eventual reward.

It should come as no surprise that his fantasy life was largely informed by systems, with his favorite system being trains. He loved the logic of life on the Island of Sodor, and looked for ways in which his life could be as classifiable as that of Thomas the Tank Engine. He was always observing, hoping to understand a potential outcome of any particular action before trying out the action himself. The motive was curiosity more than anxiety. He saw a complex world around him, and it struck him as one very worthy of getting to know.

Raising this kind of child made it easy to do the type of things that usually cause great stress to parents of young children. We could eat long meals at quiet restaurants, travel long distances, visit art museums, and count on him to endure a day of tedious errands. At night, I went to sleep less physically exhausted than many of my peers, and grateful for it. But emotionally and intellectually, I was perplexed. This child of mine, at an unusually early age, had already begun replacing instinct and intuition with reason. He saw himself as part of a larger system, and we were, whether we liked it or not, providing the building blocks of his system, the architects of his Sodor, responsible for the scaffolding to which he so determinedly clung. That's a lot of pressure.

While most parents struggled to get their kids to listen to others, my job was to get Augie to listen to himself. I wanted him to see the world on his own terms, less beholden to external factors. I wished, at least sometimes, he would just eat the damn marshmallow if he wanted the marshmallow and not worry about future consequences. In order for this to happen, I knew I would have to consciously and deliberately get out of his way. Parents are their children's guides for the world, and I needed to be a careful one, leaving lots of room for dissent and alternatives. I needed to not have it all figured out.

This was not something that came naturally to me. I was a writer in the "hot take" boom of the 2010s, and therefore strong opinions were my livelihood. Online journalism is intolerant to uncertainty and dismissive to prevarication. One needs a firm, and easily categorizable, opinion to gain clicks and sell work. When I wrote, I didn't lie so much as ignore the other truths that would have blurred the singular fact I was focusing on. I had to draw a quick and neat line separating right from wrong, and present the judgment as absolute and obvious. Breastfeeding is oppressive! Men who don't do the dishes are sexist! Liking Woody Allen is fine! And, later, liking Woody Allen is indefensible! Ask me a question or point to any news story and by the end of the day I could hand over eight hundred hard-edged words on the subject. My point of view would be well argued and, on good days, entertaining, the possibility that it wasn't the only defensible position completely ignored.

Pre-motherhood, I worried about how parenthood would ruin my ability to work, and in the end it did just that, but not in the way I expected. No, caregiving didn't make me want to stop working, or worse at it. Instead, I began to question the type of work I was doing, the kind of person I had become, and whether there could be a different, and better, way to exchange ideas. This was a slow process, one that began with Augie and intensified with Levi.

Compared to Augie, Levi is a study in contrasts. Broad-shouldered and topped with wavy, improbably blond hair, he trades almost entirely in impulse, intuition, feeling. During Levi's first five years, I am pretty sure he had more tantrums per month than Augie has had in his entire life. When not overwhelmed with big feelings, he can most likely be found making music, art, or entertaining any willing audience member with a slapstick comedy routine. Whereas with Augie I had to question my ideas, with Levi I had to question my tolerance of other people's desires—particularly when they are desires I don't think they should have. Particularly when I am trying to get everyone to bed on time. It's so easy to fear the illogic and rawness of another's desire, to harden ourselves to it and think we know better. I've done a lot of that with Levi and, I'm not proud to admit, with grown-ups.

The deeper I got into caring for these two distinct individuals, the more I began to question the certainty I paraded around in my writing. How could I be so sure of how the world was? And was how I saw the world really how others should, or could, see it? What if I led with the question, rather than the answer? I became a worse online opinion writer but better caregiver and, I hope, thinker and person all around. When talking to Augie, I could make room for possibilities and other ways of seeing the world. When tending to Levi, I could make space for his needs and perceptions, even when I found them inconvenient or irrational. Not always, with them or with others, but more often. There are, a simple and obvious and yet somehow counterintuitive truth, so many ways for a person to be. Care is how I learned this. It's why I began to say "maybe" and, eventually, see the strength in "maybe" as an opening for a deeper understanding of the people and world around me. It's how I began to allow myself more "maybes" too.

At last, I was interested in philosophy. Specifically, I wanted to better understand how we construct our realities and morals, and the role our relationships can play in that process. I wanted to know what exactly Eva meant when she said "ethic of care," "dependency," "something more than reason," and began to read her work and the work of other philosophers who wrote about care. There, often in language I still struggled to understand, was the discussion I craved. Big questions, and occasional answers, about the relationship between care and being a good person, or living a good life, from philosophers who thought that care was worth their time. Sometimes these questions were directed inward and addressed our individual, subjective experiences of care. Other times they were addressed outward, looking at our ideas of a well-functioning society and interrogating how care gets left out.

Care ethicists, as these philosophers often refer to themselves, weren't much interested in the type of philosophy I rejected after three weeks as an undergrad. They had little patience for the individualistic, rational, and independent man who has been long associated with philosophy. He's the guy who figures out everything from a distance, using abstract principles while ignoring the particulars of the people involved. He adores big rules, big ideas, and doesn't pay much attention to how they might play out in personal relationships. Instead, these philosophers of care argue that relationships and emotions belong in philosophy, and that our care relationships offer a wealth of insights into the human condition. "All along, philosophers were looking at human beings and not connections, and it is those connections that get so enriched by caring relationships," Eva told me. "I don't want us to get rid of individuals, but look only at individuals and you obscure the connectivity between us. And nowhere does that connection become richer than in care."

CAREGIVING TEACHES YOU
WHAT PHILOSOPHY CLASS WON'T

Few of us consider ourselves philosophers, but all of us think philosophically. We try to figure out what the "right" thing to do is in complicated situations, and contemplate what really matters in life. At an
early age, we are taught to separate right from wrong, and that sense
of right is supposed to come from within. In preschool, we learn the
Golden Rule: Do unto others as you would want done unto you. Taken
from a passage from the Gospel of Matthew, it tells us to use our own
feelings as a moral compass when dealing with others. Or there's the
Jewish twist on the Golden Rule: Whatever is hateful to you do not
do to any other person. It's slightly less presumptuous; one is only supposed to avoid the behaviors they find harmful and not make assumptions on what would bring another happiness. Either way, our internal
reckoning is supposed to tell us how to treat other people.

As we get older, we're often taught to rely more heavily on reason and think more broadly about right and wrong on a societal level.
Maybe, if we are ambitious, we use this reason to try to reckon with
universal truths about freedom and justice, or wrestle with highly abstract and complicated philosophical hypotheticals, like the ones I was
exposed to in Philosophy 101. The trolley problem is a popular one:

> There's a trolley heading down a track. In its direct path five
> people are tied up and unable to move. You are standing at a dis-
> tance, next to a lever that can redirect the trolley to a different
> path. But, uh-oh, there is someone standing on that other path
> and they won't have time to escape. Pull the lever and save the
> five people but kill the one? Or do nothing, allowing the trolley
> to kill the five tied up on the track?

Concocting a compelling answer to this requires intense mental gymnastics, feats of logic and reasoning that I wasn't up to at age nineteen. For a long time, I thought this was a product of my incompatibility and ineptitude with all things philosophy. But this recent return to philosophy later in life has changed my mind. These hypotheticals, with all their abstract thinking and emotionless gamification, can only tell you so much about how to live your life. The one where people aren't tied up but rather complicated, vulnerable beings who need something from you.

This is where care ethics comes in. The theory traces back to Harvard University in the early 1970s, where Carol Gilligan had been teaching classes and working alongside prominent developmental psychologists. One of these was Lawrence Kohlberg, famous for his six-stage theory of moral development, which he published over a decade before. He came up with this theory by following eighty-four white boys from their teen years through adulthood and observing their moral development. Through this process, he created a scale to measure how their moral thinking progressed over time. The lowest stage of morality, as Kohlberg saw it, was obedience and punishment— or when people make a decision based on potential negative consequences, or whether or not they will get in trouble. The highest stage, one few reached, is when someone makes their moral judgments based on a well-articulated, universally applicable ethic. Women, Kohlberg decided without having studied any women, only reached the third stage of morality. This was what he called "interpersonal reasoning," or when decisions are made based on the effect they will have on your social standing.

In 1973, Gilligan, suspecting there was more to the story, began to do her own research and ask women the kinds of questions about morality that psychologists had long been asking men: How did they determine the right thing to do? What did they see as a moral problem?

What were their rights and their responsibilities? Specifically, she asked pregnant women who were considering abortion about how they were processing the decision. What she encountered was not, as Kohlberg suggested, stalled moral development. Women weren't less advanced than men; they were, she found, just different. Their experience in the world, which tended to be more relationship oriented, had led them to a different understanding of morality; an understanding that, perhaps unsurprisingly, had not been detected in a study conducted only with boys and men.

Her findings and observations came together first in an academic paper, and then later in her 1982 book, *In a Different Voice: Psychological Theory and Women's Development*. She wrote the book in academic prose and peppered it with erudite references to the likes of Sigmund Freud and Virginia Woolf. Nevertheless, it became a major bestseller, with over seven hundred thousand copies sold and translations into over sixteen languages. Women, lots and lots of women, saw themselves in this book.

In it, she looks at how, when it comes to moral quandaries, women tend to focus on what effect their decision will have on their relationships rather than their principles. The reason to do or not do something is considered in light of how that behavior or action will impact other people—feelings are part of the equation. This is, as Gilligan defined it, an ethic of care, and is a response to the ways in which women are raised to see themselves as caregivers. Men, on the other hand, tend to rely on an ethic of justice, or a sense that there is some external moral code that applies to all people at all times and it is up to them to interpret it. "Sort of like math problems with humans," as one eleven-year-old boy she quotes puts it. Both approaches, she argues, are equally valid.

Gilligan was insistent, and has remained insistent, that "the different voice I describe is characterized not by gender but theme," as she wrote in her book. Any differences in moral orientations are not coded in our gendered DNA. Instead, they are a product of the way empathy and relational thinking have been gendered "feminine" and detached and rational thinking have been gendered "masculine."

"I called my book *In a Different Voice*, not *In a Woman's Voice*," she told me. "What's clear all these years later, through work on infants and neuroscience, is that the different voice, the voice of care ethics, is a human voice, and what it differs from is a patriarchal voice—not a male voice."

Men, she explained, are expected to be autonomous. Women, on the other hand, are supposed to be selfless—a strength bound up with a weakness. Neither makes for good relationships. "How do you care for someone if you don't have a self? There has to be a self," she said. Gilligan doesn't want women to reject independence or reason, nor does she want men to fuel their moral compasses on emotions and relationships alone. Instead, she wants to dismantle the imagined wall between these two manners of ethical reasoning, in order for all of us to see how much better life can be when they coexist.

HOW CARE ETHICS DIFFERS
FROM OTHER ETHICAL THEORIES

If I'd stayed in that introduction to philosophy course, I would have had a better context of where my sense of right and wrong came from, and how it was being challenged by care. There are a number of well-established ethical theories, or an explanation of the systems people use to separate right from wrong. Until Gilligan and other care ethicists, inventing an ethical theory was nearly exclusively a male pursuit.

The three main ethical philosophical systems are virtue based, deontological, and utilitarian. Even if you don't know them by name, you'll probably be familiar with the concepts behind them. The first, virtue ethics, goes back to Plato and Aristotle. They believed that ethics is based on our internal character: "I am honest, and therefore I don't cheat."

Dentology, or "duty ethics," largely centers around following a universal, mutually agreed-upon standard for right and wrong—like the classroom rules: "Cheating is prohibited by the teacher, so therefore I don't cheat."

Utilitarianism, on the other hand, focuses on outcomes instead of rules, and encourages individuals to calculate which decision would create the most good in the world: "How much harm will come from me cheating? How much good will come from me not cheating? Or how much good will come from me cheating?" Whatever creates the most good wins.

With care ethics, relationships are front and center. You don't cheat because you don't want to hurt someone you care about. Or perhaps you do cheat to protect someone you love. Maybe a parent generously "helps" their child with a homework assignment after a traumatizing day of bullying at school. Preserving and tending to the relationship is the motivation, and there is sensitivity to the particulars of the people involved. Decision-makers utilize reason as well as emotion and empathy.

Before Gilligan's work in the 1980s, care ethics didn't exist and philosophy wasn't much interested in caregiving. Philosophers considered care unintellectual, bourgeois—it reeked of the domestic. Serious thinking on these subjects was hardly imaginable, let alone encouraged. But with the publication of *In a Different Voice*, an opening was created and philosophers, mostly women, came and filled it. At last, relationships were the subject of thorough, well-regarded inquiry. Care ethicists never argued that relationships should be the only factor in moral decisions, only that they are a factor, and one that has long been ignored.

With this intense focus on relationships came a rising awareness of the complexity of human dependence. What is ethically okay behavior with my friends or husband, people who are my equals and independent, isn't always okay with my kids, who are my dependents. For a very long time, philosophers didn't acknowledge this distinction. Fairness, as they defined it, is something that was achieved by two equal people, whether friends or business partners. But care ethicists, many of them mothers, saw things differently. They pointed out how this definition of fairness left out caregivers, who, they argued, need an ethical code of their own. For example: If two employees of equal standing are arguing over the last bagel at work, then it stands to reason to fall back on abstract rules and precedent. If an adult child and his cognitively impaired parent are arguing over a bagel at home, figuring out what is right and wrong demands a whole other set of skills and internal negotiations. Big abstract rules aren't much help.

These types of dilemmas pepper my life on a daily basis. Sometimes a child needs punishment when they act out, and sometimes they need a hug. Sometimes the same kid needs a different response for the same bad behavior from one day to the next. Often, two different kids demand different responses for the same infractions. Levi needs a reminder that he is loved alongside his punishments. Augie needs to be left alone. Thanks to care ethics, I know better than to fall for the trap of ready-made Instagram parenting tips and treat each situation on its own, rather than following a meme formula.

CARE AS THE BIRTH OF MORALITY

The philosophical upheaval that caregiving created in my life may have something to do with my childhood. Your childhood too. Care ethicist Nel Noddings believed that our early care relationships are the initial sparks of conscious morality in our lives, the experiences that can set off a lifelong hunger for goodness. My newfound revulsion to certainty may have had as much to do with the circumstances of opinion writing as it did with the way caring for my children filled me with a longing, somehow somewhere, to return to a purer state of human connection not unlike that which I experienced when being cared for as a child. I remembered the power of one person seeing another.

Noddings, who died in 2022, isn't your typical intellectual radical. The first in her family to graduate from high school, she raised ten kids and taught junior high and high school students for two decades. Summers were spent crisscrossing the United States in a station wagon built for twelve and cooking spaghetti at campsites. She was, in her own words, "incurably domestic," liked "order in the kitchen, a fresh tablecloth, flowers on the table and food waiting for guests," and "having pets and kids around."

All of this domesticity, the stuff of still-life and Norman Rockwell paintings, alchemized into original and bold thinking about care. In 1973, at age forty-four, Noddings received her PhD in educational philosophy and theory from Stanford University. Ten years later, she published her groundbreaking book *Caring: A Feminine Approach to Ethics and Moral Education*. In it, she explores how our instinct to care, an instinct that surfaces as early as infancy, is the foundation of our obligation to be good. This is a long way away from the male psychologists of yore who thought that intimate relationships—with all their biases, contradictions, and irrational moments—could be a hindrance to moral thinking. Noddings turns this thinking 180 degrees, arguing instead that care is one of the greatest, if not the greatest, methods of ethical education.

Though not all care. In her book, Noddings works through different types of caring, isolating those instances that are most likely to shape us. She distinguishes between "caring for" and "caring about." "Caring for" means we both give attention to the recipients of our care and respond to them. "Caring about" means we give the recipients of our care attention, but we don't necessarily respond. We are, she argued, only ethically obliged to care *for* those with whom we are in intimate relationships.

As part of this explanation, Noddings stated that she didn't believe herself to be obliged to care for the starving children of Africa. This incited a lot of controversy—"Woman only cares for her own children!"—but Noddings explained that she is not capable of caring for the African children. To provide that level of care requires huge amounts of time, money, and feelings, which she necessarily did not possess. Care, real care, can't be distributed fairly or equally, and to pretend it can is to be willfully ignorant of what it entails. Therefore, to believe Noddings had an obligation to care for all children, or all underprivileged children, was to create an impossible standard. She could certainly care *about* the starving children of Africa, and maybe she could, in a very small way, care *for* them by donating money to an organization that served them. But to truly care *for* them as she cared for her own children is highly unrealistic and therefore not something she should feel obligated to do.

This provides a moral justification for the time- and resource-intensive care we bestow on our loved ones. I've probably read over a hundred trend pieces in the past decade dedicated to critiquing the way contemporary parents overinvest in care. These morally corrupt parents "helicopter," "snowplow," and "lawn mow" all so their children will never suffer and always succeed. There are absolutely parents who go too far, but sometimes it feels as though there is a fundamental misunderstanding of care behind these critiques. To care for another is to be a little selfish on that person's behalf and prioritize their well-being over others'. If we all listened to Noddings and understood this, perhaps we'd be less quick to call parents self-indulgent, and stop and consider whether they're just meeting the requirements of caregiving in today's world.

Though the inherent selfishness of caring *for* someone doesn't mean we have to give up on caring *about* others. We can try to make it easier for people to be cared for by others, through the support of policies and cultural practices that make caring well easier to achieve. Supporting universal paid leave would make it much easier for many caregivers to adequately care for their loved ones. So would, on a smaller scale, offering a burnt-out friend the gift of a night off from caregiving. We wouldn't be, according to Noddings's definition, caring for his child or her aging parent, but we would make it much more likely that that child or aging parent would be properly cared for by their rested and restored caregiver.

Noddings makes another important distinction in types of care. She separates out what she calls "virtue carers" and "relational carers." The former are caregivers who do what they think is right for the person being cared for. The latter are caregivers who attempt to understand what needs the person being cared for is expressing and then go about trying to provide that for them. All caregivers, at some point or another, have been guilty of caregiving by virtue. We did what we thought we knew was best for another when we really, really didn't. These can be small infractions, like demanding someone needs to go for a walk when what they really need is rest. Or larger infractions, like mine. I went into parenting thinking of my children like the readers of my opinion pieces: in need of a clear and firm take on the world around them. I fed them what I believed they needed to eat, comforted them when and how I thought they should be comforted, and instructed them on matters without making space for their ideas. But what they needed wasn't a steadfast guide, but someone who stopped to pay close attention to their expressed needs. On my best days, I am a "relational carer." I respond to questions with more questions, I remain curious about their desires, all the while hushing the part of me that thinks, This should be different, better; they could be different, better.

Noddings provides her readers with a handy, three-part checklist to determine if one is caring in a way that will serve the person being cared for while also inspiring personal growth. Number one, the caregiver must exhibit engrossment and have a deep understanding about the other. Two, the caregiver must exhibit motivational displacement and respond to the needs of the other. Three, the care receiver must respond in some way to the caring. When all three pieces are in place, the caregiver can form an "ethical ideal" of the kind of person they want to be, a best self that will serve as a lodestar or reference point. "I have a picture of those moments in which I was cared for and in which I cared, and I may reach toward this memory and guide my conduct by it if I wish to do so," she writes.

Noddings's last rule, perhaps the most important one, is to be skeptical of rule-based thinking in our relationships. In care, as in life, being a good person requires us not to follow some external script of morality but instead to constantly check in on the particulars of the situation. Again and again, we need to try to let go of the long series of shoulds and oughts that have accumulated over the course of our lives when they don't serve our relationships. Again and again, we need to respond to what is right in front of us. "To care is to act not by fixed rule but by affection and regard. It seems likely, then, that the actions of one-caring will be varied rather than rule-bound; that is, her actions, while predictable in a global sense, will be unpredictable in detail," Noddings writes. People over formulas. People over plans.

Critics of care ethics question what the difference really is between a relational approach to right and wrong and a rule-based one. Can't we just say it should be a rule to care about others? But care ethics doesn't just tell us we should care for others but also helps us figure out what it means to care for another. Rules are great, but we also need to think about how to sensitively and effectively translate them into our lives. Yes, we all agree it is the responsibility of a caregiver to protect the care recipient from harm. But what does protecting one particular person from harm really mean? It is, to repeat Noddings, unpredictable in detail.

RECEPTIVITY BEGINS AT HOME

June Barrett, Jamaican-born and longtime home health-care aide, has spent her life learning to care well amid all the inevitable unpredictability.

In 2003, June visited a hospital in Miami to meet an old woman she would be caring for. She was in her late thirties and had recently decided to try out a job as a home health-care worker, a gig her sister had arranged for her after June lost her nannying job in Connecticut. "I walked into the room, introduced myself, and oh my God, they called me the N-word," June told me. "I ended up spending a year with her. I knew I could reach this woman." She did. "Mela and I became the closest aide and client. When I had to travel back to Connecticut she came to the train station to say goodbye."

June's been treated poorly at work. There's the commonplace abuse, the racism, sexism, and homophobia that seep out as casual degradation or disdain. Then there's the more violent variety, the racial slurs, and, in her earlier nannying days, sexual abuse by the father, her boss. These are, unfortunately, common workplace hazards for caregivers, which take place in close quarters, often inside an employer's home, often with little oversight or recourse.

But June saw beyond the rot. Not just because caring for Mela was a job and she needed the money, which was very much the case. But also because of an early experience with caregiving that calls to mind the work of Noddings. "While taking care of Mela, something happened to me. I started having flashbacks of my grandma, who took care of me as a child," June said.

June's mom died when she was a baby due to complications from childbirth. After, she was separated from her twin sister and sent to live with her mom's sister in a rural area in Jamaica. Her aunt was tough, and June looked forward to weekend visits to her grandma's house—five miles away, and often traveled by foot. Henritha Campbell, or Ma Heny as the sisters called her, was strong, vibrant, and June's "favorite person in the world."

Years later, when June was an adult and working in Kingston, she went back to the countryside to visit her family. Her grandma had recently had a stroke, and she was left alone during the day while her daughters, June's aunts, worked as farm laborers: "My grandma developed bedsores. Every time I left, I would weep for my grandma. I didn't want to leave."

The flashbacks she had after meeting Mela were of this scene, a woman denied the care she needed and suffering as a result. "I thought, I am going to give her the care that every person deserves. I am going to care for her the way I would have cared for Grandma," June said. If only she had had the chance.

June's epiphany was in line with that modification of the Golden Rule that care ethicists were implicitly exploring. Sometimes we do unto others what we want done unto ourselves. Other times we do unto others what we, through communication and observation, understand they want done to them. On those trips home from Kingston to visit her sick grandma, motivated by justice, yes, but also by love and attention and seeing, June had become receptive.

June brought this receptivity with her to her work with all her clients. She wanted to give them what they needed, and not what she thought they needed. "It's not an easy job. Each person I came in contact with, I always wanted to learn about their background. What was their life like? Who were their fathers, their mothers, their grandmothers?" she said. "When I live with a family, I always try to see through the eyes of the family, so I can give the care he or she deserves. I learned to care from a place of empathy."

Most of June's clients are white. The world has a long history of expecting people of color to look at the world through white people's eyes while the favor has most definitely not been returned. June knows this but refuses to let this be the only explanation for her ability to care well. She's worked hard at this, and is really good at what she does. She's proud of it.

Her success is measured by the number of people's hands she has held as they died, at their request. How she has been told, time and again: "June, you make me feel safe." "June, I need you here with me." Years later, after the person she has cared for has long passed, she's still invited to family dinners: "June, you're part of the family."

"To do this work you have to dig deep inside. You have to develop patience. You have to have love," she said. "I generally power my life with love. You have to."

This not only helps her do her job well but also is why she enjoys it. She can go from moments of hostility with difficult clients to "beautiful moments, some of the most beautiful laughter you can imagine." A beautiful laughter that she could help other caregivers find, if they'd only listen.

WE DON'T SELF-ACTUALIZE; WE CO-ACTUALIZE

Philosophers have long contemplated the ways moving beyond our own perspective can bring us more fully into ourselves. Simone Weil, a philosopher who was born in France in 1909, wrote about the importance of cultivating attention to others, and why doing so is a difficult and mysterious process that is essential for the pursuit of truth, beauty, and goodness. Open-minded, tender, and compassionate attention is "the rarest and purest form of generosity," and a key ingredient of a moral life, she explained. When we step outside of ourselves, attempt to clearly see others, and explore life from their perspective, we get new insights about who we are and life itself.

Weil knew that this is a hard thing to do, and saw failure as both inevitable and an important part of the process. Attention, like love or prayer, is an imperfectible process. We can only keep going, with a longing to see, hear, and feel; waiting for those quicksilver moments when our perception shifts. "Every time that a human being succeeds in making an effort of attention with the sole idea of increasing his grasp of truth, he acquires a greater aptitude for grasping it, even if his effort produces no visible fruit," she wrote, hinting at the never-ending, philosophical unfolding that Noddings sees as part of care. To think it can or should end, that individual or global immutable truths can ever be fully grasped, is to miss the point.

Iris Murdoch, an Irish and British novelist and philosopher, was inspired by Weil when writing her 1970 book *The Sovereignty of Good*. In it, she rejects the idea that the goal of a moral life should only be about making the right choices. In addition to doing the right thing, we should also be thinking about how we pay attention to the world, for the act of paying attention can be, as she sees it, a moral act. For Murdoch, this came down to something she called "unselfing," her name for the process that happens to us when we pay such deep attention to something or someone else that we manage to escape our own egos, vanities, and blind spots and come to see things more clearly. "The self, the place where we live, is a place of illusion. Goodness is connected with the attempt to see the unself . . . to pierce the veil of selfish consciousness and join the world as it really is," she writes.

Murdoch and Weil are joined by other voices in the philosophy, many from outside the Western world, who have long directed us to the fertile spaces in between. Millennia-old Confucianism sees morality in the context of relationships rather than only rules, and emphasizes the importance of emotions, including empathy and compassion, in moral decision-making. A similar emphasis on relationships also appears in some African approaches to morality, which privilege connection over individual achievement. Ubuntu, for example, is a moral worldview that Archbishop Desmond Tutu defined as "a person is a person through other persons." Or, as twentieth-century philosopher John Mbiti described it, "I am because we are, since we are, therefore I am." The idea is that our bond to our community, and care for the people in it, are what make us who we are. This personal and political philosophy of interdependence rose in prominence in the late twentieth century, as African countries began to forge a postcolonial identity and unite citizens in a shared understanding of their past and future.

In 1923, Martin Buber, an unconventional and charismatic Jewish theologian and philosopher, published a book titled *I and Thou.* "One of the epoch-making books of our generation," the book's English translators declared in 1937. Buber's *New York Times* obituary in 1965 largely agreed. Sometimes, Buber argues, we treat another as an "it," which means seeing the person as a separate object who is only useful for the ways they can serve us. Much better to try and see the other as a "thou," a subject, a full presence, a messy, complicated entity that we experience in all their surprising, confusing, and delightful complexity. "I-It" relationships are marked by separateness and detachment. "I-Thou" relationships are marked by mutuality and reciprocity. Only through "I-Thou" can we tap into what Buber identified as the "in-between," or the otherworldly, possibly divine, current that melts the human ego and charges human connection: "All real living is meeting."

BRINGING CARE ETHICS
TO THE WIDER WORLD

Sadly, the lack of support we give caregivers and caregiving can make this "unselfing," or achieving "I-Thou" relationships, very difficult. This neglect has philosophical roots of its own, and can be traced back to the way the founders of Western nations conceived of their societies. They exalted principles like equality, independence, and freedom. Dependence, meanwhile, was relegated as a small footnote to existence that merits little attention. It's all right there in our founding documents.

"We hold these truths to be self-evident, that all men are created equal, that they are endowed by their Creator with certain unalienable Rights, that among these are Life, Liberty and the pursuit of Happiness," reads the preamble to the Declaration of Independence. What if, in addition to liberty and the pursuit of happiness, care was one of our unalienable rights? And why not, "We hold these truths to be self-evident . . . *that even though all men are created equal, they are not always equal in capability and therefore all need care*"?

"We the People of the United States, in Order to form a more perfect Union, establish Justice, insure domestic Tranquility, provide for the common defense, promote the general Welfare, and secure the Blessings of Liberty to ourselves and our Posterity, do ordain and establish this Constitution for the United States of America," reads the preamble to the U.S. Constitution. How about this small tweak? ". . . in Order to form a more perfect Union, establish Justice and *Care* . . ." Care is as fundamental to the good life as justice, but it's rarely presented in fundamental terms.

For Eva Feder Kittay, philosopher and mother of Sesha, and others, this blind spot is one of the root causes of why we don't have real care infrastructure in the United States, and why we don't value caregivers. Our society and institutions were built around the idea of ensuring our equality and protecting our independence. Both are noble values, even if they have yet to be delivered to all. But as a culture, we fail to acknowledge those times we aren't equal, like when we are young, old, or impaired in some fashion. Nor do we do much to acknowledge the times when we aren't independent, the norm for the many of us who spend the beginning and end of our lives depending on another, and much of the middle being depended on.

This is why Kittay thinks it is time for a new social contract—a political philosophy term for what we think we owe one another as a broader society. She wants one that will ensure that those who need care receive care, and those who provide care are cared for themselves. "Rather than denying our interdependence, my aim is to find a knife sharp enough to cut through the fiction of independence," she writes in the preface of her 1999 book *Love's Labor*, in which she explores what a care-aware social contract might look like.

A public reckoning with care in our values and institutions might also push us to think harder about when, and for whom, caregiving is a good thing. There are roughly 11.5 million migrant domestic workers around the world, an estimated 8.5 million of whom are female according to 2013 data from the International Labour Organization. That's millions of people who left their homes in order to work as caregivers, nearly always for financial security. Add to this the many unpaid caregivers who have to choose between caregiving and rent, or, for financial reasons, have no other choice but to be the sole caregiver for someone who abused them and yet they still feel responsibility for. While there are many Junes out there who find deep meaning in it, there are countless others who are forced to work in difficult conditions, with no Plan B.

"Some of the assumptions in care ethics derive from the experiences of fairly affluent white women and the lessons of white femininity," care ethicist Asha Bhandary told me. "We need to look at who is providing care and who is receiving it, and we need to filter that data with the races of the participants on both sides of the arrow of care. We need to see how women of color are often assumed to be caregivers, and to be other-directed—that is, to orient their attention and actions toward others." Bhandary is trying to square the harsh reality of care that many women of color and migrants experience with some of the more tender, relational theories about care that her predecessors explored. She understands why older care ethicists like Noddings distanced themselves from rules and justice in order to find a less rules-based, more emotional and subjective definition of ethics. But focus too much on intimate relationships and we can easily blind ourselves to the injustices faced by caregivers around the world. A modern care ethics, she argues, could be invested in both cultivating positive care relationships among some and protecting others from abusive care relationships. We need to make a space in care where rules matter less and a space outside care where rules protect the vulnerable. All in the name of care.

RIPPLE EFFECTS

Whether or not caring for others makes us more compassionate overall is a question that psychologists and ethicists have been wrestling with for a long time and the answer is yes and no and everything in between. I feel confident that caring *for* my kids has helped me be a better person, increasing my ability to see others more fully and care *about* their lives. Not all the way, but a few notches better than I used to be. I could easily say the same about June and many other caregivers I've met. And yet there is no shortage of examples of parents and caregivers who have been casually shitty, or committed gross atrocities, to those outside their homes while absolutely adoring the people they cared for.

We are wired to care for those we identify with—whether that's our family, people of the same religion, or our compatriots—more than those we don't identify with. This can make us biased, shortsighted, and even selfish. It's why we can at once care about our children while treating the woman we employ to care for them poorly. Or why we can care about the person caring for our children while ignoring the reality of her children living in the same neighborhood, or thousands of miles away.

And yet when a man says being a father changed him, made him more empathetic and patient, or a daughter says caring for a sick mother changed her, made her more understanding and open-minded, we believe them. When a wealthy woman says taking care of her infant made her realize how important universal parental leave is—that now she cares about all mothers—the metamorphosis strikes us as both plausible and sincere. When mothers get together to fight for gun control or peace, we accept that they have been shaped and emboldened by their experience of care and firsthand understanding of dependency and vulnerability. Yet it is also utterly conceivable to me that one of these mothers was rude to a barista or a parking lot attendant on her way to improve the world.

Care as a positive moral education happened to Julie, who requested that I didn't include her last name. Her son, Josh, was born at twenty-eight weeks and spent months in the NICU, which saved his life but could not remedy all the complications. As a baby, he was diagnosed with hearing loss, blindness in one eye, moderate retardation, and, later, Asperger's.

When Josh was twelve, Julie and her husband divorced, making her a single working mom. She loved Josh, she wanted to be with Josh, but she was also a special education teacher for a junior high in La Grange, a suburb of Chicago, and on top of that she cooked and cleaned and

made sure their basic needs were met as well as securing some necessary downtime for herself too. Julie's main pleasure, her much-deserved
sweet escape, was dancing, which morphed from a beloved hobby to a
second career while she was still teaching, and has kept her busy after
retirement in 2007.

In a perfect world, one in which a single mom doesn't always need
to be firing on all cylinders, she would have liked to spend more time
with him: "I am not saying I was a bad woman; it's just that you have
to do what you have to do to pull it all together."

Decades flew by until spring 2020, when COVID shut the world
down. Suddenly, for the first time in her life, there was nowhere else
to be but home with Josh, who was now forty-four and still living with
her. "Here I am at home, and it was either pay attention to Josh, or
clear the basement—though I have found a few interesting things in
the basement. Really, though, the more time I've spent with him, the
more I have found myself more patient, and more willing to listen. I
have changed over the past months because of this. I think I have gotten way more from Josh than he has gotten from me," she told me in
November 2020.

Julie is aware that she is lucky. She's financially secure, and healthy
herself, and therefore has the ability to simply be with her son. She
knows not everyone has this. As for Josh, he is a "polite, good person,
who never makes fun of anyone." He enjoys reading, which he does at
a roughly second-grade level, looking out the first-story bay window of
their home, from which he can see the comings and goings of their Chicago suburb, and making silly jokes like pretending his mom's hair is
orange. Josh is passionate about climate change.

"Before the pandemic he got into the habit of starting a sentence and
stopping it, assuming others will finish it," Julie said. During quarantine—
when time had, for the first time in decades, felt less scarce—she learned
to stop interjecting and allowed him to carry on with his thoughts.

Somewhere along the way, she became a more careful and observant listener. First with Josh and now with everyone. "When I slow down and listen, I discover that there are things about him that are useful and praiseworthy that I didn't see. . . . Suddenly I have this patience, and the ability to say: This is what I think; what do you think? I am a better mother, and a better human. It has allowed me to see in a much clearer way the humanity of people who are not the same as I am." In return Josh has, for the first time in his life, begun to hug Julie.

President Joe Biden also had a moral education by way of care. His campaign succeeded, in part, because of his ability to convince us that his life had made him a caring person and now he was caring to all. He spoke about "the duty to care" in speech after speech, as a way to distinguish himself from his predecessor. The catalyst for Biden was not only some broad ethical objective to be caring but also his experience of being a single dad after losing his first wife and child in a car accident.

"As many of you know, I was a single parent for five years after my wife and daughter were killed and my two boys were badly injured. Even though I had a lot more support than a lot of people going through tough times today, it was hard. . . . We care.

". . . We know so many of you are going through the same thing without the kind of help I had, but now everything, everything feels different. There's just that feeling, that sense, when you just don't know if everything is going to turn out okay," he said in a speech about his caregiving plan.

Care ethicist Sarah Clark Miller was delighted to hear Biden mention "the duty to care," as it's the central idea of a book she wrote. Many friends called to make sure she saw it. Like Biden, her personal experiences with care stirred something in her that made her more aware of our dependent sides. "When I became a parent, and had a dependent being relying on me, the dependency and vulnerability of life became much more apparent to me. I was experiencing vicarious vulnerability. The idea of that person being harmed became the worst thing that could happen in some ways," she said.

This was an awakening of sorts, but it wasn't without complexity. Miller knew that care could make her heart grow, and change how she reasons her way through right and wrong. At the same time, she knew that care can narrow one's focus, so that newfound emotional gener-osity would be limited to one's inner circle. Sometimes it's even worse than that, and can lead to hostility to anyone not in this circle. Her big philosophical question was: How do we bridge this gap? How do we make it so our intimate experiences of care, including all those insights into human dependency, vulnerability, and subjectivity, extend to the wider world and translate to a more caring society?

We could, she realized, think of care as a duty, or a collectively agreed-upon rule and obligation: Thou shalt care well, with dignity for all parties involved. When care is a duty, it tells us that we must care because it is fundamental to the good life, considering humans' inher-ent dependent nature. Care becomes something you do because it's the right thing to do, a social norm that you don't think much about. But, and this is where Noddings and others fit in, we don't have to apply rules to our intimate care relationships. We leave the big rules out of *how* we care and instead rely on our relationships, the tending to that one-and-only very particular person, to inform those decisions.

Care ethicist Daniel Engster agrees that this shift to thinking of care as both a profound intimate experience as well as a duty is an important next step in the evolution of care ethics. He himself felt transformed by his experience of receiving care after breaking his leg in college. The longtime soccer player and overall athletic guy now moved slowly and clumsily through the world in a full leg cast that he had to wear for six months. During this time, he became "utterly dependent" on others to get his basic needs met. "That was a really profound experience for me in making me understand our dependency on one another," he said. But such individual epiphanies alone will not, he realized, lead us to a world that is more caring, supportive of care-givers, or accepting of dependency.

"Back in the early days, there was great optimism in the care ethics community that we just need to care more and then we will become a more caring society, or that our ability to care has been stunted by the state or capitalism and if we can only overcome these obstacles we will open ourselves up to care," he said. "It's not hopeless, but it requires a lot more cultivation than care theorists have thought."

Cultivation can look like better government policies supporting caregivers, which, besides giving them some financial and practical relief, tell them that their efforts are acknowledged and valued, that what they do matters. It also requires a culture shift that takes us away from seeing humans as a collective of individuals and instead as a collective of relationships. In some ways, Engster says this shift is already happening, most notably in our conversation about equality. For a long time, equality meant that everyone had to follow the same rules. In this line of thought, as long as, say, Jeff Bezos isn't breaking any laws, then he is entitled to his near-immeasurable wealth, fair and square. But looking at equality through the lens of care helps us see that it shouldn't just be about fairness but also relationships, how one person's well-being compares *in relation* to another. What makes Bezos's wealth offensive isn't that he's not playing by the rules; what's upsetting is the contrast between his unimaginable wealth and the day-to-day reality of the 34 million people living in poverty in America. "In the traditional, liberal, and abstract system of equality, you can have huge disparities of wealth and status and yet still be considered equal," Engster said. "But if equality is about relationships between people, then we start to pay attention to how the difference between people harms our ability to care for one another."

If you are looking for a through line of care ethics, or a path to thinking more like a care ethicist, relationships are a good place to start. Relationships are what Eva Feder Kittay realized philosophy ignored and needed more of and what Nel Noddings sees as the foundation of our moral selves. They're what Daniel Engster believes should be at the center of how we view ourselves in relation to strangers and our broader societies. We turn to philosophy with questions about how to be a good person, how to live a good life, and how to create a fair and just world. Relationships, with all their vulnerability, dependency, and uncertainty, can inform our answer for each and every one.

You must know Auguste Rodin's sculpture *The Thinker*. A strong man, sitting down, chin resting on his knuckles; aquiline nose and tense brow drawing the viewer's attention to his eyes, which, in return, gaze downward, oblivious to his surroundings. Rodin said he intended the man to appear to be thinking with "every muscle of his arms, back, and legs, with his clenched fist and gripping toes." Rodin's goal was to make physical, visceral, the effort and anguish that go into contemplative thought.

Intellectually, I've had my *Thinker* moments—still, inward, pulsing, though lacking in muscularity compared to the original. I've also spent time with the sculpture and admired, in that gauzy, noncommittal, art museum way, how a hunk of metal had been transformed into interiority. I like the statue enough but have come to resent the story its popularity tells us about the gestures, postures, and social conditions of deep thought. There's more than one me, more than one Eva, Julie, and June, who have discovered themselves in moments of epiphany while looking into someone else's eyes, holding their hand, or rubbing their back as they laughed or cried or died. This, too, is deep thinking. Philosophizing by way of care.

_____

When Revelation Takes Place at Home

Care's Spiritual Potential and Why It's So Easy to Ignore

MARTIN LUTHER THOUGHT HOME WAS HOLY

Like many Catholics in the sixteenth century, Martin Luther began his religious career in a monastery. It wasn't his lifelong plan, but instead the result of a vow he made to God one night during a Noachian thunderstorm. Protect me, Saint Anne, and I will serve God. Serve in the way Catholicism has taught me to, by leaving my home and my family and joining a monastery. No longer will their presence or the messiness of quotidian existence cloud my reception of your divine light.

The rain stopped. Luther became a monk. Days began at 2:00 a.m. with morning prayers. Nights were spent in his spartan room, furnished with a single table and a chair. The chaos and comforts of domestic life were replaced by the strict simplicity and hush that he and his peers believed was necessary to experience God on our terrestrial plane.

It didn't work out. With time, Luther grew weary and intolerant of this narrow and overly prescribed spiritual path and, eighteen years after becoming a monk, he left. Bodily urges were, presumably, an influence. He would soon proclaim that perpetual chastity was not realistic and therefore was problematic, as a sexually unsatisfied man is a tormented man, and a tormented man would struggle to connect with God. Maybe marriage, the union between two people, can bring us closer to God. Kids too. Maybe God could be just as easily experienced in regular life, by regular people, at home with their families.

A few years later, then forty-two, he put this to the test by marrying Katharina von Bora, a former nun who was inspired by Luther to leave her convent and explore a domesticated spiritual existence. Together, they had six children, giving Luther plenty of time to test out his big ideas. His experience with his actual wife and children and his actual house did not change his opinion on the matter. God, he believed, can be found at home.

One day, a friend was over and explained that he sees God's blessings in fruit and therefore hangs a cherry branch in his dining room. "Why don't you think of your children?" Luther responded. "They are in front of you all the time, and you will learn more from them than a cherry bough." He didn't need flowers to teach him about miracles, or remind him about God. He just needed his children around. I hope this has something to do with the way children aren't just a miracle of life and beauty but are also complex and alive and demand things of us. Unlike his friend's cherry branch, children talk back.

Luther didn't take us all the way in the movement to appreciate caregiving as a spiritual experience, handicapped as he was by his belief that men should rule over women—the people who did much of the care. But he did move us in the right direction. Life at home with kids, he insisted, can be spiritually profound, true no matter how one defines their spirituality. Be it God, the divine, transcendence, awe, the universe, the majestic, or whatever you call the mystery and majesty of experience, it can all be found in care.

A THEOLOGY OF CARE

Most world religions really want you to believe they value caregivers. They talk a lot about care, even caregiving, in broad terms, praise it and celebrate it and call it holy. And they seem to really believe it. Except you know what is more holy? The discipline and study and solitude and prayer that generally only men do, all activities that lead to power and authority, while care—sweet, lovely, women-produced—does not. Care is valued as a moral ideal in these patriarchal traditions, but not a flesh-and-blood experience. The reality of caregivers? The people who give care? Throughout history, they've rarely gotten to share their ideas on life or God, or call the shots.

On a handful of occasions, I've attended Friday-night Shabbat dinners at ultra-Orthodox Jewish homes. Before we eat, there are a handful of traditional blessings and songs, one of which is "Eshet Chayil," or "Woman of Valor." It's a millennia-old poem from the Book of Proverbs, the typical melody soulful and earnest with hints of longing and even unease, which praises women for all their hard work, including what we today refer to as "invisible labor."

"A Woman of Valor, who can find? . . . She gets up while it is still night to provide food for her household, and a fair share for her staff. . . . She makes and sells linens; she supplies the merchants with sashes. . . . She opens her mouth with wisdom and a lesson of kindness is on her tongue. . . . Give her credit for the fruit of her labors, and let her achievements praise her at the gates," the song goes. This is an incredible woman, no? She's nurturing, industrious, and wise, the kind of person we should all be learning from, a beacon in the home and community. And yet, in the Orthodox homes I've been to, the woman to whom this is being sung is not allowed to publicly sing this or any other song herself, as her voice is considered a distraction to men. While her life might feel full and she might feel spiritually nourished, there is, because of her gender, a limit to how much power or influence she can have in her community. This "Woman of Valor," whose laudable wisdom is informed in part by care, can't make laws, or lead her broader community.

In Judaism and other traditions, care matters as long as it is kept in the abstract. To connect with another is to connect with the oneness of the universe. To care for others is to be good and to be good is to reflect that tiny, precious shard of the divine we all contain within us and honor that shard of the divine others contain within them. Community, both a sacred obligation and gift, is created through care. And yet the highest states of being, the greatest sources of revelation, were not, it was forever presumed, to be found at home, through care.

Nearly all religions require the holiest of holies to leave home and seek divine truth elsewhere. Buddha, Jesus, and the monks and nuns who followed them left home to find their truth in the great out there. So did the great rabbis of the Talmud, who spent their day in a house of study. Islam and Hinduism also have a tradition of casting women, which is to say caregivers, in a supporting role, while men take on the heavy lifting of a spiritual existence. We see and talk about the "Woman of Valor," Virgin Mary, and other iconic religious mothers but never hear from them. They're idealized, glorified, and, as such, kept at a distance, locked up in metaphors for goodliness and creation. Rarely does the caregiver get to be a seeking, real-life human, with a messy story to tell and a lesson to teach.

This is until she starts telling that story herself, with or without an invitation. In recent decades, more and more women have realized that it is not enough to prove that women are capable and worthy of doing what men do, spiritually speaking. They also want to explore and exalt the spiritual experiences women have long had as caregivers, while their fathers and brothers and husbands and sons were off at the monastery, temple, church, wherever, doing the official, significant work. Men, they hope, will return the favor. These fathers and brothers and husbands and sons will listen to their mothers and sisters and wives and daughters about their care-infused spiritual experiences and then, maybe, try it out themselves.

None of this requires much in the way of imagination, as caregiving and spirituality have a lot in common. Religion pushes us to grapple with the mysteries and complexities of life, and suffering, rejoicing, despairing, and hoping is all part of the process. In our spiritual lives, we toggle between feeling adrift in chaos and having a deep sense of purpose, moving through the questions and certainties that help us tell the stories of our days. Caring for a dependent human, one to whom we feel a sense of obligation and affection, is all of the above. Caregivers experience madness, doubt, and rawness alongside communion and direction, suffering and hope forever intertwined. It can feel like a test, punishment, or a higher calling, a way to go higher and lower, a reason to turn within and a reason to turn without, sometimes at the same time. All these paradoxes of human existence, the very ones we've long grappled with through religion and other forms of spirituality, are present in care.

In 2016, the Pew Research Center published data on gender and religion among six faiths in over eighty-four countries and found that "globally, women are more devout than men by several standard measures of religious commitment." One reason, according to a number of sociologists, is that women's firsthand knowledge of the beginning and end of life makes it much harder to walk around acting like one has all the answers or isn't in need of some guidance now and again. It's a lot to wrap one's head around, and my attempt to do so has made me, much to my surprise, a regular worshipper.

I want to tell you that I am religious, but in doing so I immediately feel compelled to tell you that it doesn't mean what you think. Or at least what I think you'll think. I have no firm theology or strong beliefs, and I definitely don't need other people to believe anything, let alone behave a certain way. Instead, I have questions, gaping curiosities that, in this particular moment of my particular consciousness, have been best addressed through a pursuit of faith. Sometimes only a mystery as big as God will do.

There are lots of reasons I am Jewish. Mainly, I was born Jewish, raised Jewish, and am conservative in the sense that the past has a pull on me. Though it wasn't until I became a parent, a regular caregiver, that a deeper spiritual longing emerged. It began with awe, when I birthed one singular consciousness, and then another, two very different and yet entirely whole beings who came from my husband and me, though also maybe something else. Then there was fear of time, that it was passing too fast, or too slow, that it would be too easy to lose control of it amid the rushed and yet still often tedious days, and the lightning speed at which the baby fat seemed to melt from my sons' cheeks. So I began, in the Jewish fashion, to mark time, separating out the busyness of our regular, profane life from a sacred time dedicated to reflection and connection. This happens weekly, sundown Friday night to sundown Saturday night, with the Jewish Sabbath, along with the roughly ten other Jewish holidays we observe.

I didn't know, and still don't know, where I am going with this, or what exactly I am after. Only that I'm driven by my awe and fascination with ongoingness, the curious swirl of life that I witness and take part in every day as the world around me, the people around me, my kids, and even I constantly re-create. Who is behind this? What is behind this? I really don't mean to flatter myself when I tell you that one of my answers was me. As a caregiver, I began to feel closer and closer to the act of creation, so close that I'm almost terrified, so close that I've begun to see myself as part of it.

There are lots of big ideas about creation. Some think it only happened once and now we exist in creation's aftermath. Others believe it is continual. Some believe that God alone was, or is, responsible. Others believe that humans are partners in creation, and have been since the beginning. It's hard for me to imagine that there is a caregiver on the planet who, whether they believe in God or some God-type energy, doesn't lean toward the ongoing and partnership model. What is care if not helping creation take one more step, one more breath? For whom is it not an education in the delicate balance between enabling and sustaining life, and, sometimes, getting out of life's way? A nonstop cycle of feeling large and small, an agent of change and a bit player in existence? This is a central tension experienced by the God we meet in the Hebrew Bible, and it's the central tension of any caregiver's life.

Before I became a parent, I used to see Judaism exclusively as a means to an end, a culture and community that shared my love of humor and food and ritual. I thought it was a place people went to for answers—but since the answers about why bad things happen or where goodness comes from could never be answered, they weren't really worth pursuing in any deeper or disciplined way. Now Judaism has become my place for questions, questions that are either a precursor to a more crystalline faith or, more likely I imagine for me, the essence of the faith itself. Prayer and observance is how I connect the dots between the constantly evolving creation of a vulnerable and miraculous us, all of us, bugs and trees included, and the role I play in that creation. I feel part of something so purely alive, something that other people more comfortable with their faith might even call holy.

None of this means I have a coherent answer to the question of what God is, or even whether I believe in God. In fact, I doubt I ever will. What I can tell you is that I feel a special something in the face of our beautiful and difficult ongoingness. And caring for my sons helped me arrive at this special feeling with a depth and texture I hadn't felt before.

FINDING NEW IN THE OLD,
AND OLD IN THE NEW

We tend to think of religions solely as rule books, with fixed positions on all major matters—and many minor ones too. In reality, religions are old and layered, and contain a multitude of conflicting and textured ideas and opinions on a life well lived. Among these are positive thoughts about care. "There have been blind spots to care, but, nevertheless, you can retrieve ideas about the importance of care from traditional texts. You can retrieve what has been invisible," Deena Aranoff, a professor of Jewish studies, told me. Removing these blind spots requires us to better understand how care was diminished in religion, find places where it was valued, and create new traditions, rituals, and customs that acknowledge the full roller coaster of experiences, emotions, and epiphanies that come along with care.

Most major religions have some rules that apply to a person's relationship with the divine, and others that apply to our relationships with other people. Unfortunately, these religions tend to also have leaders, generally male, who privilege the rules about interacting with the divine and dismiss, consciously and otherwise, those pertaining to our relationships with other people. But the rules on the latter are there for us to contemplate and follow.

The Hebrew Bible, sacred to Christianity and Judaism, begins with a story about people needing people. In the creation myth, the first time God points out a problem with the world is the moment when God realizes that Adam should have a partner: "The LORD God said, 'It is not good for man to be alone; I will make a fitting helper for him.'" After this follows a series of dramas in which humans struggle with other humans. There's sibling rivalry, parental favorites, grooms being tricked at the altar, and mockery of the infertile, certainly enough material to give any psychoanalyst a lifetime of troubles to sort out. Before we get rules, before Moses gets the Commandments up high on Sinai, we get insights into the relationships of messy people living messy lives.

One of these is the story of Abraham and his son Isaac. It's one of history's most harrowing requests, and also—as I read it—a surprising endorsement for the entanglement of faith and care. A Sunday school refresher: Abraham and his wife, Sarah, had their first child together at ages one hundred and ninety, respectively. They called him Isaac, Hebrew for "laughter." One day, God calls upon Abraham to sacrifice his son to demonstrate his faith. Abraham agrees to the challenge, climbs a mountain, and binds Isaac, whose age isn't mentioned. He is about to kill his son when God intervenes. "For now I know that you fear God," God says, and tells Abraham to kill a ram instead.

God is asking Abraham to choose between loyalty to God and his child. It's the ultimate test, horrific as it is. When God stops it from happening, God is sending the message that you can do both. You can love your child and love God. Abraham's fanaticism and Isaac's ensuing trauma should be a warning sign, telling us to remember, always remember, relationships and see the day-to-day, body-to-body act of parenting as spiritually important alongside worship of the divine. And, just as important, it's a reminder that negotiating these two modes of being won't be easy. I wonder why, historically speaking, so few men have taken note. The Ten Commandments, which come later, also strike a balance between the importance of our relationship with God and the importance of our relationship with one another. The idea that love for the divine and love for the people we care for are equally important and can feed each other is in the text. We just need to, as Aranoff told me, make it visible.

REIMAGINING HIERARCHIES OF LOVE

Christians are supposed to love. "By this shall all men know that ye are my disciples, if ye have love one to another," reads John 13:35. Jesus loved the people and the people should reciprocate by loving God, Jesus, and one another. The Hebrew Bible tells us to love thy neighbor. Jesus took it a step further and told us to also love our enemies. Why? Love is the answer.

But not all love is the same. Love that is divorced from self-interest is considered the most important type of love in many forms of Christianity. Other kinds of love, including *eros* (romantic love), *philia* (friendship), and *storge* (family love), all matter too, but they're not seen as a pure manifestation of God or Christ. "There is an emphasis on loving the neighbor as yourself and then making that love universal, especially in the past couple hundred years. Though this is impossible because you can't love everybody in any meaningful way," Sandra Sullivan-Dunbar, a professor of Christian ethics, told me.

Sullivan-Dunbar started her PhD program in Christian ethics in 2003 when her oldest son was three months old, and, as a result, did all her work through the lens of early motherhood. Again and again, she was assigned reading in which the ideal version of love was described as heroic and undiscriminating, and yet neither of these adjectives shed much light on how she felt about her child: "My takeaway was, 'Yeah, these guys aren't spending much time caring for kids.'"

There are two stories back to back in the Christian Bible that illustrate this. The first is that of the Good Samaritan, a well-known story in which a Jewish scholar questions Jesus about how he could make it to heaven and achieve an eternal life. Jesus responds with a parable about a Jewish traveler, who was robbed and beaten on the road. A Jewish priest walks by and doesn't help him. A Jewish priest's assistant walks by and also doesn't help the man. Then a man from Samaria stops to help the man—despite the fact that Jews and Samaritans despised each other. How to get to heaven? Love your neighbor as you love yourself, just like the Hebrew Bible says. Who is your neighbor? Everyone.

Directly after this story, we have one about two women, Martha and Mary. Jesus and his disciples were traveling when they arrived at a village. A woman named Martha invited him into her home, where her sister Mary (no relation to Jesus's mom) also lived. Mary sat at Jesus's feet and listened. Martha was "distracted by all the preparations that had to be made. She came to him and asked, 'Lord, don't you care that my sister has left me to do the work by myself? Tell her to help me!'"

"Martha, Martha . . . you are worried and upset about many things, but few things are needed—or indeed only one. Mary has chosen what is better, and it will not be taken away from her."

This passage offers empathy for Martha, but it is one-sided. Jesus wants Martha to cease her hostess duties so that she might open herself up to his teachings, but there is little respect for the work she is doing, why it matters to her, and what she might possibly be getting from it. Martha was tending to the home, doing the domestic work that makes our homes safe and comfortable places, distinguishing them, physically and psychologically, from everywhere else. Housework and hospitality are varieties of care and, often, love. How do we know that Mary has chosen better if nobody ever asked Martha about what she was doing? How daring is it to imagine that if they both share the household labor making sure the other is taken care of, then they both have ample time for contemplation and quiet conversation? What if both of these activities were seen as equally ripe for respect and revelation?

"Historically speaking, the Christian tradition devalued care by privileging ascetic traditions. The highest Christian calling was to deny the body, and follow a call to celibacy and virginity, setting aside all concerns of the flesh so as to focus only on the spiritual," Elizabeth O'Donnell Gandolfo, author of *The Power and Vulnerability of Love: A*

Theological Anthropology, told me. There's a gendered component to this: spirituality is most associated with the male, and the fleshy, corporeal nature of life is mostly associated with women. Women, beginning with Eve, are inferior to men. They were—according to one of the two creation myths in the Bible, though tellingly the best-known one—made from man, who was made by God. This makes them one step removed from the divine. Then Eve couldn't control her body around the luscious, seductive fruit (the original Hebrew suggests as much), thus ending our days in paradise.

This is why, in Christianity as well as other religions, the mother figure became more useful as a metaphor than as a real human with a body and feelings. It's cleaner, theologically speaking, to use mothers and maternal language to speak broadly about creation and the nurturing of life, rather than acknowledging head-on the messy power of women's bodies and lived experiences. This way, religious leaders can rhapsodize about maternal power, without having to give authority or voice to the actual mothers who have gone through it, or acknowledge the very demanding bodily work that motherhood entails. "The whole idea of spiritual discipline is about leaving flesh behind and ascending to a spiritual realm," or, to leave behind femininity and women's work, Gandolfo, a Catholic, explained. "And yet where does that leave the world? Who takes care of the babies and elderly and the sick?" The love a mother has for her children, in all its embodied, oozy fleshiness, doesn't belong.

Monks and nuns have, as part of their spiritual practice, cared for the needy. However, care as an act of charity and care as an act of relational or familial obligation are not treated or seen the same. For one, charity often comes with an escape route; one can opt out or pass along the dependent to another. Also, care as an act of charity is celebrated, whereas care as an act of obligation has been belittled and ignored. Mother Teresa is a saint, while the billions of other women who also spent their lives caring for children and older, sick, and disabled people are forgotten or invisible.

In the 1990s, the Vatican attempted to change this. Pope John Paul II wrote an open letter in which he described women's capacity to care and feel compassion—yes, he is assuming all women are natural caregivers, which is its own problem—as a type of genius:

> The Church sees in Mary the highest expression of the "feminine genius" and she finds in her a source of constant inspiration. . . . Through obedience to the Word of God she accepted her lofty yet not easy vocation as wife and mother in the family of Nazareth. . . . For her, "to reign" is to serve! Her service is "to reign"!

This was a well-intentioned and radical attempt to praise women, connect the dots between caregiving and spirituality, and raise up the love in care as being as important as other types of love. The needle was moved forward. Still, the Church wasn't suggesting that this care makes the women doing it men's equal, nor was there much effort to discover the complexities and challenges of this type of spirituality. The heavy emphasis on Mary didn't make it any better. "They compared women to Mary, the virgin mother. This is a high pedestal, an impossible ideal," Gandolfo said.

While Protestants have more of a tradition of reaching for great heights within the ordinary—going all the way back to Luther—there is still a reluctance to place the love experienced in care on equal standing with other types of human connection and spiritual experiences. Bonnie J. Miller-McLemore, a Protestant theologian, thinks this can't happen until we begin to see caring for our loved ones as worthy a vocation as any other. Christian theologian Frederick Buechner defines vocation as "the place where your deep gladness and the world's deep hunger meet." The "deep hunger," Miller-McLemore tells her readers and audiences, can be found in that person who needs our care. "There is a passage from Matthew that tells us that we will be judged if we don't visit the sick or help the poor, and it has been interpreted as meaning that you have to get out of the house. But sometimes the poor and unclothed, sometimes the 'sufferer,' is the child in your house," she told me. Sometimes the love you give someone you care for is as noble as any other kind of love.

For Alesia Canady, a mother, grandmother, sister, daughter, Black and women's rights activist, and Christian, care has been a vocation. Here is a list of everyone Alesia has cared for: her two kids, the first of which she had in high school; her sister's two kids, who moved in when Alesia's oldest child was seventeen; her mom and dad; her friend in her final days of cancer; and, now, her granddaughter.

The last one came as a surprise. Right when Alesia was getting ready to retire at the age of sixty she learned that her son's girlfriend was pregnant. Both were addicted to drugs, and Alesia tried to help them get off, an effort that only resulted in the couple cutting her out of their lives. She heard nothing for months until she got a phone call late one night. A baby girl had been born, and the odds were high she'd have health issues due to her parents' drug use. The hospital was not going to release the baby to her biological parents.

"I went down there and put my hands on her head and prayed for her," Alesia said. "A couple days later I brought her home with me." A decade later, they are still living together in her home in southern Seattle and Aleiyah, nicknamed Yaya, is bright, healthy, and happy.

Alesia is, predictably and understandably, tired. She could really use a break. "I'll be honest. I feel some resentment right now. I can't just have twenty-four hours to myself. I feel that I haven't gone on a vacation in a very long time," she said. But alongside the struggle and exhaustion has come what she considers a blessing—a chance for healing.

"I feel as though I was put here to do something, to help somebody. If I help somebody, then I end up helping me," she said.

For Alesia, caring for others is akin to a spiritual discipline. Most religions demand more than belief. Believers must practice their faith in a conscious way, and sometimes these ways are uncomfortable, inconvenient, even painful. They can include daily prayer practice, meditation, fasting, service, and, on the extreme end, self-flagellation. Such actions are meant to cultivate humility, and the cultivation of humility is a central aim in all major faiths.

"Caring for others makes me feel closer to God. Everyone has a journey and this is just the way my life has been," Alesia said. "I didn't get to have anybody stand with me and guide me when I was young. I looked at that and thought, because I didn't have anybody, I should do that for someone else. That was my training, as hard as it was. I wanted to use it for good and not just look at it as something horrible, even though that is what it was. That's where I get my strength, courage, conviction, and determination to make it better for someone even though it wasn't good for me. That makes me feel healed. It is a chance for me to heal myself."

Underneath it all is Jesus. She's always felt him, but care has strengthened her connection with God unlike anything else. It's a feeling she's harnessed into her personal relationships as well as her community work. In 1994, Alesia founded a group called Women United, to support caregivers who lacked support—at the time she was caring for her nieces and needed support herself. In the past decade, the organization has begun to focus on supporting grandmas, mostly other Black women, who are raising their grandchildren. There are regular meet-ups as well as yearly festivals in which grandmothers are pampered and kids get to celebrate.

Alesia wishes the love she feels would be shared by those in power. Grandparents lack the structural and financial support given to foster parents, even though they often have essentially the same responsibilities. She's working on that too, but in the meantime, she's not giving up on the love that is needed at home.

"You have to have a spirituality in you to remove yourself and go help somebody else. Anything I do is just showing his love for them."

HOMEBODIES

In her 2006 book *In the Midst of Chaos: Care of Children as Spiritual Practice*, Miller-McLemore follows in Luther's path and makes a case for finding God in the noise, mess, and excitement of domestic life. "What would happen if we considered how people discover God not just when alone, in worship, or on the mountaintop, but when with others—specifically when with children and all the turbulence and wonder they bring into our world?" she writes. Whenever she brings this up in the company of caregivers, a few are bound to cry. For so long they've held on to the guilt that their spiritual life was somehow lacking because they couldn't get to church as often as they'd like, and then Bonnie says this and they realize that there is a different way to think about it. The home, their home, has its own spiritual potential, separate from and complementary to church. The challenge of maintaining faith as a caregiver is not, then, how to prioritize leaving the house to make time and space for worship, but how to integrate the home-based experience of faith, in all its unpredictability and imprecision, with the more pristine and tightly controlled choreography of traditional religious practice.

This tension runs through all major religious traditions, though perhaps none more so than Buddhism. Beginning around five hundred years before Christianity, Buddhism was started by a young prince named Siddhārtha Gautama, "the Buddha," who left behind everything, home and family, to seek awakening on his own. He eventually found it, six years later, meditating under a bodhi tree. After this, he returned to society to praise virtues like wisdom, kindness, patience, generosity, and compassion, all of which could be achieved through meditation.

For Vanessa R. Sasson, a writer and religious studies professor who practices Buddhism, it's been a challenge to reconcile the Buddha's insistence on kindness and compassion with his treatment of his family. According to the scripture, Siddhārtha left home shortly after his wife gave birth to their son. The boy's name is Rahula, which, according to a common interpretation, means "obstacle," "fetter," or "impediment." "There has been so much idealization of Buddha as this hero who finds the answer to suffering," Sasson told me. "But the paradox is that in order to find the answer to suffering he has to break everyone's heart."

In 2020, Sasson wrote a novelized version of Buddha's wife's story called *Yasodhara and the Buddha*. It's a feminist counterpoint to Hermann Hesse's backpacker favorite novel *Siddhartha*. He celebrated the leaving. Sasson looks at how leaving affects those who stay, or more specifically those who can't leave because they are caring for others. "He had abandoned all of us when we needed him and then he came home and was hailed a hero, while I remained invisible and forgotten," Yasodhara, Buddha's wife, explains in Sasson's novel.

Buddhism is, on its face, a tradition that privileges the kind of calm and freedom of thought that caregivers can rarely achieve. Traditionally, to be a good Buddhist has meant living in a monastery as a monk or nun and spending hours a day meditating. That's how you become a leader and a teacher. Householders, or people who live at home besides dependents, have not, by contrast, traditionally been allowed to be spiritual leaders.

Care isn't absent from the Buddhist worldview. Monks often look after one another and members of the broader community. Buddhism outside the West tends to be far more invested in collective well-being than Buddhism in the United States, where it was first popularized in the mainstream in the 1960s by beatniks and others—mostly men—who tended to present it as an individual pursuit. Still, even in these more communal settings, there is little value placed on domestic life, family bonds, or caregiving as a source of religious epiphany.

In her writing and her own practice as a Buddhist, Sasson is trying to shake up this hierarchy and find a place for her home in her spiritual life and the life of others. The need for solitude and the busyness of existence are both part of life, and one is not holier than the other, she argues. Instead, they can feed into each other and enrich each other, bringing us to a higher state of being. "To set up an absolute binary is a mistake," she said. Digging into Buddhist scriptures, she has found her own answers on how to do this. There is a long history of debate over whether householders could be leaders. While the conversation didn't exactly have caregivers or parents in mind, there was an attempt to reject the historically popular notion that to be a good Buddhist was to disconnect from one's family.

Buddhism encourages its practitioners to renounce their attachments. What if this doesn't have to include renouncing relationships? Instead, Sasson believes, Buddhists could focus on renouncing their attachments to a particular model of spirituality. It may sound simple on its face, but at its heart it is a truly radical notion that pushes the act of renouncement even further than many Buddhists claim, and, in doing so, makes space for chaos and care. Such a redefinition of renouncement would better allow us to understand that Buddha's path of leaving home in pursuit of solitude came with risks and rewards, as did Yasodhara's path of staying home and raising her son. Both are valid paths, both should be ours to explore, as we free ourselves from the idea of one universal formula to awakening.

"Perhaps the real renunciation is this: that we must renounce our expectations of our lives. When it is busy, it is busy. And when there is solitude, we try to embrace it. In both cases, we must prepare ourselves. Because without preparation, solitude can be devastating and busyness can be like a roller coaster," she said.

"The question of 'Do we have to leave everything behind?' is as old as time," Sasson said. "But we are focusing on it more now, largely because of the rise of strong female voices asking these questions."

WRESTLING WITH GOD, THE BABY

As a Jew, I haven't felt much pressure to pursue solitude as a path to faith. In my tradition we have no history of celibacy vows for religious leaders. Quite the opposite. Having lots of babies is considered a mitzvah, or holy act. Acts of public worship require a minyan, or ten adults, historically only men, who pray and grieve together. The domestic space is an equal rival to the synagogue as a place where religion happens. Worship takes place at home on major holidays like Passover and Sukkot, as well as on the weekly Sabbath.

There are plenty of care-related mandates in sacred Jewish texts: Respect your elders! ("You shall rise before the aged and show deference to the old. . . . ," Leviticus 19:32.) Have kids! ("And God blessed them; and God said unto them: 'Be fruitful, and multiply, and replenish the earth, and subdue it. . . . ,'" Genesis 1:28.) Raise them well! ("And these words, which I command thee this day, shall be upon thy heart; and thou shalt teach them diligently unto thy children, and shalt talk of them when thou sittest in thy house, and when thou walkest by the way, and when thou liest down, and when thou risest up," Deuteronomy 6:6–7.) There's also a touching story ritually read once a year about a woman named Ruth who insists on caring for her mother-in-law after her husband dies and she is no longer obliged to do so. "Do not urge me to leave you, to turn back and not follow you. For wherever you go, I will go; wherever you lodge, I will lodge; your people shall be my people, and your God my God," Ruth tells her mother-in-law, Naomi.

And yet, even with all this emphasis on communal life, and all the rules about caring for one another in the holy books, I've witnessed relatively little interest in caregiving as a holy act, something through which God could be felt or whereby a person could learn. Jewish theologian Mara Benjamin felt the same way. "It was so shocking to me that when I started thinking about my own experience caring for kids and what it means religiously, that there was nowhere to turn in classical Jewish literature to find curiosity about that. It was bizarre," she told me. This realization motivated her to write what she wanted to read. In 2018, Benjamin published her book *The Obligated Self*, in which she argues that caring for children is theologically fruitful work.

Benjamin, like many other Jewish women, had grown up with lots of implicit pressure to have babies. Jewish communal leaders, her family, her friends, all expected her to become a mom. Jews were always in the business of "multiplying," as the Torah puts it, but ever since the Holocaust that obligation has intensified. Children are a bulwark against obsolescence. But for all the talk of babies, there was little interest among Jewish authorities about what it was like to raise a child: "And not just the special moments of caring for children, but ordinary life. Because ordinary life is what most people experience most of the time."

Benjamin's theology of care attempts to pull in all aspects of the experience, the joy, sweetness, anger, and frustrations, into one soul-provoking experience. The "obligated self" of her title is someone whose obligation, to God or a child, is routinely tested by the stresses of daily life, as well as a deeper yearning to be free. It's right there, in that conflict, caught between the push and pull of care, where faith can be enriched.

The outcome of this process was a reimagining of the central metaphor through which she viewed God. Benjamin shifted away from the liturgy's common metaphors, of God as Father or King, and began instead to sometimes view God as a baby, or a being that demands care. There are moments when we like providing that care and moments when we don't—and there will always be both. Imagining God "as a baby invites us to name the condition of being obligated to God as being compelled and beguiled, shackled and infatuated, all at once," she writes. Push past the thought experiment of this, and imagine it in your tired caregiver body, or maybe even your soul if you believe yourself to have such a thing. Viewing God as a baby helps us accept the imperfections in God, or the universe. Or maybe the real baby is a manifestation of God, a God with whom you are absolutely going to struggle but also a God who needs you.

"Israel" means "wrestle with God," and Jews have long seen themselves as wrestlers with the divine. The inevitability of the wrestling, in both the case of babies and God, creates an opening in which the hard parts of care and the hard parts of faith can be both predictable and potentially fruitful. When we are prepared to wrestle, when we count on it being hard, then there is nothing surprising about the moments we want to run away from our children or elderly parents or God. That includes the times when they make us scream or cry, when we wish we could be anywhere else in the world. We are supposed to wrestle with our obligations. In fact, wrestling is, itself, the obligation.

Perhaps as we mix up our metaphors with God, we might also change what we expect to get from God. If God is someone we care for, someone who expects something from us, then maybe connecting with God can bring us closer to the flesh-and-blood people to whom we give care. In her 2016 book *Nurture the Wow*, a book about the spirituality of parenting, Rabbi Danya Ruttenberg considers whether the endpoint of all the work of being religious should be our relationships with other people, rather than our relationship with God. "[W]hat if loving God . . . is actually just a set of exercises to better enable us to love the actual people in our actual lives?" she writes.

Or maybe, in the end, it's all the same and loving God and loving others is one and the same. For over forty-five years, Rabbi Richard Address has been offering support to caregivers to old, ill, and disabled people through his talks and now his podcast. He said there isn't enough ethical or spiritual guidance for this group, who, quite often, are going through some of the most complicated ethical and spiritual challenges of their lives. He helps them navigate thorny practical questions: How do I divide care between siblings? And difficult ones: How obligated am I to care for a parent who abused me? (Jewish tradition, he argues, says you are not.) Also: What happens to our souls when we care?

"Many are thrust into this role reversal. This larger-than-life person is suddenly frail. Can I bathe this person? Can I toilet this person? Can I do this with my mom and dad? This is a profoundly spiritual moment. It represents a shift in generations and a sometimes subconscious confrontation of our own mortality," he said. Care, particularly for the old, can be a one-two punch of physical and existential demands, which is something Address doesn't deny or smooth over. He's there to help not by telling caregivers everything will be fine, or that they are doing great, but by providing context for the experience that helps them make sense of their big feelings.

Maybe, like Moses, caregivers are reluctant to climb the mountain. But like Moses, the mountain will lead to revelation, a covenant between the caregivers and the great mystery beyond. Address says his go-to words of comfort are reminding caregivers that Jewish tradition tells us that we are each created *"b'tzelem elohim,"* or in the divine image. There is divinity in everyone, and care, when one singular consciousness is responsible for another, can be the easiest way to see it.

INTO THE MYSTIC

Amany Shalaby regularly lectures Muslim women and communities about the not always valued importance of caregiving in traditional Muslim texts. There are stories about listening to, valuing, and comforting children, and a passage in which caring for parents is seen as being as important as the belief in a single God—a central tenet of monotheistic faiths.

Shalaby likes to share these teachings because of the way they elevate care over rituals and judgments, both of which have long been considered the domain of men, and, often, more important. Though perhaps more inspiring than these teachings are the stories she tells about her own life, when care and faith intertwined. For Shalaby, God has been most keenly felt in those moments when self and other blur, the world takes on a new charge, and she gains access to those corners of human experience that we often label as mystic.

Religion used to be primarily about order and ritual for Shalaby. She was born in Cairo, Egypt, where, in her twenties, she got married, had two kids, and worked as an engineer. At age thirty, she moved with her husband to Florida, where she could not find work or, with time, joy in her marriage. She had one more child before she separated from her husband, a life change that led to a "deepening," as she put it, in her faith. As a married woman she had practiced and enjoyed Sunnism, a more structured denomination of Islam. But when she became a single mom, her ideas about what the world should and could be opened up, and she began to move toward a more mystical practice of Islam, Sufism. Mystics seek out God everywhere, and this is exactly how Shalaby felt in her looser, more improvised, more chaotic and energized existence. God was there in prayer, and God was there in relationships. She felt God in the work she did running an organization for Muslim women, helping the homeless as part of an interfaith effort, and caring for her children. God's presence was not just around her but in her, a fullness of feeling and spirit that many other seekers try to achieve through ecstatic prayer, psychedelics, or rigorous meditation practices.

"I remember caring for a child, not my own. She was the daughter of a friend of mine who was going through difficulties, and I watched her eleven-year-old daughter for nine months," she told me. "One time she was sick, and I remember putting my hand on her head and she said to me, 'That was so powerful. I felt the hand of God above me.' And I was feeling that too, at the same time. I was a representative of the divine at that moment."

Sometimes such mystical abandon is sweet. Other times it is painful, an act of succumbing to the unknowable force that makes our biggest decisions for us.

Vasudha Narayanan, a scholar of Hinduism, told me that for Hindus, care is deeply woven into their tradition, a well-articulated dimension of their moral order. "When we think about these things we think about them as obligatory. Caring for each other is about the duty and rightness of things," she told me. This goes for God too. In the Hindu tradition God is sometimes seen as a man and sometimes a woman and sometimes a child, who requires care. "God is seen as your baby, as a child who we have to entertain, and bathe and watch their first steps and delight in them," she said. It's this paradoxical framing of God as a being whom you must care for that gives a particular religious charge to the very common, and often challenging, work of looking after one's elderly and sick parents in her culture. Many Hindus approach this work with a mix of love, duty, gratitude, and devotion, all fortified by their faith.

There's a Hindu saying that one's parents are "the gods who you see in front of you." "It sounds grand, and of course most people treat their parents like we all treat our parents. Still, somewhere, it is locked in our consciousness that when we care for our parents, it is spiritual," Narayanan said. She felt this personally, painfully, when she cared for her dying mom and her spirituality took the form of surrender. Her mom's suffering and Narayanan's inability to make it all better, whether through a failure of her patience or the unyielding fact that human bodies don't always heal, pushed her to reckon with the limits surrounding human life: "Anytime you are doing acute, intense care, whether for a baby or adult, when you are tired beyond thinking, it pushes you to a type of state of mind that in Sanskrit I would call 'surrender.' To surrender is a form of faith; it is looking at God as the complete protector and caregiver. You submit yourself and seek the divine as a refuge. You submit yourself completely to this being."

Nate Hayes's parents were both diagnosed with Alzheimer's disease in 2015, on the same day, in the same office. Over the past year, the forgetfulness had grown more frequent and more severe. Conversations that took place in the morning vanished from his mom's memory by noon, and his father's word mix-ups became more and more common. "How are your chickens?" he'd ask Nate, meaning his dogs instead. Even if it wasn't surprising, even if he saw it coming, even if it all made sense, the change was still a shock. The tides of family life had reversed. Nate's parents, who lived two hours north of his home in Athens, Ohio, would no longer be able to care for themselves. It was his turn to care for them.

Nate had been doing Zen Buddhist meditation for twenty years at that point, and was a diligent student of concepts like impermanence and detachment. He had sat and meditated, preparing himself for moments of rupture, fortifying his ability to stay clear and calm when they happened. His parents' diagnoses, followed by years of driving back and forth to their farmhouse and helping them with tasks large and small, put this all to the test.

"Meditation is all about trying to maintain being present. What better practice is there than this?" he told me, referring to the time he spent caring for his parents. "It wasn't pretty. It wasn't storybook. It is one thing to sit on a nice little pillow in front of a candle, and all is well and all is nice, and it's another thing when your mom is fighting with you at the supermarket that she needs more lemon curd." Nobody needed any lemon curd.

His Zen practice helped him accept that things would never go back to how they were: "I wasn't looking for a silver lining. I wasn't looking on the bright side. My spiritual practice is about being present to whatever is arising in my life, so I knew I had to be present. I had to be here—for this." Still, being at peace with impermanence is hard, even for a seasoned Buddhist. Over the course of caring intensely for his parents, Nate divorced his husband and his business fell apart. Neither was a direct result of his caregiving responsibilities, but they certainly didn't help.

Like Narayanan, the spiritual education of caregiving for Nate was one of surrender. He realized that truly acknowledging impermanence demands us to go beyond acceptance and, finger by finger, release our grip on what we thought life should have been and submit to what he sees as a beautiful emptiness.

From his diary, January 30, 2017:

One of the central tenets in Zen Buddhism is the miracle of emptiness. Not as in a void or a vacuum. But the belief that everything is empty in that everything changes. The grasses die each autumn, the mountains become low. The years pass and we age and die. Even the stars wink out eventually. The miracle lies in even for one moment being a part of life, being a part of everything. And since everything changes, how amazing to be a part of all creation.

As I held my sobbing mum, I realized how fortunate I am. That I am a part of something so much bigger than I could ever comprehend. How honored I am to be a help to her and dad, how amazingly privileged I am to be a part of their journey.

Nate's dad died in August 2017. He went fast. Nate's mom died in November 2019. She went slow. "It was an intimacy I never expected to have with my parents. It was a challenging and difficult gift, but what a gift to be given. What a blessing," he told me.

A CARE REFORMATION

There's one other important element to my story about how motherhood led to me feeling more spiritual. Every Saturday at my synagogue there is free childcare, a highly desirable offering to a fatigued parent of two who very much appreciates three hours of quiet, contemplative time after a busy week of family life. There are absolutely weeks when I go to services for this reason alone, not to mention the community lunch that follows, which I never have to cook or clean up.

But the weekly childcare works on another level as well. It tells me that I, a parent, belong in religious life, that I deserve to be accommodated and included. It makes me feel welcome, and also opens a pathway for me to step up as a leader. If I want to get in front of the community and share my thoughts on life, maybe even thoughts about being a caregiver, I can do it because someone is watching my children.

Embracing care in spiritual communities means embracing everything that comes along with care: dependents, including children, people with disabilities, and dependent older adults, as well as the unexpectedness and unpredictability they may bring. The chapel or sanctuary will be less orderly than a room full of independent men with pure focus, but it will also be a lot more human. In order to make this change, religious organizations should start with top-down strategies and rules, including increased accessibility, support groups, and childcare. But if change remains only at that, caregivers will still be marginalized. The shift in the priorities of spiritual leaders and the communities they serve has to be one of sensibility as well.

When I moved to Oakland from New York in 2018, I visited a number of synagogues before I found the right one. The first time I attended services, the rabbi introduced himself not just to me but to my son as well. He looked both of us in the eyes, asked us our names, where we were from, and then he asked my son what the name of his stuffed animal was. This wasn't performative schmoozing. The rabbi's eyes weren't darting around in an effort to find a more important person to rush off and speak to next. Me and Augie, mother and son, mattered to him. I'd never seen a rabbi make a child feel so welcome. And by extension, I felt welcome.

Shalaby shared another example of this with me. "Leaders can talk about families and care, and that's good, but this is what I would describe as real care. My sheikh [prayer leader], if he hears a child cry, instead of getting annoyed, like many others, he incorporates the cry into the sermon," Shalaby said.

When caregivers are welcome, their voices can move from the margins to the center of the conversation. They become the experts and authorities, the ones who pick which ancient texts to focus on, and the ones who decide which light to frame that text in. They point out when and where care is hiding in plain sight, and encourage us to start care-inspired conversations that were systematically excluded for centuries. "What would it mean to put my bubbe [grandma] and her Sisterhood friends on the same level as a rabbi? To think of them as someone who has something that should be passed on as well?" Benjamin wonders.

I imagine those caregivers would have a lot to say. Care is about life, death, joy, strength, weakness, pain, and surrender. "There will be dark nights of the soul," Gandolfo told me, referencing a mystical sixteenth-century poem by Saint John of the Cross. It is about ambiguity, not knowing, having questions that lead to more questions, certainty or answers forever out of reach. Care brings us to a place of humility, of feeling weak, and confused about our power. How much do we really have? What should we do with it? This is care and this is faith, whether someone describes themselves as spiritual, God-ish, or God-believing.

I once heard about a group of Middle Eastern Jewish women for whom food preparation was their primary form of worship. To get ready for the holiday of Passover, the women sorted and cleaned large quantities of rice, one grain at a time, seven times each. When a researcher first stumbled upon this, she assumed some oppressive male rabbi had once demanded this of them, recently or far in the past. No, they told her, this was how they spoke to God, a prayer that came from their homebody hearts.

I suspect my grandma had a similar story to tell. She never went to synagogue, or observed the holidays or Shabbat with any regularity. There was nothing formal about her faith. Still, there was no apparent ambivalence or reluctance when she called upon God to protect her children, or praised God when learning we were safe. I suspect there was God in the food she made us, and the way she pressed her garlic-scented hands gently upon our cheeks. I suspect we were her Gods, her access point to the force of life, her care, the primary medium of her faith.

During the afternoon of her dying, she demanded the chaplain rabbi recite the Shema, the central prayer of Judaism, over and over and over again. When my brother told me this, I was surprised, as I had never heard her say the prayer once. Was it a request for forgiveness for being a non-rule-following Jew? One last attempt to get it right before she died? Or a final goodbye to God's universe that she, through care, had helped create? I suspect the latter, but sadly I'll never know because nobody ever thought to ask.

CONCLUSION

Interdependently

THE FAMILY MADRIGAL

In 2021, Disney released the animated film *Encanto*. It tells the story of the Madrigals, a Colombian family who, after a violent and traumatic episode, moved to a new city and were given special powers by a mysterious spiritual force in order to survive. One has superhuman strength, another can control the weather, and another can heal you with her cooking. Our teenage protagonist, Mirabel, however, has no gift. She's the ordinary one, overlooked and ignored, left out of the action and made to feel as though her contribution to her family's well-being matters less than others'.

But as is often the case, the outsider sees things that everyone else misses. Mirabel discovers that the Madrigals' home, the container for their family life and web of interdependence, is sick. A crack runs through the floor, moves its way up the stairs, and then spreads to the walls of the house. Lights, metaphors for the family's physical and spiritual health, flicker. Ultimately it is up to Mirabel to help her family see that they and their home are rotting from the inside, corrupted by their need to be, and appear, special—separate from their community and, increasingly, one another. Her moment of victory, and the film's climax, arrives when she persuades everyone to be open about their weaknesses, vulnerabilities, and fears. Honesty allows the family to heal and restore their bonds with one another—the magic that makes all other magic possible.

When I watched it for the first time, I failed to see what made this story so different from nearly all major children's films that came before it. I was so enamored with the humor, visuals, and music that I missed the fact that *Encanto* is a story about care. It took a few days, and a long walk with the dog accompanied by the film's soundtrack, for the story's revolutionary qualities to become clear to me. Here was the inversion of the hero's story I have been arguing for in these pages, one in which someone passes through a threshold, goes on a journey, and returns enlightened, all without ever leaving home or family. The dragon Maribel faced, the sinister curse she had to undo, was internal. Her family had forgotten how to care for one another, how to see one another as they really are. Every Disney character I have ever cheered on before did all of their hard work away from their families and away from home. Mirabel did hers by exploring the complexities of the power of interdependency, all while staying put. Best of all, and a slam dunk for my thesis, the story didn't suffer for it.

This inversion of the hero's story was more than just a novel movie plot. Here was a diagnosis not just for the Madrigal family but for all of us whose drive for independence and perfectionism is pushing us to our limits and depleting our capacity for care. Not a day goes by when I don't hear a friend or family member tell me how tired they feel. We're working too hard, accumulating too much stuff, and it's not doing much for our happiness or sense of purpose. Nobody seems to feel like they've won. Like Mirabel, we understand that we need to slow down and reconnect. We want to see who we are when not defined by work or our flimsy online personas, but rather the aspects of us that appear and evolve in intimate human relationships. We're thinking about the value of these human relationships for the relationship's sake, and not because it will advance our careers or garner likes on social media. We're questioning our treatment of the natural world, reckoning with the substantial debt to the planet we've accrued. A small but growing number of us sometimes go so far as using the term "interdependence," even if we find it a bit corny or overly sincere.

Over the past five years or so, I've noticed a spike in experts and friends talking about interdependence of all kinds. "Your brain as an individual is really determined by the brains you're connected to," explained neuroscientist Uri Hasson in a 2019 interview with *Scientific American*. For a long time, neuroscientific researchers focused on one person at a time, without much concern for how the absence of human connection was coloring their findings. In the 2010s, they began to see the error of this method and started exploring ways to observe two or more human brains interacting with each other. In one study, Hasson looked at the brain of a person telling a story and the brain of a person listening to the story. Then he mapped the whole thing out like a musical score, matching moments in the story with changes in each person's brain. He found that the brain of the listener reflected the brain of the storyteller, and there was a direct positive correlation between the similarity of the two brains and the listener's self-reported comprehension of the story.

Whenever I go on a hike with friends or family members, they ask me if I know the truth about trees. Trees appear to communicate with one another, you've likely heard by now, thanks to the popularity of research by forestry ecologist Suzanne Simard. Long seen as monuments of solitary perseverance, trees actually function a lot like family and thrive in states of mutual dependency. They speak to one another, feed one another, and protect one another, all with the help of a special type of fungus that spreads itself around the trees' roots.

Less common, but still notable, was the change of heart toward bacteria. This, too, was relayed to me via close friends and relatives as both fact and metaphor, as well as via the news. For a long time, scientists thought of bacteria as bad, invaders of our bodies' true and natural state. Now we know that our bodies host a multitude of bacteria from the outside world and how fundamental to our well-being they are. In 2012, the National Institutes of Health reported that the average body, or what they call "the human ecosystem," has a ratio of ten bacterial cells to every one human cell. These bacteria assist in our digestion, mood, and health. The question of why we are who we are, and why we do what we do, is no longer simply answered by DNA. Those instructions are in constant communication with, and shaped by, the rich, often invisible, bacterial world around us. We are the world around us.

This news shouldn't surprise us so much. "No man is an island, entire of itself; every man is a piece of the continent, a part of the main," said sixteenth-century poet John Donne. The world is "one great living organism where everything was connected," said eighteenth-century German naturalist and explorer Alexander von Humboldt. "When we try to pick out anything by itself, we find it hitched to everything else in the universe," said nineteenth-century environmentalist John Muir. "All life is interrelated. All men are caught in an inescapable network of mutuality, tied in a single garment of destiny. Whatever affects one directly affects all indirectly," said twentieth-century civil rights activist Dr. Martin Luther King Jr.

They spoke, people listened, nodded along, and yet here we are, still surprised by all these connections, still reluctant to face their truth. Even with all this promising talk of trees and our collective love for *Encanto*, we remain a society that resists interdependence.

Some of us shy away from it, like a child who matter-of-factly ignores his sticky orange palm prints on the wall. That? Huh. Interesting. Or we boldly reject it, our gaze constantly redirecting to all that separates us, and our urge to disconnect. It's an instinct that is clear in the way we see the outside world and our insatiable appetite for drawing distinctions between human beings, with far less curiosity paid to the ties that bind us together. And there it is in our inner lives, prompting us to see ourselves like specimen jars in a lab, unique entities whose truest essences are best revealed in independence. We erect and protect psychological boundaries from depending on one another or being depended on, believing, despite all evidence suggesting otherwise, that what is inside us is best cultivated when kept apart from everything else.

One of the biggest roadblocks to accepting interdependence, the reason we've been talking about it forever but have failed to internalize it, is that the conversation about it has largely left out caregiving. Whether from those gazing at the cosmos or those reimagining our government, these male prophets failed to take women's work into consideration. Care—that small act between people, the one not beholden to the rigid ethical systems that guide society but rather the fuzzier, relational ethics that exist between one person and another— makes up the building blocks of interdependence. Care by care by care is how we form ourselves into continents, or hitch ourselves to the universe of humans, to use the language of Donne and Muir, and build the human relationships that lead to all other human relationships—the relationships upon which interdependence rests.

I hope this book helps us overcome this blind spot, by showing how care and interdependence can be rich and ripe in our personal and collective lives—a not-to-be-ignored, not-to-be-missed part of the human experience. Here are a few specific ideas about how we can make that happen.

CARING FOR THE CAREGIVERS

Care is a public good that demands public investment. This is, fortunately, no longer news to a growing number of politicians or activists who have slowly moved the needle toward more guaranteed support for caregivers in recent decades. We're inching closer to becoming a society that both helps people find good care and cares for caregivers, by way of: state and city paid family leave bills, universal pre-K measures, and legislation to protect against pregnancy discrimination. On top of that, there are active political debates about additional policies that would better support all caregivers, paid and unpaid, including those for children, as well as old, ill, and disabled individuals.

The most intuitive and long overdue of pro-caregiver policies is universal, federal paid sick and family leave, which allows workers to take time off to take care of others, or to receive care themselves, without suffering financial burdens. Every other industrialized country in the world aside from the United States provides their citizens with some paid leave; the absence of a policy here is the ne plus ultra of America's systemic denial of the reality of care. Paid leave makes it so babies have a chance to be properly nurtured and new moms have time to properly recover. It helps make sure there is ample time for parent or caregiver and baby to bond and this bond can create a sense of security and emotional well-being that can serve the child for life. Parents who take paid leave report higher levels of health, lower stress, and higher rates of satisfaction in their ability to care for their children compared to those who don't take paid leave. Notably, the conversation about paid leave often omits people who care for old, ill, or disabled individuals, a big oversight considering the vast population of these caregivers who similarly need paid leave as well. People who care for older adults, people with illnesses and disabilities, also need time to connect, heal, and, sometimes, grieve without worrying about losing jobs or decimating bank accounts in the process.

In addition to taking breaks, caregivers would also benefit from sharing the load of care, an equitable possibility that requires more collective investment. Among the most damaging fictions of independence is the belief that we are supposed to be able to care entirely on our own. That if we can't muster the stamina and emotional bandwidth to provide all the care another requires by ourselves, then something must be wrong with us. We don't really care enough or we are too selfish or unwilling to sacrifice. But all caregivers—even those in relatively easy care relationships like, for example, two financially secure parents who share the load while caring for an easygoing nine-year-old—need breaks. Denying them support and making a pause from care seem like an indulgence or a special gift rather than a fundamental necessity sends the message that the job is smaller than it is and therefore less worthy of aid.

There's also this fear, particularly among mothers, that getting help with care will lessen the power or depth of the experience. As if caregiving were an ultramarathon that should deplete you completely; if you don't feel like utter shit after, you didn't really do it. But for most of us, care doesn't tolerate such extreme conditions. We caregivers need our time, too, a chance to rest, restore, and retreat within. When caregivers are given regular intervals apart from care, and thus chances for self-care, they return to care relationships stronger, ready to learn, grow, and, at least some of the time, relish the experience.

For parents, such support may look like an expansive and affordable childcare and after-school system, available to anyone who needs it, as well as allowances that give money to families with parents who wish to step up as primary caregivers at any point. Flexibility is key, Elliot Haspel, an early-childhood and K–12 education policy expert, told me. "That requires starting with the concept that family needs are pluralistic," as family structures and care capabilities vary tremendously from family to family, and sometimes within a single family, on a month-to-month basis. Help should be adaptable, meeting families where they are.

For family and friend caregivers to old, ill, and disabled individuals this could mean more breaks for full-time caregivers. Such time and energy breaks can be found through more adult daycares, accessible to all, as well as programs that bring professional caregivers into individual homes for a set number of hours a week at an affordable price—while still paying the caregiver a fair wage. Caregivers for ill and old individuals would also greatly benefit from a more unified health-care system. For too many, the burden of the actual care is nothing compared to the financial and psychological burden of chasing down doctors, diagnoses, and treatments.

Evolution among workplaces can offer helpful solutions too. The more workers have flexible and predictable schedules, decent vacation policies, the option to work remotely, the more employers are understanding of the demands of care, the better caregivers will manage. This one has to be a one-two punch of policy and culture change, as few workers are going to be eager to take advantage of policies for which they fear they'll be, often subtly or informally, penalized later down the line. For now, many of our workplaces still operate under the "glass door" fiction that in each family there is someone within the confines of the home, separate from the world at large, who provides care, and someone outside, engaging with political, social, economic systems, who works and is independent and free. There are bottom-line benefits to reap from flexibility sown into systemic change in the workplace. Flexibility fosters employee retention as well as a more productive and happier workforce.

With all these proposed changes, it remains important for people to be able to define family and kinship relationships on their own terms.

"Families determine for themselves what the structure of that family is, who that family is, and that is how policies should support them," Marjorie Sims, managing director of Ascend at the Aspen Institute and longtime advocate for women and families, told me. "Whatever the structure of their family is, the policy should support it." Care happens in all sorts of human constellations, extending far beyond the parent-child and husband-and-wife arrangements. Sometimes grandparents raise grandchildren, like Alesia and Aleiyah, or friends care for sick friends, like Joseph and Rich. Unfortunately, not all of these arrangements are acknowledged by supportive policies.

This is not a comprehensive list of what caregivers need. Historically speaking, we've just begun to think big about what it means to view caregiving and caregiver well-being as a public good. I look forward to future activists and policy makers refining all of the above and conceiving of not-yet-thought-of ways to integrate care into our collective agenda.

One of the ways to do so is by taking caregiver needs into consideration in all policy making, and not just in instances where they would be directly impacted, says Jennifer Olsen, executive director of the Rosalynn Carter Institute for Caregivers. "We are trying to move the caregiver conversation from the fringes of the discussion on policy making and employer benefits to a more central place. Starting twenty years ago, there was a big movement to get health considered in all public policies. For example, if you are going to build a sidewalk, how does that influence health and exercise?" Olsen said. "Now we should start thinking about how we get the caregiver lens into all of our policies and thinking."

This holistic approach offers an expansive view of what caregiver support might look like. Caregiving affects so many aspects of caregivers' lives, well beyond the act of caring. "Currently, a lot of support and services are tied to helping the caregiver with the caregiving and not the caregiver as a human," she said. But when policies fail to see the caregiver as a human, they miss the point entirely. Caregivers, paid or unpaid, can't do their jobs well when the systems supporting them see them only as caregiving machines.

Olsen suggests two solutions. The first is simply collecting more data. We currently have insufficient research on caregivers to inform policies and outreach efforts. The more we know, the better we can serve all who care. The second is the creation of a federal office or task force that would advocate for caregiver well-being and work out how a wide range of policies might impact caregivers. There is no aggregate body of thought considering caregivers, even as they contribute tremendously to the health and well-being of tens of millions of Americans.

Lastly, always, there's money. Unpaid caregivers deserve at the very least no risk of financial upheaval when performing care. A combination of supportive workplaces that make it possible to work and care, strong laws protecting caregivers at work, and policies that transfer funds directly to caregivers, whether through basic income or another mechanism, are all courses of action to consider. Paid caregivers need better training, better workplace protections, better hours, and better wages. In 2021, the mean hourly wage for home health aides was $14.15 and the mean annual salary was $29,430, according to the U.S. Bureau of Labor Statistics. It's not surprising, then, that a significant number of home health aides—one-sixth according to a 2019 report from PHI, an eldercare and disability services advocacy group—live below the poverty line.

I'm not a policy expert and am therefore in no position to recommend the one-and-best way to roll out universal paid family leave, or backup care for dependents, or to make sure people don't go broke from caregiving. What matters to me isn't the precise way we do it but that we try to do it, well and quickly. In the process, I hope we learn to adapt and shift in order to make sure we meet the needs of caregivers.

AN INTERPERSONAL SHIFT

What I am confident in endorsing, the main objective of this book, is a cultural, intellectual, and emotional shift in the way we see caregiving. There is no political change without cultural change, and vice versa. Without top-down laws, individual intentions can fall flat. Without a more positive narrative of care, policies may remain toothless in the face of widespread bias.

When men in some parts of Europe and Asia were offered paternity leave, few took advantage of it because of societal expectations; the professional and cultural stigma of caring as a man was too high, and made actually taking the offered paid leave unappealing. We need to be told something matters, and we need to believe it matters deep within the recesses of our minds where lessons solidify. Narrative and structural change both must shape each other until, with time, society is made anew.

A new cultural narrative on care would free itself from the confines of "saintliness" and "oppression," the pious, modest mother, painfully singular in her caregiving and unlike anyone else. Instead, we could venture into the expansive, full, and complex terrain of real lived experiences. We'd tell stories in which care was afforded curiosity and respect, in which caregivers get to be complex human beings rather than martyrs, whether blissful or ravaged. In time, caregivers would start to see themselves this way, replete with new insights about what it means to be human. To do this, we have to expose, unravel, and, eventually, dispel many of the myths around care, including ones explored through particular subjects and lives in this book.

One of the most pervasive and toxic myths is that wanting to care, and do a good job with it, is one and the same as wanting to care all day every day, without any help. This is care as inevitably complete and irrevocable sacrifice. We expect caregivers, and caregivers expect themselves, to give caregiving their all, eradicating any non-care desires, dreams, ambitions, or practical needs in the process. To care well, the story goes, is self-abnegation, to repress and dilute the self in service of the other. But anyone who has cared knows that this is an impossible and unrealistic model, even when they can't help but feel guilt or shame about being unable to achieve it. Utter selflessness in care tends to lead to exhaustion and sometimes repressed, sometimes unfurled, rage. Someone who is denied a self can't ultimately care well for another, nor would they have the chance to learn and grow from the experience. There is absolutely such a thing as too much caregiving.

I'm certain I would not have arrived at any of the care-inspired realizations I have shared in this book had I had no break from care or consistent help with it over the years. My husband, Nathaniel, along with our nannies, Carole, Janet, and Molly, gave me not only time to myself but also a break from the existential pressures related to having other lives depend on you. I had, since I've become a mother, roughly thirty hours a week during which I didn't see my children. With this, I was able to maintain my tether to my simultaneously important non-care identities. I was a wife, friend, daughter, writer, reader, culture consumer, and, when necessary, lazy and selfish. Though Carole, Janet, and Molly didn't just benefit me and Nathaniel by giving us breaks. Their caregiving gave our kids new ways to understand themselves and the world.

Carole, calm and reassuring, encouraged Augie to take risks on the playground and in life that I would have avoided. If we hadn't moved across the country and she still worked for us after Levi was born, I am sure she would have taught him the same. Janet, positive and open-minded, taught our kids that actively marking moments of joy, ideally with a piñata, is a life imperative. Molly helped my kids learn to laugh at themselves, and accept their own, and her own, mistakes. I learned from all these women, each of whom shaped me and bettered me as a mother, and they all learned too. Janet said being with Levi every day helped her heal from a broken heart.

A better story on care is one in which we see care as something to be shared, the norm for most of history, and never left to one person on their own. This will require the participation of men, who need to continue doing more care, as well as engaging in more creative housing and family structures that support the cohabitation of larger groups of caregivers who can share the load. I have one set of friends, two families each with two parents and two kids, who split one big house into two. They now live side by side and share a backyard and child-care responsibilities. Another group of friends, two parents of three rowdy children, and one child-free lesbian couple, bonded during the pandemic; now all share parenting roles for the kids. Each assemblage of family units formed under one easily perceivable truth: It is really hard for anyone, alone or coupled, to care for their children entirely on their own.

My dream: People share care more equally. They have a chance to develop a distinct self apart from care, a self they can fold back into care. And they are bettered by care, and then bring what they learn from care into the rest of their lives. They have the chance to experience the power of what Iris Murdoch called "unselfing" through care. This idea is more important than ever as simplistic formulations of self, fueled by increasing polarization, divisiveness, and social media algorithms, prevail.

Unselfing stands in marked contrast to the widespread belief in the optimized self. Popular manifestations of this fantasy include: our workaholism, our intense workout routines, our seven-part skin-care regimens, our Instagram-fueled travel lust, that productivity-oriented never-ever-enoughness that characterizes our present selves, no matter what we've accomplished, as lacking. Human relationships, particularly care, don't abide by the rules of growth metrics. Unselfing is also hard for caregivers who are stretched thin on time, energy, and resources, who work two or more jobs to pay the rent, and who struggle enough to find time for their loved ones, let alone working on an optimum self.

Attention to another, necessary for unselfing, is hard to sustain when one's mind is pulled in ten directions or has a to-do list that never ends. "The countervailing value to multitasking," or optimization, "is presence," Haspel said. "You are just there with them. It doesn't have to be superlong, but when you are there you are just there. You don't see presence lifted up in our culture or valorized."

The well-off never stop not because of material necessity but a fuzzy yet unyielding belief that somewhere out there exists a finish line, a threshold through which they will pass that will deem them successful. Except there is no finish line in life, nor is there one in imperfect, unpredictable, cyclical, and ongoing care.

Collectively embracing these qualities of care, and this is another myth, is not possible as long as care is seen as small. For too long, care has been kept in a box, a domestic prison that confined and tongue-tied those within it. Patriarchal systems, quite cleverly, held care up on just a high enough pedestal to make this confinement seem noble, but never high enough for caregivers or non-caregivers to admire the expansiveness of the experience. Let care, and caregivers, out of the box, let their benefit to society be recognized, let people listen to their stories, let men form a line around the block hungry to get a taste of what it is like to give care, and we will start to see change. A society that values care is one that acknowledges and permits this bigness, this power, and the inevitable messiness that comes along with it.

This job won't be finished until we dig deep in the furthest reaches of our psyche and accept the reality that we, you, are needy— interdependent. Philosopher Martha Nussbaum connects our struggle to see ourselves as dependent with our denial of mortality. We are "emotional beings who wish not to be emotional, who wish to withhold these acknowledgments of neediness and to design for [ourselves] a life in which these acknowledgments have no place," she writes in her 2001 book *Upheavals of Thought: The Intelligence of Emotions.* As a response to this fear of death, or "finitude," as Nussbaum puts it, we learn to reject our dependency and deny the existence of any attachments to others that might expose this dirty truth. This makes us the "only animals for whom neediness is a source of shame, and who take pride in themselves to the extent to which they have allegedly gotten clear of vulnerability."

I understand. Interdependence is scary. Collectively, it carries the whiff of ill-fated social experiments in which people were forced to suppress individual desires for the common good. When Maoists burned Mozart scores because Western music was seen as a corrupting force, or kibbutzniks in Israel had children and parents sleep in different homes because the nuclear family was seen as a threat to a broader group identity, it was done in the name of collectivity and the individual was lost.

Individually, the thought of interdependence taps into the tension surrounding one of the central paradoxes of human life. This is the simultaneous desire for freedom and communion, to detach and connect—our most central longings as human beings. We want, need, solitude, to be able to tune in to the conversation taking place in our mind without interference. We also want, need, to be part of a human family or community, to be in the company of others who depend on us and whom we can depend on. While the proportions and rhythms of these longings vary from person to person—and even within a person, over the course of a life—the vast majority of us will always be drawn, in some measure, to these two distinct poles.

A pro-care society need not be draconian, erasing the individual. With more public support and creative thinking, it doesn't have to be a zero-sum game between "me" and "us." That's not to say there won't be conflict, inextricable contradictions, eternal friction between the snow leopard self who wants to run free and the self who wants to stay and nourish and be nourished by the people he, she, or they love. But not all conflict is bad. This conflict can be fertile ground, a meaning-making exercise that pushes us to figure out just what it is we want to do with our lives. Dependence and independence will we forever toggle between. Both, together in interdependence.

I think I've gotten closer to accepting this. I haven't reached a harmony in all my relationships, a Kumbaya state in which individual and collective needs are met in a steady rhythm. My life isn't easier or smoother—denial of neediness makes for a highly effective social lubricant. But the struggle of living in and with interdependence has its rewards. I experience more love, generative provocation, and connection, fueled in part by my recent realization that all my relationships are, in part, care relationships.

With clearly defined caregiving relationships, imbalance is self-evident from the beginning. There was never a question of who was dependent on whom in my relationships with my children. I am one end of the flow of care, and they are the other, and, like magnets, we understand exactly how it is we are supposed to connect.

With less obviously dependent relationships, like my marriage or friendships, the asymmetries can be harder to see. For a long time, I entered them believing that I was one of two independent parties and that our exchange would be, or at least should be, equal. With this came a sense of justice, or, more often, injustice, when needs of the other trumped my own, or vice versa. I resented them when they took up too much space, and felt ashamed when I took up too much space. It wasn't just that I didn't want to be seen as needy. I did not want to *be* needy, the one with more questions than answers, that friend or romantic partner who just couldn't stop talking about her own life.

I don't remember the exact vows we said at our wedding, but I know we made promises to be by each other's side and hold each other up through good times and bad. In my fantasy of marriage at the time, I imagined that these would be executed in fairly equal measure and that at any given point the scorecard would be close. We'd give and get, and get and give, and give and get, and it would all blend together into one color, one substance, the raw material of our relationship. A newlywed's fantasy.

Caring for my sons has helped me see the asymmetries in my marriage, which then led me to see the asymmetries in all my relationships. Someone in some way always needs more, and that needing more always lasts longer than I want it to—no matter which side I am on. When my husband needs more, it is usually a result of his depressive tendencies, of finding the world inhospitable or unsatisfying. When I need more, it is usually a result of my insecurities, whether about my place in the world or the decisions I have made that got me here. We arrive at each other without form or direction, feeble creeks devoid of hope of ever making it out to sea.

I don't think either of us was prepared for this level of neediness, and we certainly weren't prepared to be providing each other with the level of care such neediness demands. We were supposed to be better, stronger, together, and while there is an interpretation of that that stands true, it's more honest to say that we are still weak and would have been far better off entering the marriage with the belief that we were primarily here to receive and give care in all its ongoingness, rather than to uplift or change each other in some lasting, clearly articulated, highly perfected fashion. If we'd gone into the marriage understanding this, I would have been less surprised when my care for him didn't immediately make it all better, and less disappointed when the care he gave me resulted in the same. I would have known that the goal of marital care, something I am slowly coming to understand, isn't to bring us to a state of equilibrium, let alone equality. Instead, it is only to attempt to tend to another and hope that, when the time comes, that someone will do the same for you in return.

I don't have a single relationship that is symmetrical at any given moment and couldn't benefit from this more care-based perspective. Not with my family or friends, or the driver who forgot to turn on his blinker, or even, in my trippier moments, with inanimate objects like my decade-plus-old car or our sick Earth. The care ethicists' insistence on making the preservation of relationships a cornerstone of morality applies to all our connections, which can benefit when we make our fundamental, essential neediness a part of our script. The task isn't to remedy or smooth over that neediness, but to find ways to meet it. This shifts the gravity of our identities away from who we are on our own to whom we become together. For me, building this relational identity has been no less fraught than the singular identity I worked so hard to construct throughout my youth. My care self, decentralized, unmoored, is highly uncertain and often scared. Much like my teenage self, who was in constant pursuit of individuation.

This care lens works in the mirror too. The more I see the world by way of care, the more I think about what I need in the way of care, from others, and myself. This isn't quite the same as self-care, as in time off from one's responsibilities. The refresh matters, but so does taking the time to consider what kind of care I require and finding my place in the ecosystem of care. What is the nature of my neediness? Who is okay with my neediness? Who will care for me? I am working on figuring all this out.

Still, I like it here. To have thought I figured out who we are and what life is all about, and then have a lot of that called into question by way of caring for Augie and Levi, feels like a gift. The prize is not the answers, but the questions. Questions I ask about who I am, who my kids are, who we are, how we fit together, how we stay apart. This book is a look at some of those questions and how we might answer them after breaking those glass doors, but I'm not done. There are so many more questions to ask about care, questions to ask ourselves, questions to ask one another, and questions about how care can be better seen in all its fullness and complexity by the cultures and systems within which we live. Questions I intend to ask those I care for, questions I intend to ask myself as my children and parents age, and a whole new set of questions I will face when it's my turn to receive care. So many questions, to be guided and ignited by one firm answer: A human relationship as profound and essential as care is worthy of our inquiry and deliberation.

ACKNOWLEDGMENTS

To my lovely agent, Jamie Carr, who, with Weilian attention, saw a book in my inchoate, yet very passionate, ideas about care and helped make it a reality. You've been the best advocate from the very beginning. To my editor, Hannah Braaten, who was as caring and attentive in her feedback as one would hope for a book about being caring and attentive. The book is richer, deeper, and, most important, more richly and deeply human because of you. To the rest of the Gallery team, including Jennifer Bergstrom, Jennifer Long, Aimée Bell, Sally Marvin, Eliza Hanson, Sarah Schlick, Lauren Truskowski, Tyrinne Lewis, Lisa Litwack, John Vairo, Caroline Pallotta, Emily Arzeno, Ashley Cullina, Jaime Putorti, Jamie Selzer, and Chloe Gray, for being incredibly supportive, on top of it, and whip-smart. To my fact-checker, Madysen Luebke, who improved not only the accuracy of this book but also its spirit with her careful and caring attention. Thank you.

To Nathaniel, for telling me in no uncertain terms that I can do it, I can write a book, and will do it well. Not only that, but for being devoted to the project of equal parenting, which protected me from being burnt out on care, and made room for me to be enlightened by it and write about it. Augie and Levi, my sons, I smile just writing your names. This book wouldn't exist if your two singular selves hadn't entered my life. Thank you.

To the Strauss family, Mom, Dad, Peter, Landon, Alanna, who convinced me before I ever realized I was being convinced that life is so much better when we care for one another. And even better when that care takes the shape of making each other laugh. Same to my parents' new spouses, Michele Dremmer and Howard Price, who expanded this circle of love and support. Thank you.

To my in-laws, Sally and Lewis Popper, for being the closest readers of my work since I published my first article, and gushing just the right amount to make it believable. To Miriam, Franklin, Juliana, Robbie, Flo, and Bea, for all your support and love over the years. Thank you.

To Ruth Whippman and Yael Goldstein Love, you glorious peacocks, who showed me the many faces of care possible in a friendship. Thank you.

To the Athols, Elyse Gilbert, Greg Sherman, Zoe Sylvester, and Andy McNamara, for being my pandemic, fire, and whatever disaster strikes us next survival crew. And Elyse and Greg in particular, for the *ruach*, and making years 5779 and on some supersolid ones.

To the whole LABA: A Laboratory for Jewish Culture family, around the world and over the years, especially Ronit Muszkatblit and Ruby Namdar for a decade and a half of provocation and adoration. Thank you.

To Gabrielle Birkner, Gal Beckerman, and Deborah Kolben, who, in addition to being wonderful friends, have all edited me and insisted that people want to hear what I have to say at pivotal moments. Thank you.

To the readers of individual chapters, Gabrielle Birkner, Deena

Aranoff, Sarah Clark Miller, Vanessa Sasson, Ian Hesketh, and Elissa Braunstein, I so appreciate your research, time, and insights. Thank you.

To the readers of the whole manuscript, Rima Praspaliauskiene, Anne Germanacos, Sarah Wolfman-Robichaud, Ruth Whippman, and Yael Goldstein Love—talk about care. What a gift you gave me. Thank you.

To everyone in this book who shared their personal stories with me: June, Robert, Julie, Colin, Alessia, Lourdes, Kimmi, Nate, Kevin, Eric, Melissa, Sian-Pierre, David, Joseph, Natalie, Denise, Eva, and Atalya, your stories, your acts of care, are wonderful hero's journeys, each and every one. I am so honored to share them with the world. Thank you.

To Kristina Kasper and Ricki Nolan, for decades of friendship and care and helping me survive my teenage years in the 91302. Thank you.

To Lizzie Leiman Kraiem and Joshua Ladon, for powerful conversations about care right when I needed it—and without even realizing it. Thank you.

To every single teacher my children have ever had, for taking such good care of them, especially everyone at St. Paul's and Temple Beth Abraham. And to the wonderful caregivers who cared for them one-on-one, Carole Glenn, Janet Vasquez, and Molly Cortese. Thank you.

NOTES

INTRODUCTION: WHY CARE?

2 *adoration for Rachel Cusk's 2003 early parenthood memoir*: Rachel Cusk, *A Life's Work: On Becoming a Mother* (New York: Picador, 2001), 57.

11 *"If you are ready to leave father and mother"*: Henry D. Thoreau, *Essays: A Fully Annotated Edition* (New Haven, CT: Yale University Press, 2013), 244.

12 *This is a central theme in*: Thomas M. Ratliff, Penko Gelev, and Mark Twain, *The Adventures of Huckleberry Finn* (New York: Sterling Children's Books, 2020), 1.

13 *In 2017, the most purchased photo*: Claire Cain Miller, "From Sex Object to Gritty Woman: The Evolution of Women in Stock Photos," *New York Times*, September 7, 2017, https://www.nytimes.com/2017/09/07/up shot/from-sex-object-to-gritty-woman-the-evolution-of-women-in-stock -photos.html.

15 *Movies like Maggie Gyllenhaal's* The Lost Daughter: *The Lost Daughter*, written and directed by Maggie Gyllenhaal (Netflix, 2021).

18 *Just a century ago, experts advised parents*: Therese Oneill, "'Don't Think of Ugly People': How Parenting Advice Has Changed," *Atlantic*, April 19, 2013, https://www.theatlantic.com/health/archive/2013/04/dont-think -of-ugly-people-how-parenting-advice-has-changed/275108/.

18 *we are all parenting more*: "Today's Parents Spend More Time with Their Kids Than Moms and Dads Did 50 Years Ago," *UCI News*, April 23, 2018, https://news.uci.edu/2016/09/28/todays-parents-spend-more-time-with -their-kids-than-moms-and-dads-did-50-years-ago/.

19 *older adults are expected to outnumber children*: "Older People Projected to

Outnumber Children for First Time in U.S. History," U.S. Census Bureau, October 8, 2021, https://www.census.gov/newsroom/press-releases/2018 /cb18-41-population-projections.html#:~:text=%E2%80%9CBy%20 2034%20(previously%202035),decade%20for%20the%20U.S.%20popu lation.

19 *roughly 42 million Americans . . . up from roughly 34 million in 2015*: "Caregiving in the U.S.," National Alliance for Caregiving and AARP, 2020, https://www.caregiving.org/wp-content/uploads/2020/05/Full-Report -Caregiving-in-the-United-States-2020.pdf

19 *Many have no choice*: Paula Span, "The Quiet Cost of Family Caregiving," *New York Times*, September 4, 2022, https://www.nytimes.com /2022/09/04/science/elderly-work-caregiving.html.

19 *known as the sandwich generation*: Kim Parker, "The Sandwich Generation," Pew Research Center's Social & Demographic Trends Project, Pew Research Center, July 31, 2020, https://www.pewresearch.org/so cial-trends/2013/01/30/the-sandwich-generation/.

19 *there is a shortage of paid caregivers*: Robyn I. Stone with Joshua M. Wiener, "Who Will Care for Us?: Addressing the Long-Term Care Workforce Crisis," Urban Institute (The USA Department of Health and Human Services, The Robert Wood Johnson Foundation, Institute for the Future of Aging Services, The Urban Institute), October 26, 2001, https://www .urban.org/research/publication/who-will-care-us-addressing-long-term -care-workforce-crisis.

19 *fewer paid family caregivers than ever*: Phil Galewitz, "With Workers in Short Supply, Seniors Often Wait Months for Home Health Care," NPR, June 30, 2021, https://www.npr.org/sections/health-shots /2021/06/30/1010328071/with-workers-in-short-supply-seniors-often -wait-months-for-home-health-care.

19 *"There are people going without baths"*: Ann Oldenburg, "Nationwide Caregiver Shortage Felt by Older Adults," AARP, November 10, 2022, https:// www.aarp.org/caregiving/basics/info-2022/in-home-caregiver-shortage .html.

19 *it was difficult for humans to go it alone*: Batool Zaidi and S. Philip Morgan, "The Second Demographic Transition Theory: A Review and Appraisal," *Annual Review of Sociology* (U.S. National Library of Medicine, July 2017), https://www.ncbi.nlm.nih.gov/pmc/articles/PMC5548437/; Ron Lesthaeghe, "The Second Demographic Transition: A Concise Overview of Its Development," *PNAS* 111, no. 51 (2014): 18112–18115, https://doi.org /10.1073/pnas.1420441111.

19 *It just wasn't economically or practically feasible*: James R. Wetzel, "American Families: 75 Years of Change: Monthly Labor Review," *Monthly Labor Review*, U.S. Bureau of Labor Statistics, March 1990, https://www.bls.gov /opub/mlr/1990/article/american-families-75-years-of-change.htm.

20 *single-person households were rare*: Rose M. Kreider and Jonathan Vespa, "The Historic Rise of One-Person Households: 1850–2010," (working paper, U.S. Census Bureau, April 25, 2014), https://www.census.gov/con tent/dam/Census/library/working-papers/2014/demo/paa2014-kreider -vespa.paper.pdf.

20 *second-most common household type*: George Masnick, "The Rise of the Single-Person Household," Joint Center for Housing Studies, May 20, 2015, https://www.jchs.harvard.edu/blog/the-rise-of-the-single-person-house hold.

20 *the decline of marriage over the last sixty years*: Juliana Menasce Horowitz, Nikki Graf, and Gretchen Livingston, "The Landscape of Marriage and Cohabitation in the U.S.," Pew Research Center's Social & Demographic Trends Project, Pew Research Center, November 6, 2019, https://www .pewresearch.org/social-trends/2019/11/06/the-landscape-of-marriage -and-cohabitation-in-the-u-s/#fn-26820-4.

20 *that figure was 72 percent*: Kim Parker and Renee Stepler, "As U.S. Marriage Rate Hovers at 50%, Education Gap in Marital Status Widens," Pew Research Center, May 30, 2020, https://www.pewresearch.org/fact -tank/2017/09/14/as-u-s-marriage-rate-hovers-at-50-education-gap-in -marital-status-widens/.

20 *Cohabitation has risen*: Nikki Graf, "Key Findings on Marriage and Cohabitation in the U.S.," Pew Research Center, November 16, 2019, https:// www.pewresearch.org/fact-tank/2019/11/06/key-findings-on-marriage -and-cohabitation-in-the-u-s/.

20 *fewer people having children*: Erin Duffin, "Number of Children in the U.S. 2020," Statista, September 30, 2022, https://www.statista.com/statis tics/457760/number-of-children-in-the-us/.

20 *4.7 children per woman*: James Gallagher, "'Remarkable' Decline in Fertility Rates," BBC News, November 9, 2018, https://www.bbc.com/news /health-46118103.

20 *in the middle of a loneliness epidemic*: Ezra Klein, "Coronavirus Will Also Cause a Loneliness Epidemic," Vox, March 12, 2020, https://www.vox .com/2020/3/12/21173938/coronavirus-covid-19-social-distancing-el derly-epidemic-isolation-quarantine.

20 *According to the Pew*: "Social Isolation and New Technology," Pew Research Center: Internet, Science & Tech, November 4, 2009, https://www .pewresearch.org/internet/2009/11/04/social-isolation-and-new-technol ogy/.

20 *2018 study of twenty thousand Americans by Cigna*: "The State of Loneliness in America—Cigna," Cigna, 2018, https://www.cigna.com/assets /docs/newsroom/loneliness-survey-2018-updated-fact-sheet.pdf.

20 *loneliness means social isolation*: Julianne Holt-Lunstad et al., "Loneliness and Social Isolation as Risk Factors for Mortality," *Perspectives on*

Psychological Science 10, no. 2 (2015): 227–237, https://doi.org/10.1177/1745691614568352.

20 *the effects are grave*: Kay S. Hymowitz, "Alone: The Decline of the Family Has Unleashed an Epidemic of Loneliness," *City Journal*, Spring 2019, https://www.city-journal.org/decline-of-family-loneliness-epidemic.

20 *increasingly likely to be feeling low*: Jean M. Twenge, "The Sad State of Happiness in the United States and the Role of Digital Media," chapter 5 in World Happiness Report, March 20, 2019, https://worldhappiness.report/ed/2019/the-sad-state-of-happiness-in-the-united-states-and-the-role-of-digital-media/.

20 *has declined since the 1970s*: Jon Clifton, "The Global Rise of Unhappiness," *Gallup Blog*, Gallup, September 15, 2022, https://news.gallup.com/opinion/gallup/401216/global-rise-unhappiness.aspx.

20 *increased among adolescents in recent years*: Renee D. Goodwin et al., "Trends in Anxiety among Adults in the United States, 2008–2018: Rapid Increases among Young Adults," *Journal of Psychiatric Research* 130 (2020): 441–446, https://doi.org/10.1016/j.jpsychires.2020.08.014; Michael Daly, "Prevalence of Depression among Adolescents in the U.S. from 2009 to 2019: Analysis of Trends by Sex, Race/Ethnicity, and Income," *Journal of Adolescent Health* 70, no. 3 (March 2022): 496–499, https://doi.org/10.1016/j.jadohealth.2021.08.026.

21 *A report on loneliness from Harvard states*: Richard Weissbourd et al., "Loneliness in America: How the Pandemic Has Deepened an Epidemic of Loneliness and What We Can Do about It," Making Caring Common Project, 2020, https://static1.squarespace.com/static/5b7c56e255b02c683659fe43/t/6021776bdd04957c4557c212/1612805995893/Loneliness+in+America+2021_02_08_FINAL.pdf.

CHAPTER ONE:
BREAKING THE GLASS DOORS

30 *For now she need*: Virginia Woolf, *To the Lighthouse* (Ware, Hertfordshire, UK: Wordsworth Editions, 1994), 45.

31 *"Very difficult" . . . "Let's hope so"*: Margaret A. Simons, Jessica Benjamin, and Simone de Beauvoir, "Simone de Beauvoir: An Interview," *Feminist Studies* 5, no. 2 (1979): 330, https://doi.org/10.2307/3177599.

32 *"a deep-seated fear"*: M. Rivka Polatnick, "Diversity in Women's Liberation Ideology: How a Black and a White Group of the 1960s Viewed Motherhood," *Signs: Journal of Women in Culture and Society* 21, no. 3 (1996): 679–706, https://doi.org/10.1086/495102.

32 *magazine editor Helen Gurley Brown*: Judith Thurman, "Helenism: The

Birth of the Cosmo Girl," *New Yorker*, May 4, 2009, https://www.new yorker.com/magazine/2009/05/11/helenism.

32   *thinkers like Shulamith Firestone*: Shulamith Firestone, *The Dialectic of Sex: The Case for Feminist Revolution* (London: Verso Books, 2015), https://www.google.com/books/edition/The_Dialectic_of_Sex/Um3nD wAAQBAJ?hl=en&gbpv=1&dq=firestone+%E2%80%9Cso+diff used+as+to+be+practically+eliminated.%E2%80%9D&pg=PT253&print sec=frontcover.

34   *"This vision of autonomy"*: Seyla Benhabib, "The Generalized and the Concrete Other," in *Situating the Self* (New York: Routledge, 2020), 148–177, https://doi.org/10.4324/9781003059516-8.

37   *According to the United States' labor law*: Kaitlyn Henderson, "Why Millions of Workers in the US Are Denied Basic Protections," Oxfam, November 20, 2020, https://politicsofpoverty.oxfamamerica.org/why-millions -workers-us-are-denied-basic-protections/.

37   *relic of the New Deal*: Ella Nilsen, "These Workers Were Left Out of the New Deal. They've Been Fighting for Better Pay Ever Since," Vox, May 18, 2021, https://www.vox.com/22423690/american-jobs-plan-care-workers -new-deal.

39   *in Poo's 2016 book*: Ai-jen Poo with Ariane Conrad, *The Age of Dignity: Preparing for the Elder Boom in a Changing America* (New York: New Press, 2015).

39   *Women found this experience*: Chrissy Callahan, "Meet the Moms Who Gather in a Field to Scream," TODAY.com, January 21, 2022, https:// www.today.com/parents/moms/massachusetts-moms-gather-field-scream -release-stress-rcna13055.

39   *momentum for caregiver advocacy*: Laura Bornfreund et al., "Fact Sheet: Care Economy Investments in Build Back Better," New America, November 18, 2021, https://www.newamerica.org/new-america/briefs/fact -sheet-care-economy-investments-in-build-back-better/.

42   *"You have to be scrappy"*: Kayla Webley Adler, "Being Everywoman Is Katie Porter's Superpower," *ELLE*, August 3, 2020, https://www.elle.com/cul ture/a33406349/katie-porter-interview/.

46   *"I feel really nourished . . . too"*: Noor Brara, "'It's Opened Me Up': Writer Leslie Jamison and Artist Mika Rottenberg on How Motherhood Made Them More Creative," Artnet News, April 7, 2021, https://news.artnet .com/art-world/mika-rottenberg-leslie-jamison-1955106.

47   *reminds me of Brandi Carlile's song "The Mother"*: Brandi Carlile, "The Mother," from *By the Way, I Forgive You*, coproduced by Dave Cobb and Shooter Jennings, 2018.

52   *"own the malice" . . . "persecutor"*: Melissa Benn, "Deep Maternal Alienation," *Guardian*, October 27, 2006, https://www.theguardian.com/lifeandstyle /2006/oct/28/familyandrelationships.family2.

CHAPTER TWO:
SOCIAL HOUSEKEEPERS

55   *One such woman was Rheta Childe Dorr*: Agnes Hooper Gottlieb, "The
     Reform Years at 'Hampton's': The Magazine Journalism of Rheta Childe
     Dorr, 1909–1912," *Electronic Journal of Communication/La Revue Elec-
     tronique De Communication*, vol. 4 (1994), https://cios.org/EJCPUBLIC
     /004/2/00429.html.

56   *Woman's place is in*: Rheta Childe Dorr, *What Eight Million Women Want*,
     version #12226 (Project Gutenberg, 2004), https://www.gutenberg.org
     /files/12226/12226-h/12226-h.htm.

56   *Another was Mary Church Terrell*: Debra Michals, "Biography: Mary
     Church Terrell," National Women's History Museum, 2017, https://www
     .womenshistory.org/education-resources/biographies/mary-church-terrell.

56   *her mission*: Mary Church Terrell, "The Progress of Colored Women," Co-
     lumbia Theatre, February 18, 1898, Daniel Murray Pamphlet Collection
     and African American Pamphlet Collection (Washington, DC: Smith
     Brothers, Printers, 1898), PDF, https://www.loc.gov/item/90898298/.

58   *Women's entry into public life . . . electorate*: Paula Baker, "The Domestication
     of Politics: Women and American Political Society, 1780–1920," *American
     Historical Review* 89, no. 3 (1984): 620, https://doi.org/10.2307/1856119.

59   *"Instead, the concept"*: Eileen Boris, "The Power of Motherhood: Black
     and White Activist Women Redefine the 'Political,'" in *Mothers of a New
     World*, eds. Seth Koven and Sonya Michel (New York: Routledge, 2013),
     213–245, https://doi.org/10.4324/9781315021164-7.

60   *Comprehensive Child Development Act*: Jack Rosenthal, "President Vetoes
     Child Care Plan as Irresponsible," *New York Times*, December 10, 1971,
     https://www.nytimes.com/1971/12/10/archives/president-vetoes-child
     -care-plan-as-irresponsible-he-terms-bill.html.

60   *"So crucial is"*: Richard Nixon to the Congress of the United States, Feb-
     ruary 19, 1969, "Special Message to the Congress on the Nation's Anti-
     poverty Programs," The American Presidency Project (UC Santa Barbara),
     https://www.presidency.ucsb.edu/documents/special-message-the-con
     gress-the-nations-antipoverty-programs.

60   *"would commit the vast moral"*: Richard Nixon to the Congress of the
     United States, December 9, 1971, "Veto of the Economic Opportunity
     Amendments of 1971," The American Presidency Project (UC Santa Bar-
     bara), https://www.presidency.ucsb.edu/documents/veto-the-economic
     -opportunity-amendments-1971.

61   *"the most pervasive manipulation"*: Silvia Federici, *Wages against House-
     work* (Bristol, UK: Power of Women Collective and Falling Wall Press,
     1975), https://caringlabor.files.wordpress.com/2010/11/federici-wages
     -against-housework.pdf, 2.

62 *"[W]e see the beginnings"*: The damned, *Lessons from the Damned: Class Struggle in the Black Community* (Ojai, CA: Times Change Press, 1990). Note: The collective authors of this book simply refer to themselves with the pseudonym "the damned."

63 *according to historian Premilla Nadasen*: Premilla Nadasen, "Welfare's a Green Problem: Cross-Race Coalition in Welfare Rights Organizing," ResearchGate, January 2008, https://www.researchgate.net/publication /317155496_Welfare's_A_Green_Problem_Cross-Race_Coalition_in _Welfare_Rights_Organizing.

64 *sociologist Patricia Hill Collins*: Patricia Hill Collins, "Shifting the Center: Race, Class, and Feminist Theorizing about Motherhood," *Mothering*, April 29, 2016, 45–65, https://doi.org/10.4324/9781315538891-3.

67 *In her book* Of Woman Born: Adrienne Cecile Rich, *Of Woman Born: Motherhood as Experience and Institution* (New York: W. W. Norton, 1985).

68 *queer parents set off a softer revolution*: Elizabeth Reed, "Lesbian, Bisexual and Queer Motherhood: Crafting Radical Narratives and Representing Social Change through Cultural Representations," *Women: A Cultural Review* 29, no. 1 (February 2018): 39–58, https://doi.org/10.1080/09574042.201 8.1425535.

68 *In her book* The Queer Parent's Primer: Stephanie A. Brill, *The Queer Parent's Primer: A Lesbian and Gay Families' Guide to Navigating the Straight World* (Oakland, CA: New Harbinger, 2001).

68 *In Maggie Nelson's book* The Argonauts: Maggie Nelson, *The Argonauts* (London: Melville House UK, 2016).

71 *"It is precisely because"*: Rich, *Of Woman Born*.

71 *"No one has imagined"*: Adrienne Rich, *Twenty-One Love Poems* (Emeryville, CA: Effie's Press, 1977).

CHAPTER THREE:

A NEW MAN

74 *By the end of the intervention*: Kate Doyle et al., "Gender-Transformative Bandebereho Couples' Intervention to Promote Male Engagement in Reproductive and Maternal Health and Violence Prevention in Rwanda: Findings from a Randomized Controlled Trial," *PLOS One*, April 4, 2018, https://doi.org/10.1596/30566.

77 *Today's men do more care than men have done in centuries*: Gretchen Livingston and Kim Parker, "8 Facts about American Dads," Pew Research Center, May 30, 2020, https://www.pewresearch.org/fact-tank/2019/06/12 /fathers-day-facts/.

78 *A 2016 study of parents in eleven Western nations*: Giulia M. Dotti Sani and

Judith Treas, "Educational Gradients in Parents' Child-Care Time across Countries, 1965–2012," *Journal of Marriage and Family* 78, no. 4 (2016): 1083–1096, https://doi.org/10.1111/jomf.12305.

78 *the number of stay-at-home dads*: Livingston and Parker, "8 Facts about American Dads."

78 *same-sex couple*: Shoshana K. Goldberg and Kerith J. Conron, "How Many Same-Sex Couples in the US Are Raising Children?," UCLA School of Law Williams Institute, July 2018, https://williamsinstitute.law.ucla.edu /publications/same-sex-parents-us/.

78 *The number of paid male home-care workers tripled in recent years*: Stephen Campbell, "Racial and Gender Disparities within the Direct Care Work-force: Five Key Findings," Paraprofessional Healthcare Institute, November 2017, https://www.phinational.org/wp-content/uploads/2017/11/Racial -and-Gender-Disparities-in-DCW-PHI-2017.pdf.

78 *a 2015 survey from the AARP*: Jean Accius, "Breaking Stereotypes: Spot-light on Male Family Caregivers," AARP, March 2017, AARP Public Policy Institute, https://www.aarp.org/content/dam/aarp/ppi/2017-01/Breaking -Stereotypes-Spotlight-on-Male-Family-Caregivers.pdf.

78 *The rate is even higher among millennial men*: Brendan Flinn, "Millenni-als: The Emerging Generation of Family Caregivers," AARP, May 2018, https://www.aarp.org/content/dam/aarp/ppi/2018/05/millennial-family -caregivers.pdf.

79 *A report from the Boston College Center for Work & Family*: Brad Harrington et al., *The New Dad: Take Your Leave*, Boston College Center for Work & Family, Carroll School of Management, 2017, https://www.bc.edu/content /dam/files/centers/cwf/research/publications/researchreports/BCCWF% 20The%20New%20Dad%202014%20FINAL.pdf.

79 *The Pew Research Center found similar enthusiasm among dads*: Gretchen Livingston, "Most Dads Say They Spend Too Little Time with Their Chil-dren; About a Quarter Live Apart from Them," Pew Research Center, January 8, 2018, https://www.pewresearch.org/fact-tank/2018/01/08 /most-dads-say-they-spend-too-little-time-with-their-children-about-a -quarter-live-apart-from-them/.

79 *The COVID pandemic provided*: Betsey Stevenson, "Women, Work, and Families: Recovering from the Pandemic-Induced Recession," The Ham-ilton Project, Brookings, September 2021, https://www.hamiltonproject .org/assets/files/COVID_Recovery_Stevenson_v5.pdf.

79 *Research on gay dads*: Dwight Panozzo, "Child Care Responsibility in Gay Male–Parented Families: Predictive and Correlative Factors," *Journal of GLBT Family Studies* 11, no. 3 (November 6, 2014): 248–277, https:// doi.org/10.1080/1550428x.2014.947461; Francis A. Carneiro et al., "Are the Fathers Alright? A Systematic and Critical Review of Studies on Gay and Bisexual Fatherhood," *Frontiers in Psychology* 8 (2017), https://doi

.org/10.3389/fpsyg.2017.01636; Geva Shenkman and Dov Shmotkin, "'Kids Are Joy': Psychological Welfare among Israeli Gay Fathers," *Journal of Family Issues* 35, no. 14 (May 24, 2013): 1926–1939, https://doi.org/10.1177/0192513x13489300.

79   *Another study of a cross section of American dads*: Livingston and Parker, "8 Facts about American Dads."

79   *A 2019 study from the University of Chicago and Better Life Lab*: Brigid Schulte, "Men and Work-Family Conflict: The Heavy Toll on Men Who Are High-Intensity Caregivers and/or Parents," Better Life Lab, New America, February 4, 2021, https://www.newamerica.org/better-life-lab/reports/providing-care-changes-men/iii-men-and-work-family-conflict-the-heavy-toll-on-men-who-are-high-intensity-caregivers-andor-parents/.

80   *it is far from enough to close the care gap between men and women*: "American Time Use Survey Summary—2021 A01 Results," U.S. Bureau of Labor Statistics, June 23, 2022, https://www.bls.gov/news.release/atus.nr0.htm.

80   *shoulder much of the burden of care on their own*: Sarah Jane Glynn, "An Unequal Division of Labor: How Equitable Workplace Policies Would Benefit Working Mothers," Center for American Progress, May 18, 2018, https://www.americanprogress.org/article/unequal-division-labor/.

80   *According to the U.S. Bureau*: "Employed Parents of Children under 13 Spent More Time Providing Secondary Childcare in 2020," *Economics Daily*, U.S. Bureau of Labor Statistics, February 22, 2022, https://www.bls.gov/opub/ted/2022/employed-parents-of-children-under-13-spent-more-time-providing-secondary-childcare-in-2020.htm.

81   *Things are slightly more even*: American Time Use Survey, U.S. Bureau of Labor Statistics, accessed March 2023, https://www.bls.gov/tus/charts/household.htm.

81   *The total number of hours*: Sarah Jane Glynn, "An Unequal Division of Labor: How Equitable Workplace Policies Would Benefit Working Mothers," Center for American Progress, May 18, 2018, https://www.americanprogress.org/article/unequal-division-labor/.

82   *sociologists call maternal gatekeeping*: Elissa Strauss, "Maternal Gatekeeping: Why Moms Don't Let Dads Help," CNN, December 6, 2017, https://www.cnn.com/2017/12/06/health/maternal-gatekeeping-strauss/index.html.

83   *often experience a "fatherhood boost"*: Michelle J. Budig, "The Fatherhood Bonus and the Motherhood Penalty: Parenthood and the Gender Gap in Pay," Third Way, September 2, 2014, https://www.thirdway.org/report/the-fatherhood-bonus-and-the-motherhood-penalty-parenthood-and-the-gender-gap-in-pay.

84   *phenomenon that is well-documented in studies*: Richard J. Petts, Chris Knoester, and Jane Waldfogel, "Fathers' Paternity Leave-Taking and Children's Perceptions of Father-Child Relationships in the United States,"

Sex Roles 82, no. 3–4 (May 4, 2019): 173–188, https://doi.org/10.1007/s11199-019-01050-y; Marcus Tamm, *Fathers' Parental Leave-Taking, Childcare Involvement and Mothers' Labor Market Participation* (Essen, Germany: RWI, 2018); Mareike Bünning, "What Happens after the 'Daddy Months'? Fathers' Involvement in Paid Work, Childcare, and Housework after Taking Parental Leave in Germany," *European Sociological Review* 31, no. 6 (July 29, 2015): 738–748, https://doi.org/10.1093/esr/jcv072.

84 *Sadly, 70 percent of American fathers take fewer:* "DOL Policy Brief: Paternity Leave: Why Parental Leave for Fathers Is So Important for Working Families," United States Department of Labor, 2015, https://www.dol.gov/sites/dolgov/files/OASP/legacy/files/PaternityBrief.pdf; Petts, Knoester, and Waldfogel, "Fathers' Paternity Leave-Taking," 173–188, https://doi.org/10.1007/s11199-019-01050-y.

84 *taking paternity leave . . . career:* Laurie A. Rudman and Kris Mescher, "Penalizing Men Who Request a Family Leave: Is Flexibility Stigma a Femininity Stigma?," *Journal of Social Issues* 69, no. 2 (2013): 322–340, https://doi.org/10.1111/josi.12017; Scott Coltrane et al., "Fathers and the Flexibility Stigma," *Journal of Social Issues* 69, no. 2 (2013): 279–302, https://doi.org/10.1111/josi.12015.

87 *the dad who is making breakfast:* *Reflexes at Breakfast*, Reddit, 2022, https://www.reddit.com/r/DadReflexes/comments/tdtkfl/reflexes_at_breakfast/.

87 *grab his son off a bicycle:* *Impressive Reaction*, Reddit, 2019, https://www.reddit.com/r/DadReflexes/comments/d9v2hy/impressive_reaction/.

87 *often report insecurities:* Accius, "Breaking Stereotypes."

88 *Pew Research Center poll from 2015:* Kim Parker, Juliana Menasce Horowitz, and Molly Rohal, "Parenting in America," Pew Research Center, December 17, 2015, section 2: "Satisfaction, Time and Support," https://www.pewresearch.org/social-trends/2015/12/17/2-satisfaction-time-and-support/#financial-well-being-linked-to-outlook-on-life-and-parenting.

91 *percentage of parents living with kids:* Richard Fry, "More Adults Now Share Their Living Space, Driven in Part by Parents Living with Their Adult Children," Pew Research Center, January 31, 2018, https://www.pewresearch.org/fact-tank/2018/01/31/more-adults-now-share-their-living-space-driven-in-part-by-parents-living-with-their-adult-children/.

92 *It is not so strange:* Richard Marius, *Thomas More: A Biography* (Cambridge, MA: Harvard University Press, 1999), 225.

92 *Over history, men have been far:* Brett and Kate McKay, "The History and Nature of Man Friendships," The Art of Manliness, September 26, 2021, https://www.artofmanliness.com/people/relationships/the-history-and-nature-of-man-friendships/.

92 *sit on each other's laps:* Brett and Kate McKay, "Bosom Buddies: A Photo History of Male Affection," The Art of Manliness, September 26, 2021,

https://www.artofmanliness.com/people/relationships/bosom-bud
dies-a-photo-history-of-male-affection/.

93 *far more hands-on*: Jill Siegelbaum, "The Role of the Father: Past, Present and Future," Michigan News, University of Michigan, June 14, 2000, https://news.umich.edu/the-role-of-the-father-past-present-and-future/.

93 *"As men entered the paid"*: Roman Krznaric, *The Wonderbox: Curious Histories of How to Live* (London: Profile Books, 2012), 38.

94 *Rilling decided . . . compared to non-fathers*: Carol Clark, "Five Surprising Facts about Fathers," Emory University, 2019, https://news.emory.edu/features/2019/06/five-facts-fathers/index.html.

95 *from Northwestern University tested the testosterone levels*: Lee T. Gettler et al., "Do Testosterone Declines during the Transition to Marriage and Fatherhood Relate to Men's Sexual Behavior? Evidence from the Philippines," *Hormones and Behavior* 64, no. 5 (2013): 755–763, https://doi.org/10.1016/j.yhbeh.2013.08.019.

95 *fathers experience an oxytocin boost*: Xiaomei Cong et al., "Parental Oxytocin Responses during Skin-to-Skin Contact in Pre-Term Infants," *Early Human Development* 91, no. 7 (2015): 401–406, https://doi.org/10.1016/j.earlhumdev.2015.04.012.

95 *an activation in the same care-related parts*: Zheng Wu et al., "Galanin Neurons in the Medial Preoptic Area Govern Parental Behaviour," *Nature* 509, no. 7500 (May 14, 2014): 325–330, https://doi.org/10.1038/nature13307.

95 *Fathers who were the primary caregiver showed more activity*: Eyal Abraham et al., "Father's Brain Is Sensitive to Childcare Experiences," *PNAS* 111, no. 27 (May 27, 2014): 9792–9797, https://doi.org/10.1073/pnas.1402569111.

96 *explains a report by Brigid Schulte*: Brigid Schulte, "Executive Summary," Better Life Lab, New America, February 4, 2021, https://www.newamerica.org/better-life-lab/reports/providing-care-changes-men/executive-summary.

96 *"APA Guidelines for Psychological Practice with Boys and Men"*: American Psychological Association, Boys and Men Guidelines Group, "APA Guidelines for Psychological Practice with Boys and Men," American Psychological Association, 2018, https://www.apa.org/about/policy/boys-men-practice-guidelines.pdf.

97 *Often enough . . . "behaviors"*: Stephanie Pappas, "APA Issues First-Ever Guidelines for Practice with Men and Boys," *Monitor of Psychology* 50, no. 1 (2019): 34, https://www.apa.org/monitor/2019/01/ce-corner.

97 *as manly men avoid*: Kristen W. Springer and Dawne M. Mouzon, "'Macho Men' and Preventive Health Care," *Journal of Health and Social Behavior* 52, no. 2 (2011): 212–227, https://doi.org/10.1177/0022146510393972; James R. Mahalik, Shaun M. Burns, and Matthew Syzdek, "Masculinity and Perceived Normative Health Behaviors as Predictors of Men's

Health Behaviors," *Social Science & Medicine* 64, no. 11 (2007): 2201–2209, https://doi.org/10.1016/j.socscimed.2007.02.035.

97 *A meta-analysis of seventy-four studies found*: Y. Joel Wong et al., "Meta-Analyses of the Relationship between Conformity to Masculine Norms and Mental Health–Related Outcomes," *Journal of Counseling Psychology* 64, no. 1 (2017): 80–93, https://doi.org/10.1037/cou0000176.

98 *Research shows that the majority of men*: Juliana Menasce Horowitz, "Americans' Views on Masculinity Differ by Party, Gender and Race," Pew Research Center, May 30, 2020, https://www.pewresearch.org/fact -tank/2019/01/23/americans-views-on-masculinity-differ-by-party-gen der-and-race/.

98 *most say they are not masculine enough*: Andrew Smiler, "Are You Man Enough?," *Change Becomes You*, August 25, 2021, https://medium.com /change-becomes-you/are-you-man-enough-ac27528f00fc.

99 *The more unpaid care*: Anne Manning, "Study: Men Doing More Family Caregiving Could Lower Their Risk of Suicide," Colorado State University, June 13, 2021, https://natsci.source.colostate.edu/study-men-doing -more-family-caregiving-could-lower-their-risk-of-suicide/.

CHAPTER FOUR:
LOVE AND MONEY

105 *During the early part . . . home*: Jessica Grose, "Why Do We Call Them 'Stay-at-Home Moms'? There Must Be a Better Term," *Slate*, March 26, 2013, https://slate.com/human-interest/2013/03/housewife-homemaker -or-stay-at-home-mom-what-should-we-call-women-who-don-t-do-paid -work.html.

107 *the care Smith's mom gave him her entire life*: Katrine Marçal and Saskia Vogel, *Who Cooked Adam Smith's Dinner? A Story about Women and Economics* (Brunswick, Victoria, AU: Scribe Publications, 2015).

111 *a 2015 report from UN Women*: "Progress of the World's Women 2015–2016: Transforming Economies, Realizing Rights," UN Women, 2015, http://progress.unwomen.org/.

111 *2018 report from the International Labour Organization*: Laura Addati et al., "Care Work and Care Jobs for the Future of Decent Work," International Labour Organization, June 28, 2018, https://www.ilo.org/global/publica tions/books/WCMS_633135/lang--en/index.htm.

111 *entire retail industry contributes*: "The Economic Impact of the US Retail Industry," National Retail Federation, May 2020, https://cdn.nrf.com/sites /default/files/2020-06/RS-118304%20NRF%20Retail%20Impact%20 Report%20.pdf.

111 *report published in 2019*: "Family Caregivers Provide $470 Billion in Un-
paid Care as Role Becomes More Complicated," AARP, November 14,
2019, https://press.aarp.org/2019-11-14-Valuing-the-Invaluable-Series.

112 *costs our economy $57 billion*: Sandra Bishop-Josef et al., "Want to Grow
the Economy? Fix the Child Care Crisis," Council for a Strong America, ReadyNation, January 2019, https://strongnation.s3.amazonaws.com
/documents/602/83bb2275-ce07-4d74-bcee-ff6178daf6bd.pdf
?1547054862&inline;%20filename=%22Want%20to%20Grow%20
the%20Economy?%20Fix%20the%20Child%20Care%20Crisis.pdf%22.

112 *analysis from the AARP in 2021*: "The Economic Impact of Supporting
Working Family Caregivers," AARP, 2021, https://www.aarp.org/content
/dam/aarp/research/surveys_statistics/econ/2021/longevity-economy
-working-caregivers.doi.10.26419-2Fint.42.006.pdf; Kenneth Terrell,
"More Support for Older Caregivers Could Boost U.S. Economy," AARP,
March 29, 2021, https://www.aarp.org/caregiving/life-balance/info-2021
/caregiver-support-could-boost-economy.html.

113 *Research on programs that offer no-strings-attached cash transfers*: Randall
Akee et al., "How Does Household Income Affect Child Personality Traits
and Behaviors?," *American Economic Review* 108, no. 3 (January 2018):
775–827, https://doi.org/10.1257/aer.20160133.

113 *cash can boost the well-being of the child in the long run*: Christopher Pul-
liam and Richard V. Reeves, "New Child Tax Credit Could Slash Poverty
Now and Boost Social Mobility Later," Brookings, March 9, 2022, https://
www.brookings.edu/blog/up-front/2021/03/11/new-child-tax-credit
-could-slash-poverty-now-and-boost-social-mobility-later/; Tiffany Phu,
Pilyoung Kim, and Sarah Watamura, "Two Open Windows Part II: New
Research on Infant and Caregiver Neurobiologic Change," Ascend: The
Aspen Institute, 2020, https://ascend.aspeninstitute.org/wp-content/up
loads/2020/12/two-open-windows-part-ii-new-research-on-infant-and
-caregiver-neurobiologic-change.pdf; Irwin Garfinkel et al., "The Costs
and Benefits of a Child Allowance," Center on Poverty and Social Policy at Columbia University, August 2, 2021, https://static1.squarespace
.com/static/610831a16c95260dbd68934a/t/6113e8255527661a46d
1c3eb/1628694566648/Child-Allowance-CBA-Brief-CPSP-Au
gust-2021.pdf.

113 *are less likely to seek mental health treatment*: "Mental Health of Children
and Parents—a Strong Connection," Centers for Disease Control and Prevention, April 19, 2022, https://www.cdc.gov/childrensmentalhealth/fea
tures/mental-health-children-and-parents.html.

116 *Time Use survey*: Adrian Bauman, Michael Bittman, and Jonathan Ger-
shuny, "A Short History of Time Use Research; Implications for Public Health," *BMC Public Health* 19, no. S2 (June 3, 2019), https://doi
.org/10.1186/s12889-019-6760-y.

116 *Hildegarde Kneeland*: "Hildegarde Kneeland 1889–1991," April Third Movement, n.d., http://a3mreunion.org/remembrance/kneeland-h.html.

117 *"How Much Time to Care for Small Children"*: "How Much Time to Care for Small Children: A Radio Talk by Miss Hildegard Kneeland" (Washington, DC: Bureau of Home Economics, May 21, 1931).

117 *data collected by the Bureau*: Hildegard Kneeland, Selma Evelyn Fine, and Janet Helen Murray, *Family Expenditures in the United States: Statistical Tables and Appendixes* (Washington, DC: U.S. Government Printing Office, 1941).

118 *British economic historian named Phyllis Deane*: Luke Messac, "Outside the Economy: Women's Work and Feminist Economics in the Construction and Critique of National Income Accounting," *Journal of Imperial and Commonwealth History* 46, no. 3 (2018): 552–578, https://doi.org/10.108 0/03086534.2018.1431436.

119 *"At present" . . . "food"*: Phyllis Deane, "Measuring National Income in Colonial Territories," in *Studies in Income and Wealth* (London: NBER, 1946), https://www.nber.org/system/files/chapters/c5697/c5697.pdf.

119 *"The welfare of a nation"*: Daphne Wysham, "The Dawning of GDP's Hegemony," Institute for Policy Studies, May 2, 2014, https://ips-dc .org/the_dawning_of_gdps_hegemony/#:~:text=Simon%20Kuznets%20 warned%20that%20GDP,for%20the%20entire%20global%20economy .&text=The%20evidence%20was%20clear%2C%20yet,as%20a%20 whole%20was%20faring.

119 *including caregiving*: Jeremy L. Caradonna, ed., *Routledge Handbook of the History of Sustainability* (Oxfordshire, UK: Routledge, 2017).

120 *Perhaps, they wonder . . . shrunk*: Duncan Ironmonger, "Household Production and the Household Economy," (research paper, University of Melbourne, Department of Economics, 2001), https://fbe.unimelb.edu .au/__data/assets/pdf_file/0009/805995/759.pdf.

120 *"Parental altruism" . . . "decisions of families"*: Gary Becker, "Family Economics and Macro Behavior" (speech, American Economic Association, Chicago, IL, December 29, 1987), http://www2.um.edu.uy/acid/family _economics/family%20economics%20and%20macro%20behaviour.pdf.

121 *as Marianne A. Ferber*: Marianne A. Ferber, "The Study of Economics: A Feminist Critique," *American Economic Review* 85, no. 2 (May 19, 1995): 357–367, https://www.aeaweb.org/content/file?id=743; Marianne A. Ferber, "A Feminist Critique of the Neoclassical Theory of the Family," *Women, Family, and Work*, January 1, 2003, 9–24, https://doi.org/10.1002/97804 70755648.ch2.

122 *"Now, how about the women . . . count at all"*: Marilyn Waring, "The Unpaid Work That GDP Ignores—and Why It Really Counts" (speech, TEDx-Christchurch, NZ, January 2020), https://www.ted.com/talks/marilyn _waring_the_unpaid_work_that_gdp_ignores_and_why_it_really_counts /transcript.

123 *where Hillary Clinton gave her*: Hillary Rodham Clinton, "Remarks for the United Nations Fourth World Conference on Women" (speech, Beijing, China, September 5, 1995), https://www.un.org/esa/gopher-data/conf/fwcw/conf/gov/950905175653.txt.

124 *was worth $3.8 trillion in 2010*: "What Is the Value of Household Work?," U.S. Bureau of Economic Analysis (BEA), June 11, 2012, https://www.bea.gov/news/blog/2012-06-11/what-value-household-work.

124 *this increase helped us avoid a recession*: Benjamin Bridgman, Andrew Craig, and Danit Kanal, "Accounting for Household Production in the National Accounts: An Update 1965–2020," U.S. Bureau of Economic Analysis (BEA), February 18, 2012, https://apps.bea.gov/scb/issues/2022/02-feb ruary/0222-household-production.htm.

125 *A 2009 report written by top economists*: Joseph Stiglitz, Amartya Sen, and Jean-Paul Fitoussi, "Report by the Commission on the Measurement of Economic Performance and Social Progress," January 2009, https://ec.eu ropa.eu/eurostat/documents/8131721/8131772/Stiglitz-Sen-Fitoussi -Commission-report.pdf.

125 *the Organisation for Economic Co-operation and Development*: Gaëlle Ferrant, Luca Maria Pesando, and Keiko Nowacka, "Unpaid Care Work: The Missing Link in the Analysis of Gender Gaps in Labour Outcomes," OECD Development Center, December 2014, https://www.oecd.org /dev/development-gender/Unpaid_care_work.pdf.

126 *International Conference of Labour Statisticians*: "Measuring Women's Paid and Unpaid Work under ICLS 19," International Labour Organization, 2013, https://data2x.org/wp-content/uploads/2019/08/PolicyMakerBrief _Online-WR-181003.pdf.

126 *The World Bank too*: Glenn-Marie Lange, Quentin Wodon, and Kevin Carey, "The Changing Wealth of Nations 2018: Building a Sustainable Future," World Bank, 2018, https://openknowledge.worldbank.org/bit stream/handle/10986/29001/9781464810466.pdf?sequence=4&isAl lowed=y.

127 *Sen's work*: "Amartya Sen—Biographical," NobelPrize.org (Nobel Prize Outreach, 1999), https://www.nobelprize.org/prizes/economic-sciences /1998/sen/biographical/.

127 *saw his father*: Isaac Chotiner, "Amartya Sen's Hopes and Fears for Indian Democracy," *New Yorker*, October 6, 2019, https://www.newyorker.com /news/the-new-yorker-interview/amartya-sens-hopes-and-fears-for-indian -democracy.

128 *Quality caregiving*: Diann Cameron Kelly, "Parents' Influence on Youths' Civic Behaviors: The Civic Context of the Caregiving Environment," *Fam ilies in Society: The Journal of Contemporary Social Services* 87, no. 3 (2006): 447–455, https://doi.org/10.1606/1044-3894.3550.

129 *pay off economically and socially in the long run*: Lange, Wodon, and Carey,

"The Changing Wealth of Nations 2018"; Sam Abbott, "The Child Care Economy," Washington Center for Equitable Growth, September 17, 2021, https://equitablegrowth.org/research-paper/the-child-care-economy/.

129 *We spend less*: "Public Spending on Childcare and Early Education," Organisation for Economic Co-operation and Development, 2021, https://www.oecd.org/els/soc/PF3_1_Public_spending_on_childcare_and_early_education.pdf.

130 *in her 2006 paper on the subject*: Kelly, "Parents' Influence on Youths' Civic Behaviors."

130 *Good early-childhood education*: Guthrie Gray-Lobe, Parag A. Pathak, and Christopher R. Walters, "The Long-Term Effects of Universal Preschool in Boston" (working paper 28756, NBER, Cambridge, MA, May 2021), https://www.nber.org/system/files/working_papers/w28756/w28756.pdf.

131 *She has spent decades*: Becca R. Levy et al., "Positive Age Beliefs Protect against Dementia Even among Elders with High-Risk Gene," *PLOS ONE* 13, no. 2 (July 2018), https://doi.org/10.1371/journal.pone.0191004; Becca R. Levy et al., "When Culture Influences Genes: Positive Age Beliefs Amplify the Cognitive-Aging Benefit of Apoe ε2," *Journals of Gerontology: Series B* 75, no. 8 (2020): e198–e203, https://doi.org/10.1093/geronb/gbaa126; Becca R. Levy et al., "Active Coping Shields against Negative Aging Self-Stereotypes Contributing to Psychiatric Conditions," *Social Science & Medicine* 228 (2019): 25–29, https://doi.org/10.1016/j.socscimed.2019.02.035; Becca R. Levy et al., "Association between Positive Age Stereotypes and Recovery from Disability in Older Persons," *JAMA* 308, no. 19 (2012): 1972, https://doi.org/10.1001/jama.2012.14541.

131 *negative effect on the well-being of older adults*: Michael Greenwood, "Harmful Effects of Ageism on Older Persons' Health Found in 45 Countries," Yale School of Medicine, January 16, 2020, https://medicine.yale.edu/news-article/harmful-effects-of-ageism-on-older-persons-health-found-in-45-countries/.

131 *represents a substantial chunk of overall health-care spending*: Berhanu Alemayehu and Kenneth E. Warner, "The Lifetime Distribution of Health Care Costs," *Health Services Research* 39, no. 3 (2004): 627–642, https://doi.org/10.1111/j.1475-6773.2004.00248.x.

131 *lower these costs by $63 billion*: Becca R. Levy et al., "Ageism Amplifies Cost and Prevalence of Health Conditions," *The Gerontologist* 60, no. 1 (2018): 174–181, https://doi.org/10.1093/geront/gny131.

132 *the extremely high loneliness rate*: "Loneliness and Social Isolation Linked to Serious Health Conditions," Centers for Disease Control and Prevention, April 29, 2021, https://www.cdc.gov/aging/publications/features/lonely-older-adults.html#:~:text=A%20report%20from%20the%20National, considered%20to%20be%20socially%20isolated.

132 *A national survey led by a team*: Anne Colby et al., "Purpose in the Encore

Years: Shaping Lives of Meaning and Contribution," Stanford Graduate School of Education and CoGenerate, 2013, https://encore.org/wp-con tent/uploads/2018/06/EXECUTIVESUMMARY.pdf.

133   *includes one in four Americans*: "Disability Impacts All of Us Infographic," Centers for Disease Control and Prevention, October 28, 2022, https:// www.cdc.gov/ncbddd/disabilityandhealth/infographic-disability-im pacts-all.html.

135   *"The Independence Myth: People with Disabilities Are Interdependent Too"*: Denise Lance, "The Independence Myth: People with Disabilities Are In terdependent Too" (speech, TEDxKC, Kansas City, MO, 2016), https:// www.youtube.com/watch?v=7PD04yP4n-A t.

CHAPTER FIVE:
SURVIVAL OF THE MOST SYMPATHETIC

146   *"test, or further test, his conquest of sexual desire"*: Soutik Biswas, "Manu Gandhi: The Girl Who Chronicled Gandhi's Troubled Years," BBC News, September 30, 2019, https://www.bbc.com/news/world-asia-in dia-49848645.

146   *He showed equal sensitivity to his children . . . "but in not being so"*: Randal Keynes, *Darwin, His Daughter & Human Evolution* (New York: Riverhead Books, 2002), 12, 101, 308.

147   *"the dependence of one being on another"*: Charles Darwin, *On the Origin of Species by Means of Natural Selection, or The Preservation of Favoured Races in the Struggle for Life* (London: J. Murray, 1859), 62.

148   *In his memorial of Anne*: "The Death of Anne Elizabeth Darwin," Dar win Correspondence Project (University of Cambridge), June 5, 2015, https://www.darwinproject.ac.uk/people/about-darwin/family-life /death-anne-elizabeth-darwin.

149   *"About this time"*: "Darwin's Observations on His Children," Darwin Cor respondence Project (University of Cambridge), June 25, 2015, https:// www.darwinproject.ac.uk/people/about-darwin/family-life/darwin-s-ob servations-his-children.

149   *come into this world primed to cooperate and connect*: Gareth Cook, "The Moral Life of Babies," *Scientific American*, November 12, 2013, https:// www.scientificamerican.com/article/the-moral-life-of-babies/.

149   *"Parental and filial affections" . . . "number of offspring"*: Charles Darwin, *The Descent of Man*, vol. 1 (New York: American Home Library, 1902), 77, 79, 145, 162.

150   *"The point is, ladies and gentlemen"*: *Wall Street*, directed by Oliver Stone (Twentieth Century Fox Film Corporation, 1987).

151 *"Life"* . . . *"battle of life"*: Arabella Burton Buckley, *Life and Her Children: Glimpses of Animal Life from the Amoeba to the Insects* (New York: D. Appleton, 1904), 301.

151 *saw cooperation, not competition, as the primary engine of human survival*: Lee Alan Dugatkin, "The Prince of Evolution: Peter Kropotkin's Adventures in Science and Politics," *Scientific American*, September 13, 2011, https://www.scientificamerican.com/article/the-prince-of-evolution-peter-kropotkin/.

151 *"The mutual-aid tendency"*: Peter Kropotkin, *Mutual Aid: A Factor of Evolution* (New York: Warbler Classics, 2023), chapter 7.

151 *similar ideas about cooperation to field research on animals*: W. C. Allee, *The Social Life of Animals* (New York: W. W. Norton, 1938), https://www.biodiversitylibrary.org/item/30872#page/1/mode/1up.

152 *a science educator published an academic paper*: Abour H. Cherif, "Mutualism: The Forgotten Concept in Teaching Science," *American Biology Teacher* 52, no. 4 (January 1990): 206–208, https://doi.org/10.2307/4449085.

152 *A very, very long time ago . . . pass these care genes on to the next generation*: Stephanie D. Preston, "The Origins of Altruism in Offspring Care," *Psychological Bulletin* 139, no. 6 (2013): 1305–1341, https://doi.org/10.1037/a0031755; David C. Bell, "Evolution of Parental Caregiving," *Personality and Social Psychology Review* 5, no. 3 (2001): 216–229, https://doi.org/10.1207/s15327957pspr0503_3.

152 *developed neurological wiring for these tasks*: James W. Sonne and Don M. Gash, "Psychopathy to Altruism: Neurobiology of the Selfish-Selfless Spectrum," *Frontiers in Psychology* 9 (2018), https://doi.org/10.3389/fpsyg.2018.00575.

152 *species with longer childhoods tend to be more empathetic overall*: Preston, "The Origins of Altruism in Offspring Care."

153 *"[The] recognition of kin"*: Steven Pinker, "The False Allure of Group Selection," Edge, June 18, 2012, https://www.edge.org/conversation/steven_pinker-the-false-allure-of-group-selection.

153 *Eldercare, for example*: Megan Arnot and Ruth Mace, "An Evolutionary Perspective on Kin Care Directed up the Generations," *Scientific Reports* 11, no. 1 (July 8, 2021), https://doi.org/10.1038/s41598-021-93652-4.

155 *she argued that humans' success . . . be able to care*: Sarah Blaffer Hrdy, *Mothers and Others: The Evolutionary Origins of Mutual Understanding* (Cambridge, MA: Belknap Press, 2011); Sarah Blaffer Hrdy, "Meet the Alloparents," *Natural History Magazine*, April 2009, https://www.naturalhistorymag.com/htmlsite/0409/0409_feature.pdf.

156 *What's happening there . . . descendants, mammals*: Catharine Paddock, "Could 'Mirror Neurons' Explain Brain Mechanisms of Empathy?," *Medical News Today*, April 15, 2019, https://www.medicalnewstoday.com

/articles/324974; Patricia Smith Churchland, *Braintrust: What Neuroscience Tells Us about Morality* (Princeton: Princeton University Press, 2018).

157 *Ruth Feldman conducted an experiment*: Ruth Feldman, Ilanit Gordon, and Orna Zagoory-Sharon, "The Cross-Generation Transmission of Oxytocin in Humans," *Hormones and Behavior* 58, no. 4 (2010): 669–676, https://doi.org/10.1016/j.yhbeh.2010.06.005.

158 *"Our findings show"*: Dani Bar On, "The Five Months That Determine Your Kids' Future Happiness," Haaretz.com, October 18, 2018, https://www.haaretz.com/israel-news/2018-10-18/ty-article-magazine/.premium/the-five-months-that-determine-your-kids-future-happiness/0000017f-e980-dc91-a17f-fd8d90650000.

158 *The brains of new mothers . . . Fathers too*: Ruth Feldman, "The Adaptive Human Parental Brain: Implications for Children's Social Development," *Trends in Neurosciences* 38, no. 6 (2015): 387–399, https://doi.org/10.1016/j.tins.2015.04.004.

158 *never a sure thing*: Jennifer A. Bartz et al., "Social Effects of Oxytocin in Humans: Context and Person Matter," *Trends in Cognitive Sciences* 15, no. 7 (July 2011): 301–309, https://doi.org/10.1016/j.tics.2011.05.002.

158 *hormones, biology, and circumstances*: "Longer Maternity Leave Lowers Risk of Postpartum Depression," Division of Research: Sponsored Program Accounting and Compliance, University of Maryland, December 12, 2013, https://spac.umd.edu/news/story/longer-maternity-leave-lowers-risk-of-postpartum-depression; Bridget F. Hutchens and Joan Kearney, "Risk Factors for Postpartum Depression: An Umbrella Review," *Journal of Midwifery & Women's Health* 65, no. 1 (2020): 96–108, https://doi.org/10.1111/jmwh.13067.

159 *"moral foundations theory"*: Moral Foundations Theory, YourMorals.org collaboration, June 2021, https://moralfoundations.org/.

159 *Research on children, including infants, supports this idea*: Daniel Goleman, "Wired for Kindness: Science Shows We Prefer Compassion, and Our Capacity Grows with Practice," *Washington Post*, October 27, 2021, https://www.washingtonpost.com/news/inspired-life/wp/2015/06/23/wired-for-kindness-science-shows-we-prefer-compassion-and-our-capacity-grows-with-practice/.

160 *"admit the possibility that in the development"*: Charles H. Smith, James T. Costa, and David A. Collard, *An Alfred Russel Wallace Companion* (Chicago: University of Chicago Press, 2019).

160 *"I hope," he replied*: Keynes, *Darwin, His Daughter & Human Evolution*, 292.

160 *"It is surprising how soon"*: Charles Darwin, *The Descent of Man, and Selection in Relation to Sex* (New York: Penguin, 2004), 159.

CHAPTER SIX: THE FEELING IS MUTUAL

163 *Like roughly one out of three veterans*: Kim Parker et al., "The American Veteran Experience and the Post-9/11 Generation," Pew Research Center, September 10, 2019, https://www.pewresearch.org/social-trends/2019/09 /10/the-american-veteran-experience-and-the-post-9-11-genera tion/#fn-26608-1.

164 *"Positive affect and enjoyment"*: Daniel Kahneman et al., "A Survey Method for Characterizing Daily Life Experience: The Day Reconstruction Method," *Science* 306, no. 5702 (March 2004): 1776–1780, https://doi .org/10.1126/science.1103572.

167 *"They fuck you"*: Philip Larkin, "This Be the Verse," Poetry Foundation, n.d., https://www.poetryfoundation.org/poems/48419/this-be-the-verse.

167 *Research shows that parentified children*: Jennifer A. Engelhardt, "The Developmental Implications of Parentification: Effects on Childhood Attachment," *Graduate Student Journal of Psychology* 14 (2012): 45–52, https://www.tc.columbia.edu/media/centers-amp-labs/gsjp/gsjp-vol ume-pdfs/25227_Engelhardt_Parentification.pdf.

167 *had a very close relationship with his mom*: Dalya Alberge, "Newly Seen Letters Show Philip Larkin's Close Relationship with Mother," *Guardian*, January 15, 2018, https://www.theguardian.com/books/2018/jan/15 /philip-larkin-mother-newly-seen-letters-writers-and-their-mothers-.

170 *"I once said"*: Donald W. Winnicott, "The Theory of the Parent-Infant Relationship," in *The Collected Works of D. W. Winnicott*, vol. 6, *1960–1963*, online edn (New York: Oxford Academic, December 2016), https://doi .org/10.1093/med:psych/9780190271381.003.0022.

171 *"The good enough mother"*: Donald W. Winnicott, *The Collected Works of D. W. Winnicott*, vol. 4, *1952–1955*, online edn (New York: Oxford Academic, December 2016), 159–174, https://doi.org/10.1093/med: psych/9780190271367.003.0034.

171 *"the infant and young child"*: Robert H. Bremner, "Mental Health," in *Children and Youth in America: A Documentary History* (Cambridge, MA: Harvard University Press, 1974), 1489.

171 *essential for the child's future well-being*: John Bowlby, *A Secure Base* (London: Routledge, 1988), 165.

171 *"The occurrence of altruistic care"*: Marga Vicedo, *The Nature and Nurture of Love: From Imprinting to Attachment in Cold War America* (Chicago: University of Chicago Press, 2013), 228.

173 *"Clinical observation"*: Richard Schulz and Paula R. Sherwood, "Physical and Mental Health Effects of Family Caregiving," *American Journal of Nursing* 108, no. 9 (2008): 23–27, https://doi.org/10.1097/01 .naj.0000336406.45248.4c.

176 *Scientists call this a helper's high*: Elissa Strauss, "Don't Just Look for

the Helpers. Be a Helper," CNN, April 3, 2020, https://www.cnn.com /2020/04/03/health/parenting-look-for-the-helpers-wellness/index.html.

176 *loneliness is connected to cognitive decline and increased mortality:* "Strengthen Relationships for Longer, Healthier Life," Harvard Health, January 18, 2011, https://www.health.harvard.edu/healthbeat/strengthen-relation ships-for-longer-healthier-life.

176 *"I thought, what on earth"*: Paula Span, "Caregiving's Hidden Benefits," *New York Times,* October 12, 2011, https://archive.nytimes.com/newoldage .blogs.nytimes.com/2011/10/12/caregivings-hidden-benefits/.

176 *2019 study that she and her colleagues published in the* Gerontologist: Lisa Fredman et al., "Caregiving Intensity and Mortality in Older Women, Accounting for Time-Varying and Lagged Caregiver Status: The Caregiver-Study of Osteoporotic Fractures Study," *Gerontologist* 59, no. 5 (2019) 461–469, https://doi.org/10.1093/geront/gny135.

177 *better memories and think faster than their non-caregiver counterparts*: Rosanna M. Bertrand et al., "Caregiving and Cognitive Function in Older Women: Evidence for the Healthy Caregiver Hypothesis," *Journal of Aging and Health* 24, no. 1 (September 20, 2011): 48–66, https://doi.org /10.1177/0898264311421367.

177 *don't have higher levels of inflammation than their non-caregiving peers*: David L. Roth et al., "The Transition to Family Caregiving and Its Effect on Biomarkers of Inflammation," *PNAS* 117, no. 28 (June 24, 2020): 16258–16263, https://doi.org/10.1073/pnas.2000792117.

177 *Research on parents*: Kieron Barclay, "How Children Influence the Life Expectancy of Their Parents," Max-Planck-Gesellschaft, October 23, 2019, https://www.mpg.de/14064449/children-influence-parents-life-expec tancy.

177 *link between caring for children and living a longer life*: Sonja Hilbrand et al., "Caregiving within and beyond the Family Is Associated with Lower Mortality for the Caregiver: A Prospective Study," *Evolution and Human Behavior* 38, no. 3 (May 2017): 397–403, https://doi.org/10.1016/j.evol humbehav.2016.11.010.

177 *A number of polls . . . at once*: "Infographic—Long-Term Care and the Impact of Caregiving on Familial Roles (2014)," AP-NORC, n.d., https:// apnorc.org/infographic-long-term-care-and-the-impact-of-caregiving -on-familial-roles-2014/; Jennifer Benz et al., "Long-Term Caregiving: The Types of Care Older Americans Provide and the Impact on Work and Family," The Long-Term Care Poll, AP-NORC, n.d., https://www .longtermcarepoll.org/long-term-caregiving-the-types-of-care-older -americans-provide-and-the-impact-on-work-and-family/#3; "Caring for Aging Parents," Pew Research Center, May 21, 2015, https://www.pewre search.org/social-trends/2015/05/21/4-caring-for-aging-parents/; Catherine Quinn and Gill Toms, "Influence of Positive Aspects of Dementia

Caregiving on Caregivers' Well-Being: A Systematic Review," *Gerontologist*, December 28, 2018, https://doi.org/10.1093/geront/gny168; Schulz and Sherwood, "Physical and Mental Health Effects of Family Caregiving," 23–27; Melanie Wagner and Martina Brandt, "Long-Term Care Provision and the Well-Being of Spousal Caregivers: An Analysis of 138 European Regions," *Journals of Gerontology: Series B* 73, no. 4 (December 11, 2017): e24–e34, https://doi.org/10.1093/geronb/gbx133.

177   *the inability to work a job and have time to make the soup*: Leah Ruppanner and Georgiana Bostean, "Who Cares? Caregiver Well-Being in Europe," *European Sociological Review* 30, no. 5 (August 12, 2014): 655–669, https://doi.org/10.1093/esr/jcu065; Claire Dujardin et al., "Does Country Influence the Health Burden of Informal Care? An International Comparison between Belgium and Great Britain," *Social Science & Medicine* 73, no. 8 (August 2, 2011): 1123–1132, https://doi.org/10.1016/j.socscimed.2011.07.016.

178   *according to one large-scale study that defined caregivers broadly*: Naomi Lightman and Anthony Kevins, "Bonus or Burden? Care Work, Inequality, and Job Satisfaction in Eighteen European Countries," *European Sociological Review* 35, no. 6 (May 2019): 825–844, https://doi.org/10.1093/esr/jcz032.

178   *A survey of American home health-care workers and certified nurse assistants*: Galina Khatutsky et al., "Understanding Direct Care Workers: A Snapshot of Two of America's Most Important Jobs—Certified Nursing Assistants and Home Health Aides," ASPE, February 28, 2011, https://aspe.hhs.gov/reports/understanding-direct-care-workers-snapshot-two-americas-most-important-jobs-certified-nursing.

178   *"Watching aides interact"*: Clare L. Stacey, *The Caring Self* (Ithaca, NY: ILR Press, 2011), ix.

179   *published a study for which they examined*: David Blanchflower and Andrew Clark, "Children, Unhappiness and Family Finances: Evidence from One Million Europeans" (working paper 25597, NBER, Cambridge, MA, February 2019), https://doi.org/10.3386/w25597.

180   *Sociologist Jennifer Glass came to a complementary conclusion*: Jennifer Glass, Robin W. Simon, and Matthew A. Andersson, "Parenthood and Happiness: Effects of Work-Family Reconciliation Policies in 22 OECD Countries," *American Journal of Sociology* 122, no. 3 (November 2016): 886–929, https://doi.org/10.1086/688892.

180   *The ability to share the burden of care matters a lot too*: Claire Cain Miller, "Why Unpaid Labor Is More Likely to Hurt Women's Mental Health Than Men's," *New York Times*, September 30, 2022, https://www.nytimes.com/2022/09/30/upshot/women-mental-health-labor.html?smid=nytcore-ios-share&referringSource=articleShare.

180   *One study that considered parental burnout in forty-two countries*: Isabelle

Roskam et al., "Parental Burnout around the Globe: A 42-Country Study," *Affective Science* 2, no. 1 (March 18, 2021): 58–79, https://doi.org/10.1007/s42761-020-00028-4.

181 *Another found that the less parents feel supported by their partner*: Klaus Preisner et al., "Closing the Happiness Gap: The Decline of Gendered Parenthood Norms and the Increase in Parental Life Satisfaction," *Gender & Society* 34, no. 1 (2019): 31–55, https://doi.org/10.1177/0891243219869365.

184 *as well as parents who report*: Wendy Wang, "Parents' Time with Kids More Rewarding Than Paid Work—and More Exhausting," Pew Research Center, October 8, 2013, https://www.pewresearch.org/social-trends/2013/10/08/parents-time-with-kids-more-rewarding-than-paid-work-and-more-exhausting/.

184 *"Satisfying one's needs . . . not happiness"*: Roy F. Baumeister et al., "Some Key Differences between a Happy Life and a Meaningful Life," *Journal of Positive Psychology* 8, no. 6 (August 20, 2013): 505–516, https://doi.org/10.1080/17439760.2013.830764.

184 *parents rate themselves as happier*: K. J. Dell'Antonia, "Survey Says: Parents Are Happy, but Tired," *New York Times*, October 8, 2013, https://archive.nytimes.com/parenting.blogs.nytimes.com/2013/10/08/survey-says-parents-are-happy-but-tired/.

CHAPTER SEVEN:
A PHILOSOPHY OF CARE

192 *"I too needed to be someplace"*: Eva Feder Kittay, *Learning from My Daughter* (Oxford, UK: Oxford University Press, 2019), 8.

201 *"Sort of like math problems with humans"*: Carol Gilligan, *In a Different Voice: Psychological Theory and Women's Development* (Cambridge, MA: Harvard University Press, 1993), 26.

205 *She was . . . "having pets and kids around"*: Kathleen O'Toole, "What Matters to Nel Noddings and Why," *Stanford News*, Palo Alto, CA, February 4, 1998, https://web.archive.org/web/20040326081522/http://news-service.stanford.edu/news/1998/february4/noddings.html.

205 *In her book, Noddings*: Nel Noddings, *Caring: A Feminine Approach to Ethics and Moral Education* (Berkeley: University of California Press, 2003).

207 *She separates out what she calls "virtue carers" and "relational carers"*: Nel Noddings, "Caring as Relation and Virtue in Teaching," in *Working Virtue: Virtue Ethics and Contemporary Moral Problems*, ed. Rebecca L. Walker and Philip J. Ivanhoe (Oxford, UK: Clarendon Press, 2013).

211 *Simone Weil, a philosopher . . . and life itself*: Tony Lynch, "Simone Weil

(1909–1943)," Internet Encyclopedia of Philosophy, n.d., https://iep.utm
.edu/weil/.

212   *"Every time that a human"*: Simone Weil, *Waiting for God* (New York:
      Harper and Rowe, 1951), 107.

212   *"The self, the place . . . as it really is"*: Iris Murdoch, *The Sovereignty of Good*
      (London: Routledge, 2014), 93.

213   *"a person is a person through other persons"*: Samuel Willard Crompton,
      Desmond Tutu: Fighting Apartheid (New York: Chelsea House, 2007), 39.

213   *rose in prominence in the late twentieth century*: Fainos Mangena, "Hunhu/
      Ubuntu in the Traditional Thought of Southern Africa," Internet Encyclo-
      pedia of Philosophy, n.d., https://iep.utm.edu/hunhu/.

213   *"One of the epoch-making books of our generation"*: Adam Kirsch, "Moder-
      nity, Faith, and Martin Buber," *New Yorker*, April 29, 2019, https://www
      .newyorker.com/magazine/2019/05/06/modernity-faith-and-martin-bu
      ber&sa=D&source=docs&ust=1672361967956215&usg=AovVaw3hS
      dtB3pRaofVJiHPo-xSt.

215   *There are roughly 11.5 million*: Elisa Mosler Vidal, "Can Data Help Im-
      prove Migrant Domestic Workers' Lives?," Migration Data Portal, April 24,
      2020, https://www.migrationdataportal.org/blog/can-data-help-improve
      -migrant-domestic-workers-lives.

219   *"As many of you know . . . to turn out okay"*: Joe Biden, "Child and Elder
      Care Plan Speech," New Castle, DE, July 21, 2020, rev transcript, https://
      www.rev.com/blog/transcripts/joe-biden-child-and-elder-care-plan
      -speech-transcript-july-21.

221   *34 million people living in poverty in America*: Jessica Semega et al., "Income
      and Poverty in the United States: 2019," Census.gov, September 15, 2020,
      https://www.census.gov/library/publications/2020/demo/p60-270.html
      #:~:text=In%202019%2C%20there%20were%2034.0,and%20Table%20
      B%2D1).

CHAPTER EIGHT:
WHEN REVELATION TAKES PLACE AT HOME

223   *Like many Catholics in the sixteenth century . . . with their families*: Ro-
      land Herbert Bainton, *Here I Stand: A Life of Martin Luther* (Peabody, MA:
      Hendrickson, 2017).

225   *"A Woman of Valor, who can find . . . praise her at the gates"*: Lori Palat-
      nik, "Eishet Chayil," Aish.com, December 19, 2021, https://aish.com
      /48966686/.

227   *Pew Research Center published data on gender and religion*: Conrad Hack-
      ett, David McClendon, and Anne Fengyang Shi, "The Gender Gap in

Religion around the World," Pew Research Center, 2016, https://www
.pewresearch.org/religion/2016/03/22/the-gender-gap-in-religion
-around-the-world/.

227   *One reason, according to a number of sociologists*: Marta Trzebiatowska and
Steve Bruce, *Why Are Women More Religious Than Men?* (Oxford, UK:
Oxford University Press, 2014); "Has Religion Shaped Our Understanding of Gender?," *Life Examined*, hosted by Jonathan Bastian (Los Angeles:
KCRW, January 16, 2021), https://www.kcrw.com/culture/shows/life-ex
amined/religion-evangelical-history-women-empowerment/religion-gen
der-ann-braude-interview.

230   *"The LORD God said"*: Joshua Rodriguez, "Genesis 2:18 «a help AGAINST
Him»," Sefaria, n.d., https://www.sefaria.org/sheets/333823?lang=bi.

231   *"For now I know that you fear God"*: Genesis 22:13 (The Contemporary
Torah, Jewish Publication Society), Sefaria, n.d., https://www.sefaria.org
/Genesis.22.13?lang=bi&aliyot=0.

232   *"By this shall all men"*: John 13:34–35, Bible.com, n.d., https://www.bible
.com/bible/compare/JHN.13.34-35.

232   *The first is that of the Good Samaritan*: Luke 10:25–37, Bible Gateway, n.d.,
https://www.biblegateway.com/passage/?search=Luke+10%3A25-37
&version=NIV.

233   *Martha and Mary*: Luke 10, Bible Gateway, n.d., https://www.biblegate
way.com/passage/?search=Luke+10&version=NIV.

235   *The Church sees in Mary*: Pope John Paul II, *Letter of Pope John Paul II to
Women* (Vatican City: Libreria Editrice Vaticana, June 28, 1995), https://
www.vatican.va/content/john-paul-ii/en/letters/1995/documents/hf
_jp-ii_let_29061995_women.html.

238   *"What would happen"*: Bonnie J. Miller-McLemore, *In the Midst of Chaos:
Caring for Children as Spiritual Practice* (Minneapolis, MN: Fortress Press,
2019), xiv.

239   *"He had abandoned"*: Vanessa R. Sasson, *Yasodhara and the Buddha* (London: Bloomsbury, 2021), 278.

241   *"You shall rise before the aged and show deference to the old"*: Leviticus 19:32
(The Contemporary Torah, Jewish Publication Society), Sefaria, n.d.,
https://www.sefaria.org/Leviticus.19.32?lang=bi&aliyot=0.

241   *"And God blessed them"*: Genesis 1:28 (The Contemporary Torah, Jewish Publication Society), Sefaria, n.d., https://www.sefaria.org/Genesis.1.28?ven=The
_Holy_Scriptures%3A_A_New_Translation_%28JPS_1917%29&vhe=Miqra
_according_to_the_Masorah&lang=bi&aliyot=0.

241   *"And these words, which I command"*: Deuteronomy 6:6 (Koren Jerusalem
Bible), Sefaria, n.d., https://www.sefaria.org/Deuteronomy.6.6?ven=The
_Koren_Jerusalem_Bible&vhe=Miqra_according_to_the_Masorah
&lang=bi&aliyot=0.

242   *"Do not urge me to leave you"*: Ruth 1:16 (The Contemporary Torah, Jewish

Publication Society), Sefaria, n.d., https://www.sefaria.org/Ruth.1.16 ?lang=bi.

243   *"as a baby invites us"*: Mara H. Benjamin, *The Obligated Self: Maternal Subjectivity and Jewish Thought* (Bloomington, IN: Indiana University Press, 2018), 14.

244   *"[W]hat if loving God"*: Danya Ruttenberg, *Nurture the Wow: Finding Spirituality in the Frustration, Boredom, Tears, Poop, Desperation, Wonder* (New York: Flatiron Books, 2016), 40.

251   *sorted and cleaned large quantities of rice*: Susan Starr Sered, "Women, Religion, and Modernization: Tradition and Transformation among Elderly Jews in Israel," *American Anthropologist* 92, no. 2 (1990): 306–318, https:// doi.org/10.1525/aa.1990.92.2.02a00030.

CONCLUSION:

INTERDEPENDENTLY

255   *Uri Hasson in a 2019 interview with* Scientific American: Lydia Denworth, "'Hyperscans' Show How Brains Sync as People Interact," *Scientific American*, April 10, 2019, https://www.scientificamerican.com/article/hyper scans-show-how-brains-sync-as-people-interact/.

255   *Trees appear to communicate with one another*: Diane Toomey, "Exploring How and Why Trees 'Talk' to Each Other," *Yale Environment 360* (blog), Yale School of the Environment, September 1, 2016, https://e360.yale .edu/features/exploring_how_and_why_trees_talk_to_each_other.

256   *the National Institutes of Health reported*: "NIH Human Microbiome Project Defines Normal Bacterial Makeup of the Body," National Institutes of Health, U.S. Department of Health & Human Services, June 13, 2012, https://www.nih.gov/news-events/news-releases/nih-human-microbi ome-project-defines-normal-bacterial-makeup-body.

258   *Parents who take paid leave*: "Paid Leave Fact Sheet," Zero to Three, June 27, 2022, https://www.zerotothree.org/resource/paid-leave-fact-sheet/.

260   *The more workers have flexible*: Elizabeth Harrington and Bill McInturff, *Working While Caring: A National Survey of Caregiving Stress in the U.S. Workforce*, Rosalynn Carter Institute for Caregivers, 2021, https://rosalynn carter.org/wp-content/uploads/2021/09/210140-RCI-National-Surveys -Executive-Summary-Update-9.22.21.pdf.

262   *according to the U.S. Bureau of Labor Statistics*: U.S. Bureau of Labor Statistics, "Occupational Employment and Wages, May 2021, 31-1120 Home Health and Personal Care Aides," March 31, 2022, https://www.bls.gov /oes/current/oes311120.htm.

262   *one-sixth according to a 2019 report from PHI*: U.S. Home Care Workers: Key

Facts, PHI, 2019, https://www.phinational.org/resource/u-s-home-care-workers-key-facts-2019/.

263 *When men in some parts of Europe and Asia*: Katie Doucet, "Sweden's Maternity and Paternity Leave," Yale School of Public Health, June 1, 2018, https://ysph.yale.edu/news-article/swedens-maternity-and-paternity-leave/; Kenjiro Takahashi et al., "Towards Equality: Paternity Leave Still a Tricky Issue in Japan's Staid Mindset," *Asahi Shimbun*, June 28, 2021, https://www.asahi.com/ajw/articles/14379538.

263 *the professional and cultural stigma*: Barclay Ballard, "Governments Must Encourage Men to Use Paternity Leave—Here's Why," European CEO, June 25, 2019, https://www.europeanceo.com/business-and-management/governments-must-encourage-men-to-use-paternity-leave-heres-why/.

267 *"emotional beings who wish"*: Martha C. Nussbaum, *Upheavals of Thought: The Intelligence of Emotions* (Cambridge, UK: Cambridge University Press, 2009), 137.

ABOUT THE AUTHOR

Elissa Strauss has been writing about the politics and culture of parenting and caregiving for more than fifteen years. Her work appears in publications like the *Atlantic*, the *New York Times*, *Glamour*, and elsewhere, and she was a former contributing writer at CNN.com and *Slate*, where her cultural criticism about motherhood appeared weekly on Doublex. She lives in Oakland, California, with her family.